# The Force of

## *The Shadowed Kingdom Part 2*

## By Pira Sudham

# The Force of Karma

*The Shadowed Kingdom Part 2*

## By Pira Sudham

DCO Books

The Force of Karma
The Shadowed Kingdom Part 2
Copyright © Pira Sudham, 2022
4th Edition 2022
First Published 2002

DCO Books
This eBook edition published by
Proglen Trading Co., Ltd.
Bangkok Thailand
http://www.dco.co.th

ISBN 979-8-8482-6400-5

At the age of 14, Pira Sudham left his home village in the northeastern region of Thailand to be a servant to monks at a Bangkok Buddhist monastery. There, he was permitted to attend classes at the monastery school. To see himself through high school and the first year at the Faculty of Arts, Chulalongkorn University, he sold souvenirs to tourists until he was awarded a scholarship to study in New Zealand.

While reading English at Victoria University, the young student had his short stories published by New Zealand's leading quarterly, *Landfall*. Since then his literary works have appeared in Australia, USA, Hong Kong and Thailand.

Pira Sudham's books include *Tales of Thailand* and *People of Esarn – The Damned of Thailand* & *The Kingdom in Conflicts*.

In 2014, *It is the People*, an anthology of his short stories, was published as an ebook.

# Contents

# The Jealously Guarded Treasures

Dhani Pilaskulkosol had received a total of 80 million pounds from a series of bank transfers.

Furthermore, his parents reserved an undisclosed sum to purchase prime properties in and outside London.

Following Charles Tregonning's recommendation, the millionaire bought a three-bedroom flat on the fourth floor of a grade II listed Regency building in St James's where the art-dealer also had his town residence.

"The value goes up all the time," Charles mentioned. "Those who left St James's for Belgravia would turn in their graves."

Here, at St James's Square, Dani Pi was not far from   wine merchants, men's fashion shops, Fortnum and Mason, Christie's, his club in Pall Mall, St James's Palace, The Theatre Royal Haymarket, The Ritz, Brown's, Claridge's and The Connaught.

While keeping an eye on a premier league football club, the family considered that the priority was to purchase a country house.

For this venture, once again Dani relied on the antiquarian.

"Of course, Danny," the old Etonian expatiated. "I've an ulterior motive. When you own Wealdshire Park, we'd be neighbours."

Wealdshire Park was, as the sale literature described, *a palace fit for a prince*. Held as one of the great treasure troves, this architectural masterpiece was magnificently set in landscaped gardens, an expansive deer park, peaceful woods, and a superb serpentine lake at the heart of the 3,200 acre estate.

Dani gloated over the majestic period pile, steeped in history. Yes, the charming bachelor went for history as well as magnificence and hoarded treasures. As for history, King Henry VIII had made several visits, and later his daughter, Queen Elizabeth I, had also graced the stately home with her stay in 1571, passing several nights in the Great Bedchamber.

In 1768 the 1st Earl had the stately home remodeled and enlarged in the grandest manner by Robert Adam. John Nash had redesigned and extended the library, and Soames did the picture gallery. In the middle of the 19th century, a colossal conservatory, *the Palm House*, was added.

Wealdshire Park was up for grabs after Lord Wealden, the last of the line, had died from drug abuse at the age of 25.

Having purchased Wealdshire Park, Dani deemed that he had made a mark on British history. But in some highly respectable quarters, it was seen that the sale had hammered down another nail. It threatened the survival of the aristocracy and the existing stately home owners.

On this account, Viscount Scarsdale, at Kedleston Hall, had been quoted: *The days have gone, when families like mine lived a grand and isolated life, jealously guarding their possessions against the outside world.*

Indeed Dani was fortunate to own the stately home that boasted a regal 80 foot reception hall, 12 state rooms, a collection of priceless furniture, paintings by Van Dyck, Gainsborough and Reynolds, ancient and neo-classical sculpture, 17th century Flemish tapestries, magnificent chandeliers, exquisite carpets and two complete Sevres dinner services.

The new custodian seemed satisfied, taking into account the manorial rights and the odd extra which included an aviary, a 120-acre vineyard, six farms and cottages in Great Waldron-in-the Weald.

For the time being, Wealdshire Park had been entrusted to a property management company to turn the country house into a hotel and the estate into a game reserve.

On the other hand, a generous sum was allocated for a Rolls-Royce. It should be mentioned also that Dani had engaged not only a chauffeur but also a butler. So then the equipage was satisfactorily arranged for him who, due to the sheer power of wealth, could claim the status of an Oriental prince and the lord of the manor at the same time.

But the recently acquired town flat still had wall space that called for works of art by old masters. The billionaire set his mind on a Gainsborough and a Reynolds which were due to be auctioned at Christie's.

Before going to a preview at Christie's, Dani, in a bespoke suit, sauntered up Duke Street to meet Charles Tregonning.

From the shop front, the dapper young man could see the antiquarian talking with a customer. Charles's hair had turned snow white. Yet the grandee of the old school still retained a balance of sensuality and nobility in his distinguished features.

Dani remembered having told his former flatmate Prem Surin that Charles Tregonning was highly respected in the world of art and antiquities.

The dandy also remembered the circumstances in which Surin and Tregonning met in Soho as well as the antiquarian's first visit to Hyde Park Square.

"I say! I've read about you in a magazine," DP had claimed on that occasion.

As opposed to Charles Tregonning, Elizabeth Durham was *non-u*. Nevertheless, the professional student had always been polite to her when she had come to spend time with her lover at the Hyde Park Square flat.

Several months after the failed student had left London for Isan, the billionaire had accidentally come face to face with the beautiful blond in Piccadilly as he emerged from a bookshop. It was indeed a pleasure to bump into the Bradford butcher's daughter. From her business card, he learned that she earned her keep as an executive in a public relations firm.

Dani reflected that he had referred to her as *that Yorkshire female, a butcher's daughter*. Fate had not allowed him to know that one day he might be in need of her, as he had an urgent need of Charles Tregonning now.

Now, while loitering in front of the antique shop, Dani glanced through the shop front to see whether there was a *piece de resistance* among the showpieces. His calculating mind ran at the same speed as his gleaming eyes.

*My word! A Louis 16th ormolu-mounted tulipwood, amaranth, fruitwood and walnut marquetry secretaire. A Horace Walpole pendule a la Geoffrin... A late Louis 15th bronze and ebony pendule!*

"Sorry those have been reserved," said Charles, having stepped outside. "Good morning, Danny."

"I say, Charles! That pendule would look superb in the hall, what? How much did it fetch?"

"100,000 pounds. Come!"

At the auction house, examining the exhibited painting of Gainsborough's *The Byam Family*, Dani asked:

"How much do you expect the highest bid to be?"

"It might run up to three million. As for Sir Joshua Reynolds' portrait of Sir Charles Seymour, it could reach two million. By the way, I heard that there has been a strong move to make the Austrian government release a huge collection of art and antiques stolen by the Nazis from the Austrian branch of the Rothschilds. For so long the collection has been prevented from leaving Austria. I happen to know that among the treasures there are several portraits by Hals whose painting of Tielemann should be a whale of a catch. It's likely that the auction would be at Christie's."

"Dash it, Charles! I want something now!"

"In that case, bid for the Gainsborough or the Reynolds. You've only six days to wait. But if you can wait 12 days more, you should fly to New York with me. This is the auction of the century which you cannot afford to miss. You're sure to find the one to kill or die for."

"Yes, I will, Charles. When is it exactly? Will you be flying Concorde? Which hotel? My butler will make all the arrangements. But now, let's go to my canteen."

They left Christie's for The Ritz.

Approaching the hotel entrance, Dani resumed a princely air and walked past the doorman without acknowledging the polite greeting and welcome. Then he held up his handsome head, for he wished to observe the ceiling rather than those lesser beings in the foyer. He would not glance at those who were taking their tea in the tearoom as he glided ahead of Charles towards the restaurant.

As if he owned the hotel, the magnificent son of Siam went straight to the preferred table.

"I'm glad that the tables are kept far apart here," Dani stated as soon as they sat down. "I've something in particular to say to you. First of all I meant to ask why you stopped smoking."

"I coughed so much in bed that David threatened to leave me."

"You're the first person I know who has given up smoking for fear of loneliness. By the way, it's my treat to thank you for freighting those mahogany commodes, French bureaux, Chippendale card tables and chairs to my parents. Papa and Mama were delighted. Perhaps that's why I received another bank transfer of 10 million pounds to make Wealdshire Park an unrivalled spa, with an 18-hole golf course, of course. Meanwhile, let's have a vintage Krug."

It was imperative that the champagne be served before making their choices from the menu.

4

"To our trip to New York! When I had to go to New York some time ago, I was granted a visa that permits me to enter and remain indefinitely in the USA. By the way, Charles, am I correct in thinking that, having bought the manorial rights, which make me the lord of the manor, the members of my staff may answer me or refer to me as *My lord* and *His lordship*?"

"Only if you ordered them to."

"And snigger behind my back?"

Charles smiled at the menu.

"Why our Little Primo fled from his farewell party that you kindly hosted. I've meant to ask you this for some time."

"I was offering drinks to other guests when David said Primo had bolted as soon as Lord Bewly arrived."

"The blighter has a thing about Lord Bewly. He fled from us too, in Bavaria, one Christmas. Not a word of apology to Willie or to me. Have you heard from him?"

"No, I haven't. Have you?"

"Neither have I. Wouldn't you say our little man is dashed odd? I often wonder why he hardly looked at me in the eye. Of all the years we lived together, he hardly looked at me in the eye."

"He's frightfully shy. It's so refreshing to see someone so naïve and unsullied. I envy him. To him everything in London is new, exciting and inspiring."

"I don't think he's shy. Avoiding eye contact makes one look shifty. I suspect that he has a secret or secrets to hide."

"I don't believe the little fellow has secrets. The problem is he's too sensitive."

"Rather! I remember his sheer exuberance listening to Beethoven's 9th. Would you believe the blighter blubbed through the Elvira Madigan movement of Mozart's Piano Concerto No. 21. It must be his Isan upbringing. Those simple souls don't hide their feelings. As for his naivety, I'm rather sceptical. On the other hand, he's secretive. That's for sure. I wonder what secrets he's hiding from us. Then again he could be a bally bounder when visiting some country houses. When he made the first visit to your manor house, did he dash here and there inspecting your rooms, pictures and furniture?"

· "Yes. As a matter of fact, he did. I thought it was an Oriental way of showing interest in the place, paying compliments to the host."

5

"My dear Charles, no decent human being, Oriental or Occidental, would have done that. But, leave it to our little clod. The blighter did just that at Crest Castle. Lord Bewly had to follow him into a State Bedroom and pin him down."

"At my place, I followed him too."

"Did you pin him down?"

"No."

"Did he pinch anything?"

"No. All he did was shaking his head."

"Lord Norbury said the same. Very dashed odd indeed! That's for having been twisted and turned and starved in childhood, I presume. Come to think of it, I actually miss him, my dashed odd but perfectly obedient Isan boy."

"I miss him too."

Though Dani had been ignorant of the two souls' fast bonding in the past-life, he was not totally in the dark in this life. For the sake of grace, Dani purported a surprise.

"You too! Don't tell me that you're one those who went to extraordinary lengths to make him drop his trousers. You know, Charles, our little chap has become my little brother-valet-butler at Hyde Park Square. I hugely enjoyed having him. It was rather handy when entertaining visitors. Talking about visitors, my German brother, Reinhard von Regnitz, is coming tomorrow to stay for a few days. Charles, come to the flat tomorrow at six for drinks. Then we'll totter to the club. Do come. Of course, it goes without saying that David is also invited."

Over luncheon, when DP temporarily ceased talking, CT had a moment to entertain his own thoughts. Now, he was mentally making a comparison between Dani Pi and Little Primo.

Charles Tregonning had been dealing with sultans and princes, who had taken over famous jewellers and prime London properties; and with potentates who came to England in their own jumbo jets with their entourage to occupy several floors at Claridge's. So it was no surprise that he was not concerned with the source of great wealth which the Pilaskulkosols had been accumulating.

Dhani Pilaskulkosol, who had recently been listed by *Fortitude* the 44th richest men in the world, did not bother with the source of his parents' astonishing wealth either. It would not be far wrong to say that he took their rapidly rising riches and awesome power for granted. To him, the transfers made to his bank accounts in the U.K., Switzerland and Liechtenstein were solely the wishes of his parents.

*A gentleman does not bother with balances in bank accounts*, he had expounded in the manner of Oscar Wilde.

When he was called to the Siamese Embassy to sign various documents, some of which involved directorships of companies, share transfers, and title-deeds, he signed them as a matter of course. Furthermore, he was delighted to have an opportunity to see his surrogate father, the Ambassador.

The Very Illustrious Minister Prakarn Pi's instructions were followed promptly by one of the high-ranking diplomats at the Embassy, whether they were concerned with the acquisition of properties or the requirement of Dani's signature.

It was obvious that the senior diplomat had been his father's trusted collaborator for quite some time. But, alas, that admirable man had eventually been apprehended at Heathrow for having 20 kilogrammes of 'Grade A Drug' in his suitcase.

The Embassy had to yield to pressure from the Home Office as well as the Foreign Office to lift diplomatic the immunity so as to enable the British Narcotics Squad to proceed with the case.

Then, at New York's JFK Airport, Dani Pi was refused entry. The rejected visitor could argue as much as he wanted. In the end, he was escorted to the departure lounge, to await the return flight.

# Shocking News

Being informed that his son was refused entry at JFK Airport, Minister Prakarn suffered a stroke and had to be hospitalised.

A few hours later an assassin, disguised as a doctor, entered the intensive care unit. If it had not been for the dirty shoes, suspicion might not have been aroused. One of the security men had proved his worth, making a fast draw, killing the gunman with a single shot.

Meanwhile, in England, the millionaire student believed that the US Immigration had committed a grave mistake. So long as his passport was still valid, the visa obtained from the US Embassy in London, would have validity as well. Besides, he had previously entered the US at JFK Airport before.

*I'll see to it that the Siamese Embassy makes a protest in the strongest terms and demands an official apology from US Immigration,* Dani thought as he entered his flat at St James's Square.

The butler was not at all surprised by the master's early return.

"A glass of champagne, Taylor," Dani demanded in the manner of Algernon Moncrieff in *The Importance of Being Earnest.*

Entering the living room with a glass of champagne on a salver, Taylor mentioned: "The Daily Telegraph pertains to the arrest of a senior diplomat of a certain Embassy. Would you care to read the paper before going through your mail?"

Despite the purported subservience of which Taylor was most capable, the Oxonian sensed that it was a sneer.

"Will that be all, sir?"

"Yes, that will be all."

Dani checked the time, wondering whether to telephone his parents or not but the time difference of seven hours stopped him, thinking that his Papa and Mama would be fast asleep at that hour.

*It can wait*, he decided.

The following day, at 11 o'clock, DP reached the Siamese Embassy and found the place in an uproar. The Deputy Head of the Mission was barking on the telephone: "You cannot lift the diplomatic immunity!"

*O yes they can!* Dani silently responded and decisively left the Embassy, not wishing to waste his time, waiting to air his grievances against US Immigration while the Embassy officials were in such a state that his complaint was nothing in comparison.

When the billionaire entered his residence, Taylor informed him that a team of drug squad men had made a thorough search.

Perhaps the search was brought about by having a lot to do with the Siamese diplomat who was caught red-handed at Heathrow with a suitcase stuffed with heroin.

Then, on the butler's face, the master saw a damning sneer that seemed to say: *We knew it all along that your great wealth is from a tainted source. Now cop it!"*

When the telephone rang, Dani did not wait for Taylor to do his job for the last time prior to terminating his contract.

"Son, come home as soon as you can. Papa is gravely ill," vibrated his Mama's harsh voice which the great distance and her simulated emotion somehow failed to sheathe.

Yes, it would be good for him to leave London for a while.

In Bangkok, he would ask his parents whether they knew of a reason as to why Immigration at that confounded airport had barred him from entering the US.

# Back to the Fold

While on a house tour, Dani Pi paused, looking out of the window.

Below, three black Mercedes were progressing towards the majestic gates.

The lone observer wondered in which car his father sat. All three limousines were absolutely identical.

DP knew that there had been several attempts on his father's life. Hence, stringent precautions were necessary. At all times there was a bodyguard to protect the great man.

As for the heir, the presence of subservient servants irked him. It also vexed him, being watched most of the time. Too often, one or two of the obsequious members of the staff would crawl towards him and grovel.

At one time he entertained an urge to shout: *Dash it! Stand up straight! Don't you have spines? Behave as if you are upright human beings, not slithering reptiles!*

Even though he wanted to transform his thoughts into words, he had not yet been able to express them in fluent Siamese.

Moving to another window to have a better view of the well-drilled procedure of opening the grand gate, Dani watched a troupe of perfectly choreographed security men in action when the limousines approached.

Curiosity caused the visitor to the kingdom to continue the exploration.

He remembered the house in which he was born, a two-storied mansion, a tenth of the size of this imitation of Buckingham Palace. Since his arrival, he had met both parents only once. On that occasion, it was not possible to ask whether they had any idea why he was refused entry into the United States.

It appeared that his parents had ceased to have meals together. Madame Vichitra reigned over in her own quarters in the other wing. To gain access, the heir had to go downstairs to a reception hall and then out to a cloister which was guarded by a team of armed men day and night.

*They must have become extremely paranoid,* young Pi presumed, making his way along the corridor. Coming upon an opened door, he entered the room.

Due to the dimness, he stepped on a woman as she was on all fours, going over the floor with a cloth.

"Dash it! Mops and dusters are useless in this house! The damned thing prefers to slither rather than being on its feet."

With that utterance swirling in the air, he stood stiffly until the damned creature crept out of sight, leaving behind a fusty odour.

Windows had not been opened after the room had been turned into the Ancestors Chamber. This room hoarded ancient cabinets and gilded console tables and commodes containing heirlooms, relics, valuable porcelain, gold ornaments, carved ivories, and priceless jade and innumerable artifacts bequeathed to the Pis by their ancestors.

Against the opposite wall, two sets of intricately inlaid rosewood tables of various sizes and heights were placed from the smallest and lowest in the front to the tallest and biggest at the back. They served as an altar on which antique blue and white urns and bowls and vases were placed along with the pictures of individuals and group photographs of the deceased clan members.

Now the ancestors gazed on their precious descendant, seemingly saying: *Welcome back, darling. These treasures are ours. We worked so hard for them for you.*

Dani took a quick glance at some of the sepia photos, and was alarmingly aware that he was their blood relation, that he was a true-blue Chinese like all of them.

The young Pi recalled that his great-grandfather on his mother's side came from South China, earning his passage on a cargo ship as an unpaid coolie.

Long ago Madame Vichitra had told her son: "Due to sheer hard work and thrift the immigrant who could not speak a word of Siamese quickly became prosperous as opposed to the lazy, fun-loving and spendthrift Siamese counterparts. A lot of them couldn't even count, didn't even know how our weighing machines work!"

She had also repeated some of the ancestor's written words in one of the letters to a brother in China. The late patriarch of the Hungs, whilst alive, had regularly written to his brother as well as remitting funds.

When the grand dame had gone to China to trace her origins, she had found that most of the letters had been kept intact. The letters from Siam revealed fascinating accounts of her ancestor's life and observations on the Siamese. But to translate and publish them, certain comments and references made on the *stupid, lazy and venal* natives might offend some authorities on which the family's business empire relied.

Whether his parents had been keeping bundles of those letters in one of the antique cabinets or not, Dani did not care to look for them.

He made a quick exit to get away from the eyes of the dead to whom he did not feel a sense of belonging. Since 11 years old, he had been closer to his surrogate German father, Helmut von Regnitz, and his German brother, Reinhard, than anybody of the two illustrious houses.

Though he was born a Siamese of Chinese extraction, he did not speak, behave, eat, and look at the world like a Chinese.

For instance, he would neither loudly clear his throat and spit nor loudly slurping noodles and quickly gulp the mouthful down the gullet nor noisily squawk like a gander when talking. On the contrary, he had an absolute distaste for vulgarity and money-grubbing.

He had studied at Oxford, read hundreds of books, acquired and cherished good taste and refinement. Eventually he had rubbed shoulders with many members of titled families of England.

*It must be a ploy to make me leave London for this highly polluted and seething city*, Dani von Regnitz mentally moaned, going downstairs.

He lingered briefly in the hall to look up at the grand marble staircase.

Dani marvelled, touching the balustrade.

*Carrara!*

Then the sensation and the association of ideas transported him in a flash, in his mind, back to London.

In his mind's eye, he was walking towards Marble Arch, with Little Primo by his side on their way to Selfridges.

*Prem Surin! My little brother Primo! Wait till I tell him of the flat in St James's and Wealdshire Park in Sussex!*

The billionaire seemed keen to catch up with the Isan pauper now that the distance between them had been reduced to 300 miles.

Turning round, he observed two sets of huge ebony tables and sturdy armchairs of the same wood, all inlaid with mother of pearl, arranged spaciously in the grand hall. The Londoner shook his head, sneering silently.

With both hands clasped behind him, the charming man regally glided along the forecourt paved with golden bricks and lined with *bonsai* trees.

He went farther, taking the golden driveway towards the fountain. There, he stopped, inspecting a pair of dragons constricting Laocoon.

He paused to look in amazement at the grandiose amalgam of East and West, shaking his handsome head. Then he went on his way to the gigantic gates. There, a team of security men saluted him.

*Reiner would not believe a word about this copy of Buckingham Palace. Absolutely unbelievable!*

However he became tongue-tied in front of the armed men.

It took several seconds to translate *Where is the garage?*

"Rongrodyounai?"

One of the security men used a walkie-talkie to call the Chief of Security.

Marching towards the heir, CoS stopped abruptly, clicking his heels and saluted the young master.

Tannai Dhani tried his best to speak Siamese. Falteringly at first, he managed to eke out foreign words that meant he wanted to inspect the garage.

"Which garage, sir, *tanpor's, tanmae's*, or your own?"

For a moment the heir was nonplussed. A few seconds later he could say that he wished to see them all, and while they were doing the tour, he wished to see *Tanpor's* apartment as well.

Hence, the guided tour began with the CoS leading the way to an underground garage beneath the Grand Hall. The drive dipped towards a large electronically operated steel door in front of which stood to attention an armed guard who smartly clicked his heels and saluted.

Leading the way, the security officer indicated a Jaguar, a Mercedes and a Rolls-Royce.

"These are yours, sir. And your chauffeur is on the ready at any time."

"I want to go out later. But now I want to have a look at my father's cars."

Dani turned and saw four identical Rolls-Royces and four identical Jaguars lined up at the deeper end of the garage.

"Why four of each?"

"Because His Excellency uses three cars at a time, the fourth is in reserve in case of breakdown or maintenance procedures. Then the fifth is extra."

"Who chose which car for my father to…"

"Himself, sir."

"The drivers don't know in advance which car he will get inside," Dani remarked. "Good! Now I want to go inside and look around."

A moment later, the huge steel door at the end of the underground garage opened, and Dani alone entered.

Inside, he met an elderly woman and her younger companion.

Both women performed the *namuskara* greeting, bending their heads low to touch the tips of their cupped hands to show their utmost respect to the son and heir.

The elderly housekeeper led the way up the steps, jingling a bunch of keys in her hand along a marble corridor.

In the Grand Hall, DP eyed the coupled columns with Corinthian capitals.

"Capital! If this pseudo Buckingham Palace has a mock Grand Hall, it should have the Grand Staircase as well."

The spoken thought in a foreign tongue seemed to have frightened the women so that they kept their eyes fixed on the floor.

"I say! There it is!"

The master rushed up the red carpeted marble steps of the first landing. The mock Grand Staircase of the mock Buck House lured him on.

He dashed to the second flight, passing on the left huge portraits of Father and Mother and Himself (instead of the Kings and Queens of England), and up farther to the last flight until he reached a grand doorway.

He was too fast for the housekeeper and her assistant to catch up.

For now they were panting at the second landing.

When Dani turned to look at them, the rotund housekeeper was heaving heavily while the thinner and younger assistant coughed and coughed.

*Catch me, if you can*, the master mused, and opened the gilded door.

For a brief moment, he was happy; it seemed as if he were a child again, playing hide-and-seek back in Europe.

By the time the flustering and coughing women caught up with him, DP was already looking into the second room where a winsome girl was sitting on a pouffe, having her hair curled by an older companion.

The confined concubines were taken by such surprise that their mouths gaped and eyes dilated.

Equally surprised, the billionaire quickly closed the door and turned to face the maids.

"*Kao….kao,*" he tried to produce a question of 'who are they?'

The servants seemed embarrassed.

Some seconds later the housekeeper muttered that one of the two females was a ready woman of *tannaiyai*, the big master, and the other was the masseur kept exclusively to massage His Excellency whenever he wished.

"I want to see my father's bedroom," the son demanded, resuming the air of being *tannainoi*, the junior master.

They obeyed.

Their immediate obedience astounded *tannainoi* for he had forgotten the absolute power of the masters.

Then they bent low to pass him, leading him farther, passing several doors before entering another vast hall.

From the colour of the carpet and the crimson walls, Dani surmised that this was a copy of the State Dining Room of Buck House. He recognized the long mahogany dining table, the chairs, side tables, commodes, large rococo mirrors and splendid portraits of Dukes and Duchesses freighted by Charles Tregonning. But, what really gave true grace and splendour to the room were the four magnificent chandeliers from which the light sparkled and shimmered.

Meanwhile his guides appeared agitated, moving quickly on to the next room, which was supposed to be a copy of one of the drawing rooms of Buck House.

Again, the predominant colour was red -- red carpet, red curtains, red damask upholstered furniture and red walls. However, two huge glittering crystal chandeliers saved the room from being overpowered by red and gilded bronze and plasters.

*Perhaps this is The Red Drawing Room*, he checked his memory of the rooms in Buckingham Palace: *The Blue Drawing Room, The Bow Room, The Carnarvon Room, The Centre Room, The Chinese Room, The Green Drawing Room, The Music Room, The Picture Room, The State Banquet Room, The State Ballroom, The Throne Room, The White Drawing Room.*

But then the servants were awaiting him in the Mighty Master's bedroom.

The chamber failed to please him. Nevertheless, there was a glint of delight in his eyes, seeing the Chippendale table and chairs acquired for the Pilaskulkosols by Charles Tregonning.

*Good old TC!*

# Sins of the Parents

Having inspected his father's bedchamber, Dani lost interest in exploring further.

Concerning the servants, the heir had no mind to be civil. But for the time being he let them lead him along the corridors and down the stairs and out at the entrance of the Grand Hall, where the Chief of Security awaited him.

"I want to see my mother," the lord and master stated.

A Rolls-Royce was chosen to transport the adorable bachelor to one of Siam's tallest office buildings in which Madame Vichitra operated the family's commercial enterprise.

Sitting alone in the back seat, Dani assumed that the man who sat next to the driver was his bodyguard.

*So be it*, he thought. *I'll let them run my life for a while.*

Cars, trucks, buses, vans, pick-ups, taxis, pushcarts, armies of motorcycles jammed the road. It was stop and start. At times, a halt lasted over five minutes.

Indeed, patience should be upheld as a virtue in coping with the infernal traffic congestion. But such a virtue was a radical scarcity in Dani's mind. Soon he began to fidget, averting his eyes from the sight of the crowd moving to and fro in front of drab shop-houses on both sides of the street.

For the first time, he regretted being so far away from Piccadilly.

Everything seemed to collide with his sense of *bon gout*.

Besides, Dani von Regnitz intensely disliked being reminded that, not long ago, those dead blood relatives had been shopkeepers, making money in cluttered and fusty places similar to these roadside shops.

Having parked the limousine in a space reserved for VIPs, the driver emerged to open the door. Then the bodyguard escorted DP into the lift. It took some minutes to reach the 88th floor on which Madame VP presided as the President of The VP Group of 120 Companies (40 of which were in China, 10 in Burma, three in Vietnam and two in Lao).

As Dani entered the reception hall, two security men saluted him. The clicking sound of their heels bounced off the steel and glass.

But the world's 44th richest man was no longer amused.

16

However, he nonchalantly followed the bodyguard to the reception counter and let the man talk on his behalf to Executive Secretary Suprapada Sukesan.

The alluring girl smiled sweetly, seemingly brimming with happiness, having fallen love with him while studying in London.

Would he remember her? No, it did not seem so.

"*Tanmae* is in the meeting."

Charmingly she performed a *namuskara,* saying '*sawasdi ka*' to *tanluke* – the heir apparent, a majority shareholder of all the companies under The VP Group.

So then Siam's loveliest lass led the way to a waiting room.

"Please take a seat. I'll inform the President."

Taking leave, she took the guard away with her.

"Good morning," the other visitor greeted.

Dani's civility could not be extended further than the brief response.

Heinz Gerd Hermann, Vice President – Hotels & Resorts, knew that the young man was the son from the photos he had seen. HGH had also kept a copy of *Fortitude* in which Dhani Pilaskulkosol was listed among the 100 richest men on earth.

Meanwhile DP made it quite obvious that he preferred reading the newspaper rather than conversing. In so doing, his eyes caught a headline on the lower right-hand section of the front page: **Teacher murdered by hired gunmen.**

*The headmaster of Hauykaew School in the northern district of Chiangmai was fatally shot on 15th December in front of the school. He was leading his students and a group of Hauykaew villagers to protest against the hand-over of Hauykaew forest reserve to Mrs. Vichitra Pilaskulkosol.*

*The cold-blooded gunning down of the conservation activist, Nid Chaiwana, was witnessed by the students and the supporters who opposed the lease of the province's dwindling rain forest.*

*The deceased had been working selflessly to preserve the rights of the ordinary people in his province as well as protecting the environmental heritage of the country already so severely damaged by the greed of unscrupulous officials in charge and the incompetence and corruption of those whose duty is to protect it.*

*Before his murder, Mr Nid Chaiwana was subject to harassment and threats from local officials...*

The young billionaire looked rather grim, having discovered that his mother intended to turn a tract of rain forest into the *Switzerland of*

*Siam*, one the grandest development projects, schemed by The VP Group.

When he looked up, Dani's eyed met those of the   European's which seemed to say: *I am absolutely delighted that you have read it.*

Coming out of the conference room, Madame VP waddled into the waiting room.

Being rather short and remarkably rotund, she resembled a female version of Napoleon. Unfortunately the president could not be described as beautiful. Only sycophants would unashamedly do that. Feared, worshiped and much adored, she had also been mocked behind her back in some quarters for being a mobile diamond chest due to her penchant for diamonds.

The grand dame displayed a delightful surprise that her darling should have dropped in on her. But what should she do now? There was Hermann to smack.  Swiftly she solved the awkward situation by inviting both men to the Presidential Office.

By then the news of the visit had spread. As a result, several female executives and top-flight secretaries were busily doing something with the lovely executive secretary as their heartthrob followed his mother into the Grand Hall of Immense Wealth.

The hall was mostly steel and glass with a touch of brass here and there. To impose an awesome subjugating power, it employed its great space, which took half of the whole floor, and enormous size of most things in it, including her square steel desk. The lack of wood, flowers, curtains and upholstery emphasized the steely, impersonal air of the suite.

*Even a big fat European shudders in here*, thought DP, glancing at HGH who seemed to be anticipating an unmitigated verbal abuse for which the pugnacious president was renowned.

Madame V did not mince her words.  No kid gloves. No time for Hermann to sit down on a steel chair, the Chinese shopkeeper's daughter made a swift atrocious attack.

"Sack Karl Wittenberg today! And from now on you must make sure that General Managers and Executives of all our properties don't talk to journalists. No one may divulge information on the take-over. I don't want to see the interviews or comments in the media like that again. But, before you fire him, find out from whom he got the information that VP had an eye on the property in the Golden Triangle, and phone me immediately. Go!"

"Yes, Madame," Heinz affirmed, bowed.

Dani was amazed to see Hermann bow.

The son did not know that *tanmae* had succeeded in belittling and stomping on most men, white men in particular.

"Hermann has gone native," the mother huffed. "He has a Siamese wife, speaks Siamese and eats Siamese food and drinks too much beer. He has no gumption left. I want to replace him with a real German or a spunky Swiss to run the hotel and resort side of the business."

Her sibilant hissing bounced off glass and steel.

Soon the son would be told that 51 per cent of the total assets of the empire had been put under his name.

Conveniently the funds transferred to the son's bank accounts in Switzerland, Liechtenstein and England had been made through several banks in the Far East.

At the time the term *money laundering* had not been spread. Hence, the transactions could be viewed as normal bank transfers. On the other hand the young man's insistence on remaining in England had turned into an advantage when huge sums of cash needed to be stashed away outside Siam. By sheer luck, Dhani Pilaskulkosol, being non-resident, did not have to pay tax on the interest of his vast deposits in bank accounts in Great Britain.

"I was bored stiff being alone in the house, so I had a look around," Dani mentioned. "By the way, I saw two women in one of father's rooms. Who are they?"

"You saw his masseurs. I found them for him. I annually replace the pair. It is easy to find young virgins, beauty without brains. They are all over the country. He doesn't want their brains. In this way I can control him and them. Look at the beauty with brains sitting in front of this office. I don't let your father come near her. I can keep an eye on her while she is working for me."

Dani was aghast, observing that his dear mother could hiss and squawk like a low-class Chinese.

In that awkward situation, he blurted out:

"Have you any inkling why I was refused entry at JFK Airport?"

As if such a question had been expected, the formidable Napoliana phlegmatically responded:

"Some time ago your father and I wanted to go to New York to inspect a five-star property. Our applications for US visa were turned down. No official explanation was to be had from the US Embassy here. So we thought that we had been blacklisted because during the

Japanese occupation of Siam in the Second World War, your father and his clan traded with the Japanese, selling scrap metal and providing women and land to them. On my side, one of your aunts became a mistress of General Nakawaki. We were accused of colluding and profiteering."

"Then why am I blacklisted too?"

"It's our surname, I presume."

At the time, Dani seemed satisfied with the explanation but when he was in the lift on the way down, a question occurred in his mind: *Why could I previously enter the US, but not this year?*

# More Sins

Despite the presence of the driver, who had been known to the security officers at the gates, gaining access to the minister was tiresome. When Dani stepped out of the car, he had to go through another clearing post, as if another attempt on Minister Prakarn's life would be imminently from his own son.

"Just take me to him!" Dani growled.

The vehemence seemed to have produced the desired result.

An officer obediently led the infuriated visitor to the Grand Ministerial Office. It seemed that the mighty minister and his inner circle had been warned of the irate son's approach. Then the heir saw his father inside the reception room with several henchmen standing by him.

The pear-shaped minister waddled forward to welcome his darling.

Standing next to the elegant Londoner, the stubby powerhouse was aware that he was dwarfed. So then the dwarf, nicknamed *Aitia* (Shorty), vehemently proclaimed:

"Isn't he tall and handsome, higher and handsomer than I!"

Everyone present agreed wholeheartedly.

His Excellency took the surprise visit as an auspicious occasion for he was about to bestow 150,000 acres of *degraded* forests in Isan on a eucalyptus planting company.

"You arrived just as I was going to grant a concession to turn degraded forest reserves into eucalyptus plantations to those gentlemen," stated the proud father and led the charming visitor and the high-ranking minions to the other end of the immense room where four be-suited businessmen and an astute lawyer and a pretty executive secretary were seated at the long table.

Thus the world of bureaucrats and the world of commerce met, with the academic excellence represented by Dani Pi, a graduate of Oxford and the London School of Economics and currently a research fellow at the School of Oriental Studies, acting as an observer.

Now it was the turn of the entrepreneurs to perform the *namuskara* greetings when the professional student was being introduced. The charming man responded likewise, saying at the same time: *Sawasdi krap* as a good Siamese should.

DP did not know that he or one of his companies was launching a large-scale eucalyptus-planting project. The pulp and paper industry required vast tracts of land for the mono-culture plantations. The gigantic pulp mills were built for the ever-expanding VP Group by a Swedish industrial giant, with financial support of 95 million pounds of British tax-payers' money through Britain's bilateral aid agency.

The signing ceremony began as soon as everybody sat down at the table. The contract papers had been at the ready in front of the minister and the firm's Chief Executive Officer. Just then Dani recognized Suprapada Sukesan, Executive Secretary to President of The VP Group.

Suprapada was not there merely to adorn the contract signing ceremony in a manner of an alluring model posing by an automobile at a motor show, but as a well-oiled cog in the mammoth machine that moved forward the multi-billion dollar undertaking.

She made a coy glance at the insouciant son who, if she had whispered in his ear regarding the reward from his father's signature, would think the hyperbole was a joke.

Joke or no joke, the most beautiful girl in Siam was smiling sweetly at one of the world's richest men. If, by pure chance, *Fortitude*'s source had acquired the latest figures which derived from those signatures, Dani's position in the publication's list of the richest men on earth would probably be the 40th in the following year.

When the magnanimous deed was done, all rose to their feet.

With a righteous air, the minister shook hands with the CEO. Everyone present smiled against the blinding flashes from the photographers' cameras. Thus, the businessmen and the corporation lawyer and the executive secretary and the bureaucrats left the scene, leaving the son with the father.

"Well, son, you saw how it was done," said the omnipotent minister. "Aren't you happy now that you're home? We don't know why you like to live in England. The weather and the food are dreadful! Now that you are here, your mother wants you to be her number three."

"Who is number two, then, Papa?"

"Who? Me, of course! By the way, I noticed that you looked at that pretty girl of hers. Your mother wouldn't let me go near her. What a beauty! A beauty with brains is a rare combination. She wouldn't let you have her, either. Don't tell your Mama that I gave away a secret. She has already picked your fiancée. You'll meet your wife-to-be at the welcome-back party your mother and I will give to introduce you to the people who should know you."

"My fiancée?"

Before the perplexed son could have a reply and ask why he had become a *persona non grata* of the US, his father hurriedly made an excuse.

"I must go now, or I'll be late for the cabinet meeting."

# A New Friend

Instead of returning to VP Place, Dani told the chauffeur to head for The Imperial Palace, the flagship of the family-owned hotels. There, the master forbade the bodyguard to follow him into the restaurant.

Having sat at a table by the window that looked onto a well-tended garden and a swimming pool, the billionaire became aware that he did not have his wallet with him. Hence, he asked for the General Manager, but was told that the GM, who had just been sacked, was not available.

"Call Mr Hermann. Say Dr Dhani wants to see him."

When the Vice President - Hotels & Resorts entered The Bordeaux Grill, he warmly greeted the hotel owner.

But DP did not rise to his feet.

"Welcome, Dr Dhani. This is the best grill room in town."

The visitor to the kingdom almost blurted out: *Cut out the crap. I merely want you to sign my bill later.*

"Sit down. I don't have my wallet with me, and your waiters don't know who I am. But I want a bottle of the finest champagne on the wine list. I'll have Foie Gras as a starter, followed by Lobster Mornay. Have you cracked the whip yet? Is the offending Wittenberg still around?"

"Packing in his room this very minute," said the well-seasoned hotelier who, in 25 years as a hotel manager in the kingdom, had worked for many ruthless, arrogant, vulgar and rapacious owners of several hotels before this one.

"Do I get it right? Karl Wittenberg is or was the General Manager of this hotel, and you are the EVP Group of Hotels?"

"Correct, Dr. Dhani."

"How many hotels?"

"Eight for the moment. Very soon the ninth shall be in the bag."

"Is the one in the pipeline in the Golden Triangle?"

"Yes, Dr Dhani."

"The one that got Wittenberg fired."

"That's the one. We've had an eye on it for some time, a very good property, Dr. Dhani. It's by the Mekong River, on the Siamese side, with an enormous potential."

"Then why it's up for grabs?"

"I cannot say."

"For you may have to pack and go with your tail between your legs like Karl Wittenberg. Talking about the unemployed, have you found out why he divulged vital information to the press?"

"He said he did not say anything of the kind. It was all made up by the reporter who then quoted him as having said so. He's too young and inexperienced to cope with nasty journalists from the gutter press."

"Do you think that he has been unfairly treated? Will you vouch for him with Mama to save his job?"

"It's too late for that now."

"I say! Let's cheer the jobless up a little, what? Ask him to join us. There's a good chap. Champagne will do him a world of good. Tell him to stop packing and come."

Having instructed the *Maitre d' Hotel* to telephone KW, HH aired:

"With respect, Dr Dhani, I don't think it's a good idea to see Karl. The President wouldn't be pleased."

"She wouldn't know."

But Hermann was aware that Madame V had her eyes and ears everywhere.

"Do you get along with Karl all right? He hasn't been a thorn in your side, has he?"

"We got on fine. To tell you the truth, I'm sorry to lose him. He managed to keep the bottom-line well in the black."

"Then we shall drink to the black bottom-line."

So they did, when Karl-Michael von Wittenberg joined them.

Compared with Hermann, Wittenberg was much lighter in weight, 20 years younger, had thicker golden hair and deeper blue eyes. One could say that the young European was blessed with good looks as well as rude health.

Indeed K-M had come a long way. Luck came his way when the orphan was adopted by Frau Linda Maria von Wittenberg. She had not only endowed him with a degree of nobility derived from the 'von' in the family name but also the family fortune. But, unfortunately the said fortune seemed to have had its vicissitude later on, causing the adopted one to leave the fatherland in search of adventure as well as new fortune in the Far East.

He ended up in Bangkok as a chef. Though the job was below the dignity of the von Wittenbergs, he took the position as a stepping stone, and omitted the 'von' from the name on his business card.

Seeing that the young hotelier looked lugubrious, the Europeanized Siamese of Chinese extraction cajoled: "Zum Wohl." A moment later, he added: "You look like my German brother, Reinhard *von* Regnitz, who is high up in politics in Germany. Karl, you have a friend here. Heinz brilliantly defended you, and I will support him. I'll see my mother this evening, and I dare say you can unpack your suitcase."

Heinz Hermann smiled his knowing old man's smile, glancing at the young colleague who would be able to sign the bills on the heir's behalf later on.

# The War to Win the People

Meanwhile, in the heart of Isan, the insurgents made an attack at Fungshu Creek Crossing where the track dipped into a shallow stream. Deep in the mud, the jeep revved. At that moment guns were fired. The driver and the passengers did not have a chance to scream.

Emerging from the bushes, the partisans took their time to relish the triumph, for this remote territory was one of their strongholds.

Following that victory, the outlaws preyed on draconian village chiefs, tyrannical thieves and rapacious usurers. The latter had sought protection from the police instead of lessening their greed and strong-arm tactics. Some of these money-grabbers went further to urge an insurgent suppression regiment to take control of the region, claiming that the attacks were assaults from the Communists.

The military reacted swiftly when the headman of Napo and three henchmen were butchered.

The presence of the force in the district promised a sense of security. But, when the troops retreated, the onslaught resumed. Police stations were among the casualties.

At night, fearful inhabitants huddled within their huts. Only at daybreak did they dare to come out into the open.

Early in the morning Pundit Piksu, the learned monk of Napo Monastery, went out for alms along the village lanes. He sensed the emptiness, a void made by the absence of most men. Napo had become a village of the aged and the very young when able men and women had gone away to cities, factories and seaside resorts.

Many men had disappeared without trace.

The sound of laughter became rare.

The warmth from the steamed rice in the begging bowl assured the holy one that the spirit of Napo remained.

On returning to the sanctuary, the little monk took the contents out of the begging bowl, and discovered that a little piece of paper was attached to a boiled egg.

Having detached and unfolded it, the monk read: *Guru Kumjai is alive.*

Toon Tinthaisong (formerly Puthaisong) had given him the boiled egg that morning.

Then the monk recalled Lord Buddha's dictum: *Images, taste, scent and sound should not touch a perfect priest.* Therefore, the elation brought about by the tiny piece of paper must be suppressed. An attempt to keep his head above the flood of feelings had to be made while appearing calm in the company of the old abbot and the village elders congregating in the hall.

After the two monks had finished their breakfast, Singhon Homhaul, the new village chief, cleared his throat and raised his voice for the benefit of the ordained and the lay people.

"From the very first month of my tenure as the headman of Napo, I've been trying to bring electricity to our district. Now we will have it in less than three months."

Singhon paused to observe how the venerable abbot would react to the news, expecting at the same time to receive praise from the audience.

But the old holy man merely said one word which sounded more like a grunt than 'Good!'

"Without electricity, we cannot have television sets, electric rice cookers, refrigerators, electric fans and washing machines," the chief proclaimed.

A septuagenarian, who managed to catch a few exotic words from the chief's declaration, wanted to ask what electric rice cookers and refrigerators and washing machines were like, but he dared not.

Several Napotians had seen a television set when they went to Muang to sell their produce. The buyer had turned it on loudly the day another *coup d'etat* took place.

"And I've more **good news!**" Singhon paused to allow the emphasized words to sink in. "We're going to have a bitumen road to Muang."

Certainly these vital development projects under his authority would boost his power base, but when there was neither sound of delight nor praise, he turned to the abbot who was rinsing his mouth.

Glancing at the submissive, mild-mannered men and meek women, Prem the priest recalled Guru Kumjai's soliloquy: *Changes are inevitable; they can be sudden and brutal at one time or they can steal upon us like thieves in the night at another. I want to prepare you to face the changes in your lives.*

*Yes, changes are unavoidable*, silently confirmed the learned priest. *All is transient. Nothing is permanent.*

Trying to muster the attention of monks and men, the headman resorted to speaking Siamese, the language of the masters, instead of

Lao, the language of the Isan people, in addressing the illiterate peasants:

"Lately, I've sent 30 men from our district to work in the Middle East. Soon they'll come back with a great deal of money. Yes, their pockets will be full of cash when they return. They'll want to have television sets, electric rice cookers, refrigerators, sound equipment, electric fans and a good road, not just a rough track that makes Napo inaccessible in the monsoon season. Some of them will be rich enough to buy vehicles. They won't think of becoming communists then."

The audience tacitly accepted the announcement and later quietly departed, leaving the village chief to confer on some other matters with Abbot Boon.

Despite his long priestly life, the abbot had not ignored worldly affairs.

Money had always been so irresistible a temptation.

Budgets, public funds, grants and foreign aid became irresistible lures. At the mention of 'World Bank loans', 'accelerated development projects', 'regional irrigation schemes', 'dam construction', 'the Green Isan Project' or even the mundane sound of 'road construction and maintenance', Abbot Boon's heart withered with an awareness of graft involved.

*Men and venality go hand in hand,* he believed.

He knew that the previous headman and his collaborators had done extremely well for themselves when the era of 'intensive development projects' dawned on the Isan Region. They were not satisfied with creaming off the funds, taking bribes and kickbacks from the purchases of materials at inflated prices. They had also schemed two projects called *Agro-Aid to Farmers* and *Rice Pledging* to enlist members. Under the schemes, Montree Disakul, Sanan Rakchat and Kriangkrai Chavalitpakdipol, the three henchmen, had zealously collected membership fees. Then they sold fertilizer of inferior quality or in some cases fake stuff to members at an exorbitant price.

As for the Rice Pledging Scheme, members were required to contribute their rice to the recently established Napo Co-operative instead of individually selling their produce to the buyer in town. In this way, the 'co-op' could command higher selling price than the on-going suppressed price. At first the pledge sounded laudable. However, the contributors had not been paid for their rice after a year had passed, causing several farmers, in dire need, to commit suicide to escape debts.

To help him swindle and take as much as possible out of his powerful position, the late chief had trained his henchmen in the art of rapacity. These were his exact words at the beginning of the training: *In whatever you do, be sure there is a perfect fit, no loose ends, that all is clear. Have them come to meet you and write the amounts on paper. Don't go and say: For this 10,000 and for that 20,000 and for those 30,000...*

Using Kriangkrai as a front, an agency had been established to round up workers from Napo and other villages to labour overseas. The chief could have seen that the business was a gold mine when each aspiring applicant had to pay a fee of 100,000 baht up front even before they could obtain their passports. This was so huge a sum that most of the job seekers, using land title-deeds as collateral, had to borrow money from loan sharks at 10 per cent per month. Then after half a year had gone by, the headman had claimed that the agency in the Celestial City took the money and did not produce the passports, the air tickets and the jobs.

Kiang Surin and Tongdum Tinthaisong (Toon's husband) were among the cheated men who had lost not only their paddy-fields but also their livelihood. As a result, the destitute men disappeared one night to join Kumjai and the band of *K-Force* fighters in Srisurachwood.

A few months later, when the outlaws were ransacking the headman's house, Tongdum roared: "Wait! Don't kill him yet! He's for me! The chief's head is for me!"

Kiang stepped aside. Tongdum pierced the wicked man's heart not once but several times with a vengeful cry: "For Father Sa's life! My knife for their bullets!" before the head would be severed.

"I hope you haven't forgotten why and how your predecessor and his jackals were murdered," said the abbot to the successor, who was on his way to become Mr. Ten Percent.

"I knew who did it. I've given their names to the Insurgency Suppression Unit."

Despite half a century spent in the priesthood, the abbot was quite capable of sarcasm.

"How clever you are! Have you anything else to say to me?"

"Oh yes, Your Venerable. This evening a military propaganda unit will hold an exhibition and show films. Perhaps the temple ground would suit the purpose, if you'd give permission."

"I don't like any kind of propaganda or entertainment here, but if I say no to you, you'll hold it against me and put my name down in your little black book as being anti-government or as a communist sympathizer. I'll have to say yes."

The steaming cup of tea soothed the disciple of Lord Buddha.

When all left, the abbot felt a relief, but peace might not last long, for he would have to contend with the deafening sound, blasting from loudspeakers.

In late afternoon, men in fatigues and armed with war weapons were seen installing a huge screen and rows of large display boards.

Meanwhile a white van crept along village lanes, turning on at full blast its public address system to tell the wary dwellers of the coming event.

"Highly respected fathers and mothers, most beloved uncles and aunts, dearest brethren, we are pleased to have an opportunity to come to Napo. We hope all of you will show your support and your love for the king and the country by attending the exhibition and the film show at seven o'clock this evening at Napo Monastery. Seven o'clock this evening, at the monastery, altogether, most revered fathers and mothers and most beloved brethren."

A patriotic song punctuated the announcement at regular intervals.

A group of squatting Napotians under a rain tree followed the vehicle with their eyes.

After the cacophony was lessened by the distance, one of them said:

"Isn't it nice to be their most beloved brethren? When I was in the City of Angels last summer, one of the angelic people shouted 'idiot' at me from inside his car. Mind you, I took care crossing the street, but all of a sudden I heard a frightful screeching so close to me. A car nearly hit me. It stopped only a few inches from me and scared the hell out of me."

"Cars do have priority over pedestrians. Only rich people have cars, and money is power. If you had been hit by that car, you'd have died like a run-over dog in the middle of the road," a wiser peasant claimed.

"While working at a silo on a river bank, I was called Stupid," another yokel contributed.

"You must be very stupid to work as a coolie all day for almost nothing!" said a former factory hand who had been called Cretin by his foreman.

"They called me *Kika* (Shitty Slave)," confessed another man.

"Now it's fantastic to be their most revered and dearest, isn't it? If I had been their most beloved when I was a slave in a soft toy factory a few years ago, I'd never have quit the job," piped one of the women.

She did not know how lucky she was to be alive, when 188 of her co-workers, mostly women, had been burnt to death, and over 400 slaves were injured during a fire that razed the factory to the ground a day after her departure.

The group ceased conversing when the same vehicle returned, blasting them again, but this time with the national anthem. Hence, they rose to their feet for they had been ordered by the village chief to do so every time they heard it.

In total obedience, they stood ramrod.

At Napo Monastery, adults and children alike crowded around the display boards, looking at propaganda materials. These were posters depicting the atrocities of the Communist take-over in Cambodia. They were more or less the same display seen time and again every time the propaganda unit came to Napo.

But then one could always gawp in awe at the pictures of the fleeing refugees, of the piles of skulls and bones, at the images of the destruction of houses and of the horrible death and at photographs of landlords, merchants, middlemen, and money lenders being publicly executed.

At seven o'clock, the speeches on the importance of unity and love for the king and the country commenced.

In his room, Prem the priest endured the ear-splitting sound from the loudspeakers, blasting out messages of conflicts between the rich and the poor, the masters and the oppressed, the exploiters and the exploited, and of the left and the right.

Due to Kiang's disappearance and the loss of the paddy-fields as well as the land on which Kiang's house stood, Poon and her children had come to live with the Surins.

No one wished to talk of these happenings for fear that the young monk would want to disrobe and take on duties and heavy tasks at home and in the paddies. Simple as they were, they could guess that he would be safe, clothed in a yellow robe, residing in the sanctuary.

Piang and Poon, the two women without their men, toiled unabatedly while Grandpa Kum had been bedridden with a recurring illness. Grandma Boonliang, who had become bent, wizened and wobblier than before, was coping with an increased number of grandchildren. She accepted the predicament with her great capacity to care and to endure.

Without complaint, the grandmother tended to the sick and the young.

Bae Charoenpol, Piang's husband, had gone to the Middle East. Hopefully he would return in a few years with his pockets full of money, as Chief Singhon had proclaimed.

Pundit Piksu often thought of disrobing in order to return to the world of men, to toil on the land as well as taking care of the old and the ailing. On top of that he wished to take on the role of the surrogate father to his nephews and nieces so that they would have proper food.

But then he was concerned with the question of how the nonagenarian could keep the monastery going on his own without a younger monk to help him. There was not a single young man in sight to be ordained.

In the midst of his thoughts, the little monastery boy came into the room and knelt.

"The *falang*, who came with the military propaganda unit, wants to see you, Venerable Brother."

The monk sat silently as if he did not hear, while the boy retreated.

A moment later the visitor knocked and entered.

Despite his enormous physique, the brown-haired, hazel-eyed American did not seem awkward to sit deferentially on the wooden floor just like a native in the presence of the ordained. The *advisor*, who had turned 40 whilst on the road, wore a dark blue short-sleeved shirt and black trousers. Big-boned and handsome, the CIA agent reminded the priest of a German policeman who escorted him to be interrogated in Munich.

The learned monk's heart suffered a quick, sharp pang, while the images of Helmut von Regnitz and Wilhelm Hagenbach loomed.

For a moment the little monk forgot that he was a Buddhist priest, allowing a certain longing to pry into his mind.

*If only I had a decent height and a stalwart body like Welhelm's or similar to this good-looking American's... If I had not been raised in dire need, not having to struggle so hard to survive, not having been mentally maimed and abused ... If only I had been born an American or a European and developed my mind to the full ...*

Why must he be reminded of European values and well-developed minds at such an awkward moment? He had already shorn his head and put on a yellow robe to turn his back on the world of procreation and artistic creativity. He had burnt his European clothes, the notebooks of poems and *The Monsoon People*.

*Yet this longing of mine assail me time and again.*

Pundit Piksu realised that Napo was not remote enough.

He had believed that in an insignificant monastery of a forgotten hamlet in impoverished Isan, he was beyond reach.

*How wrong one could be!*

For now an enormous American was sitting in front of him.

"I was told that you have been to Europe."

"I went as a hopeful student but returned as a degenerated drop-out because the learning in England was not based on rote learning as in Siam. I failed miserably, and became a hippy."

"You certainly have what the British call a *posh* accent."

*If you had known the British well, you'd have said 'la-di-da'.*

Instead the monk mentioned:

"That's from having been forced by my flatmate to speak with stiff upper lip and listen daily to audio memoir of Lord Cuthry. Lord Cuthry is an old Etonian. You've heard of Eton College, I'm sure."

*Danny von Regnitz pressed me daily to mimic the accent of the aristocrats, and be familiar with their idiosyncrasies. 'What?" not 'Beg your pardon'... 'luncheon' not 'lunch'... 'rich' rather than 'wealthy'; in speaking, 'yes' not 'yeah' ...'bottle' not 'bo-el' ... 'here' ...not 'ear' ... 'house' not 'ouse' ... 'later' not lay-er'... is it not? not innit? And never utter 'Oi!' or 'Cor!' or 'Blimey!' He made me go to The Berkeley's Blue Bar where I must talk with a fellow drinker there. He convinced me that I'd gain confidence and poise as well as putting into practice my newly acquired Etonian accent. That was where I met Lord Bewly for the first time. Of course, the tryst was pre-arranged without my knowledge. I must admit that His Lordship played his part so well.*

*Yes, it was a nasty trick to make me walk into the trap. There, in the opulent hotel, His Lordship instantly took the peasantry out of me as I stammered and quivered, unable to switch on Lord Cuthry's accent.*

*It was indeed Dani's nastiest prank.*

*Yet I continued mimicking the accent. To what end, I had no idea at the time, but only to be silent, fearful and in hiding, in a Buddhist sanctuary now.*

Fred Schultz Anselm had obviously been briefed on Siamese etiquette, sitting like a polite Siamese layman, showing respect in conversing with a Buddhist priest. Obviously he was pleased to find, in a troublesome spot in Isan, a monk with whom he could speak with the fluency of his own tongue.

Pundit Piksu resumed a monkish demeanour, reminding himself not to argue in the manner of the laymen when the subject of insurgency was raised.

"Would you believe that 30 per cent of the villagers in these parts have become communists and 50 per cent their sympathizers?"

The monk did not appear alarmed. He calmly replied:

"To me, they're my people. I know most of them well."

*Has the CIA gathered the information that Kiang is my brother?*

"Communists are against religion," FSA kept up the subject. "You won't be able to remain a monk a day longer under the communists."

"It won't come to that. A straggling band of poorly-armed peasants cannot defeat the mighty Siamese military forces and those of the Americans. I speak of what I know locally, of course."

"With respect, Honourable Brother, you should have known what have happened in Vietnam, Cambodia and Laos."

*My dear fellow*, the priest itched to say, *the original spelling is L-a-o.*

But the confrontation called for solemnity, not flamboyance; therefore, the erudite priest adhered to the severity of tone.

"I know. But, obviously we could barely behave like the Vietnamese. First of all, Siam has never been colonized. The Siamese harbour no hatred for the colonial powers like the Vietnamese do. Here, the outlaws and the survivors of the October 6th massacre don't fight to win. However, they fight on *for vengeance is theirs*. Also they don't want the powerful thieves, the eminent crooks, the invincible murderers, the exceedingly venal politicians and bureaucrats, the terrible tyrants to get away with their exploits, with murders, bribery, kickback-grabbing, vote-buying, asset-hiding, money laundering and drug trafficking all the time. As for you, it's perfectly clear that you haven't learned anything from your defeat in Vietnam and from supporting the dictators, the tyrants and the most corrupt. You go on supporting them as long as they claim to oppose socialism and uphold capitalism regardless of how corrupt and tyrannical they can be. You were defeated in Vietnam in spite of the loss of over 60,000 American lives and the death of millions of Vietnamese, Cambodians and Lao people, at the cost of billions of dollars. And yet it seems you haven't learned your lesson and become wiser. Even today innumerable survivors in these war-torn countries are still being killed or maimed by land mines. They continue to suffer from blanket bombings, napalm bombs, contamination derived from exploded and unexploded bombs as well as the so-called 'agent orange', the defoliant chemicals that cause health havoc for generations to come. You seem to have convinced yourself, the world's police force, the defender of capitalism, that the bombings and the killings were just. I don't have to be a clairvoyant to see that more wars will be waged on new grounds and against new enemies. The atrocities created by both sides will not dissipate into thin air. They will bounce back at all perpetrators. It's the force of karma, my good man. But for you, the talk of *karma* may sound absurd. As a Christian you may appreciate that *as a man sows, so shall he reap*. It's the same thing. I may live to regret saying this but you've sowed a hell of a lot of missiles and bombs over many countries, not heeding the force of karma. What we sow will catch up with us even within our lifetime. Some non-Buddhist fanatics, or I should say *extremists,* may not take your missiles and your bombs and bullets lying down as most good Buddhists do. The more the warriors sow missiles and bombs and bullets, the faster they bring Nostradamus' predictions to reality. Now, at this very moment, I can hear a voice warning me to speak compassionately or not at all. Being concerned with your safety and the lives of millions of innocent bystanders, Americans as well as their 'enemies', who shall suffer abominably though they have no part in the atrocities, I must speak. Stop bombing, killing, passing on the violence! Are you aware of what Nostradamus foresaw?"

Despite his effort to sound compassionate, the age-old sentiment, which had lain deep in the heart, had thus emerged. The disciple of Lord Buddha could see, in his mind's eye, the rearing fiery head that should have been rid in the earliest phase of priesthood so as to make the ordination pure and holy.

Hence, he must lose no time in subsiding it.

*I've failed as a compassionate follower of the Enlightened One,* Pundit Piksu realised. *I have failed utterly.*

"Nostradamus, my…" *Foot* was on the tip of Fred's tongue, but then he was aware that he was addressing a priest. "In this day and age, you shouldn't believe in silly seers or grasping fortune-tellers. We Americans are so great that there is no one who can make a tiny dent in our pride. But would your people, who claim to be Buddhists, cease to commit further atrocities or bad *karma* and be compassionate enough to lay down their arms to be pardoned and so come back to society? You might have heard that the military has announced an amnesty campaign. If the insurgents surrender and lay down their weapons, they'll be pardoned. They can return to their homes."

"Unconditionally?"

"There are certain conditions, of course. For example, they must not be politically active for the rest of their lives."

At that point one of the armed military personnel with a walkie-talkie came to take the American away.

After the visitors had gone, the monk spread a rush mat on the floor and then set up a mosquito net. At that moment a piece of paper landed on the floor. He went for it, and having closed the door, he read:

*Venerable Brother,*

*I have much to tell you, but hardly know where to begin. The last time we saw each other was when I went to Wat Borombopit before taking to Srisurachwood. Please forgive me for not having properly explained my action.*

*I escaped in order to save my life but then I got involved with a Chinese splinter group of bandits, the Chin Haws, who fled from the battle at Kaoko in Petchaboon. After the October 6th massacre of thousands of students at Dhamasart University and in the streets of Kroongtep, a number of survivors joined us. As we moved around the countryside, there have been frequent clashes with the police force and insurgent suppression units, but we have advantage over our enemies due to our knowledge of the terrain and we could often inflict heavy casualties on the military forces.*

*Often, we run out of food supplies. Once we fell into a trap in a Nadhone village where we went in to collect food and medicine. During the fighting, one of our men fell next to me, and I quickly put my ID card in the dead man's pocket so that those who wished me dead would be satisfied. Only later I realised the effect the news would have on our people. For one, the Venerable Brother Sungwian whom you served, disrobed and came to join us. He is with us still, despite the fact that I am still alive. You might not know that he and I were born in the same village and became 'siaw', bonded with a vow of brotherhood.*

*It is best for you that I should not discuss here my ideology so that you are free to choose your own kind of struggle. But whatever you want to do, don't do it now. Stay safe as a monk in the monastery. Please believe me and do as I ask at any cost until it is safe to leave the sanctuary.*

*My friend Sungwian took this course because we are bonded by the vow of fellowship. You and I have a bond too, but with your intelligence, you'll know what to do. There are many kinds of struggle. As for me I have no choice except to choose armed struggle. Your brother, Kiang, and Toon's husband, Tongdum, and several Napotians including Panya Palaraksa, the village's versatile musician, joined us out of sheer necessity to survive as free men. Kiang and Tongdum have their bitterness and hatred. I don't know about Panya. Do you remember Panya? You took first place and he came second then Toon third in your final year at The Napo Primary School.*

*It still amazes me how musical he is. He can put a leaf between his lips and make a delightful sound to soothe us in the depths of Srisurachwood when we feel so weary.*

*I have intentionally kept your name and our relationship out of every liaison so that you shall not be linked and get involved and punished. I want you to know this. Please do not react impulsively to this letter out of gratitude. Your reaction will bring danger not only to yourself but also to your family members who are still in the village. You're not in England where you may walk freely no matter what your political beliefs, ideologies and orientations are.*

*Once, when we stopped in a place after a trek through the forest, I told Kiang, Tongdum and Panya what I truly believe in, and I am pleased to say that they have changed a great deal from when they first set out to take their revenge.*

*Among us, Panya seems to be the only one who can occasionally laugh. If he had been allowed, he would have made a flute from bamboo and enchanted the woods with music.*

*Destroy this letter as soon as you have read it, so that it will not cause any harm to yourself and to others. I long for the day I can walk into Napo and teach again.*

# A Terrible Beauty

Having extinguished the candle, the monk went inside the mosquito net and lay on his back.

*I shall follow Guru Kumjai's advice,* he determined. Then the image of the CIA agent entered his mind.

*It is indeed amazing to have a visitor from another continent in this austere room. It is not only the American's charm that had drawn me out of the enclosure of my mind but also a need to speak in the manner of an educated European.*

Images of Dani, Reiner and the late Helmut loomed, arguing with sheer conviction over a political issue in their Bavarian house in Heeringen.

*But, being pugnacious, contentious and aggressive is not me.*

Against the hum of insects, the world of Dani Pi; the world of the intellect; the world of Lord Bewly, Lord Norbury and Charles Tregonning, the world of nobility, art, fashion, fine dining and sophistication; the world of Wilhelm Hagenbach, the musical world of Europe, seemed to revolve around him.

Now the fretful priest felt a sharp pang in the heart, thinking of the famous conductor-composer-singer. He sighed, reflecting on the ruse used to have *An Isan Lad* turned into a song.

As opposed to the Hagenbach involvement, the bonding with Elizabeth Durham was not only pleasurable but also the happy reunion of souls, for she was the 'white-haired woman' seer Tatip Henkai foresaw in a trance.

During the prime of their present life, the two soul mates had been driven by unbridled sexuality, which was fashionable at the time.

Thinking of Elizabeth, the priest sensed alarmingly a lusty growth in the groin. After a frugal period of priesthood and the strict observation of the 227 tenets, lust had not been quenched! At a thought of his old love, he had unwittingly aroused a desire and thus caused an erectile tension which must be emasculated without ejaculation.

The monk resorted to meditation.

Next morning, after breakfast, he left the sanctuary to visit his ailing father.

Napo looked deserted.

Chinaman Ching's shop remained closed since the gruesome murder of the previous headman and his henchmen.

The wary shopkeeper and his family feared the bandits for being much richer than most inhabitants. Indeed, old Ching had been hoarding cash, gold ornaments and a collection of antique Khmer pottery and silverware and sacred images which desperate farmers severely hit by hard times, had pawned.

In the family hut, Pundit Piksu found that Toon Tinthaisong was there, sitting silently holding her youngest child near Sister Piang.

Poon, Kiang's wife, had been weeping but now the priest's presence put a stop to her tears.

Lying on a home-made kapok mattress, Kum, the ailing patriarch, turned his haggard face towards his son while Bae Charoenpol's children and Kiang Surin's boys and girls sat timidly together in a corner.

The sick tried to free a few words from his parched throat, heaving and coughing.

Mopping her husband's quivering lips and chin with a piece of cloth, Boonliang moaned.

"If I could take your pain into me to make you well again I would, old man."

For a while no one spoke.

Later, in the poignant silence, Piang asked her brother:

"Have you heard that the propaganda people have been killed?"

"Killed? The American too?"

"Yes, all!" Toon cried.

Her dilated eyes glared with the tragic flames of her sorrow.

Glancing at Toon, Pundit Piksu saw that his childhood friend had changed immeasurably.

Now Mrs Tinthaisong, a malnourished mother of a horde of skinny children in rags, looked weary and forlorn, living in fear of the masters, the army and the police force.

"They were ambushed at Fungshu Creek Crossing," Piang explained.

'So near to Napo," the priest deplored.

"I'm afraid the killing will be in the village next!" Toon proclaimed. "Having short-changed us, cheated us with his weighing machine and beating us down when he buys from us, and for so high a price when he sells, Jek Ching is living in fear of an attack. If he had been honest, less mean and not so greedy, he would still be able to open the shop. One day old Ching will have his comeuppance!"

(Indeed, the Chinese clan did suffer from the karma, clashing head on with TESCO when the British chain of stores opened its TESCO *Express* in Napo, in May 2013, causing the slow, painful end to the Ching Dynasty.)

Presently the priest perceived much bitterness and sorrow in Toon's heart.

*Poor woman…she does not know that for hundreds of years peasants all over Siam have never had any bargaining power, and she is not going to be the first to have it.*

Meanwhile, Poon Surin wept once more.

Unknown to the monk, Kiang and Tongdum had entered the village. And Panya, hiding in the bamboo grove, had waited for the right moment to jet Kumjai's letter.

Panya, the reluctant guerrilla, had whistled softly, walking away from the monastery.

"Bae sent a draft of 500 US dollars," Piang was saying. When we could cash it at a bank in Muang, we'd take Father to the hospital. Here is his letter. Toon has just read it."

Pundit Piksu heard the fluttering wings of change when his sister uttered a foreign word. It sounded peculiar being spoken by his kin who had hardly ventured far from Napo.

As for Toon, her hope of having bank drafts in US dollars had dissipated into thin air after her husband had been robbed of the chance to earn high wages overseas.

Having been swindled, the Tinthaisongs lost the farm to the moneylender. However, like most landless peasants, they could survive as casual labourers, working on the rice fields of other farmers.

But that was not to be.

For one day an informer saw Toon's man talk with a leftist recruiter. Hence, it was assumed that Tongdum had become a Communist.

Chief Chid and his gang had stormed Toon's home early one morning and killed her father who, in his drunken state, raised his hand to strike the intruders. The murderers would have shot her and perhaps her children too, had she remained inside the hut, unseen by neighbours.

Outside, while her children were clinging to her, she had been pleading for mercy.

A single shot had shattered the old man's skull.

Having discovered a collection of books, which were Kumjai's gifts to one of his prizewinning students, together with Kumjai's own, being kept for his return, the headman believed that he had discovered an archive of communist propaganda.

If Tongdum had not escaped, they would have killed him on the spot. While repairing a chicken coop, he saw a band of armed men, led by the village chief, coming from afar. Instinctively the man had foreseen danger. Hence, he had crawled among the mulberry bushes and fled.

*But my husband should not have taken the headman's life,* Toon bemoaned in silence, *for karma will eventually catch up with my father's murderers.*

*What an awful deed Tongdum and Kiang have done! They have picked up knives and guns to avenge my father who, for merely lifting his hand, had his face blasted point-blank by the man who had paid the people to vote for him. He, who has spent so much money to buy votes, would want much more in return. After having been in power, Chief Chid not only preyed on the inhabitants, but also learned so quickly how to use his powerful position for personal gain*

*But Tongdum and his friends should not have murdered the vile man and his henchmen. For now the law of men will overtake the force of karma. Tongdum, Kiang, Panya, and the rest of the outlaws will be hunted and killed. I may never see my husband again.*

Then Toon wept.

Meanwhile the little monastery boy arrived. Remaining outside the hut, Luke-nam said:

"Venerable Brother, sir, the abbot wants you to go with Chief Singhon to bless the dead at Fungshu Creek Crossing. He's waiting for you at the monastery."

Bracing himself to face the scene of carnage, the monk led the boy back to the sanctuary.

# The Lure of Money

Piang Charoenpol remembered vividly the day her husband left to labour for Rock Moving Company, contracted to lay pipelines across a desert to a port at Yanbu.

She had been hugely amused, looking at him trying on a pair of shoes. Bae's splay feet would not easily yield to the tight-fitting mock leather.

Prior to leaving Napo for the Middle East, Bae had gone to the monastery to bid farewell to his brother-in-law. Prem the priest had wondered how such a simple, illiterate tiller of the earth could cope with the formalities and complexities of international travel.

But the lure of money had been irresistible.

So then the learned monk could expect that soon age-old huts would be dismantled, giving way to new houses of brick and mortar.

At that instant Chief Singhon's proclamation had resonated: 'Electricity, television sets, refrigerators, washing machines, electric rice cookers, electric fans and a tar-sealed road!"

*The man did not say a word about rebuilding The Napo Primary School. Not a word.*

When the hopeful wayfarer had taken leave, Pundit Piksu left the precinct to observe the truck taking the 'successful applicants' away.

After the vehicle had left, the monk moved towards the edge of the village where a team of workers had been erecting a tall concrete pole. There, without being told, the lone observer had understood that shortly electricity would reach this outpost. What he had not known was that a few kilometres away another group of men, using tractors and other heavy machines, had already been at work to provide Napo with a bitumen road to Muang.

That was some months ago.

Now Piang read Bae's letter for the third time.

*C/o Rock Moving Co.*
*P.O. Box 1977*
*Riyadh*
*Saudi Arabia*

*My dearest Piang,*

*In Muang we waited at the branch office of the Agency for more recruits from other villages. Eventually they arrived, truck by truck. Then one of the Masters put us into a ten-wheeler. I was not sure whether I was actually leaving even though the thing was speeding so fast on the highway. We travelled through the night and arrived in the capital early in the morning.*

*At the Agency's big office we were given many papers to sign. Then we were allowed to rest in a back room. All of us sat or slept on the floor, almost on top of each other. We spent the night there. I am sure all of the men, like me, have wives and children at home.*

*It is for money that we left our loved ones behind, and for a better life when we return.*

*Some of the men in our group could not read or write. They had their fingerprints taken. But they have muscles and the will to work.*

*We were taken to the airport the following day. There, in a huge hall full of people, we appeared as if we were a herd of cattle, compared to the rest of mankind. Even then I still could not believe that I would ever have a chance to go up in a flying machine.*

*One of the Masters, who led us to an airline counter, said that we must not move away from the group. Even without his warning, I would not want to walk about for fear of getting lost in such a huge place.*

*I was becoming very nervous. Dapper Siamese, big built foreigners and nice looking women eyed us. My feet have been badly blistered. The shoes are to blame.*

*It seemed so long before we could get into the flying machine. When it took off, the furious sound was mortifying. I became deaf for a while, while it went up and up. Up in the sky, the clouds looked like gigantic cotton wool. Eventually it went up higher than the clouds. I could not see anything below. We seemed to be suspended in the air. The clouds far below were not moving. At times I felt some vibration, but mostly it was smooth and we could get out of our seats to walk about. Now and then good looking young women in uniform came and gave us food and drink. But I could eat very little, feeling absolutely wild in the stomach.*

*At one time I stopped one of these nice looking girls and asked her whether she could tell in which direction we were flying. She looked as if she could not believe her ears that a buffalo could speak, but then she smiled sweetly.*

*Heavens must be a long way above us. Looking out of a window, I saw nothing but empty space. Below, layers of clouds looked as if they were white skins of the earth. After so many hours in the air, the plane landed at sunset.*

*A man met us after we came out of the airport. This man looked exactly like any Siamese but strangely enough he could not speak our tongue. Later I found out that he was a Filipino.*

*A big cool van took us out to a camp.*

*I am now working in a rock-blasting unit, though in my life I have never handled dynamite.*

*In our camp there are a number of men from Isan. We, from the Plain of Napo, are a minority. There are a lot of Filipinos too. Our master is Swedish. He comes to check on us regularly. I was told that his name is Rogay. An Isaner, who had been here long before me, said that Rogay is a good master. He likes the Isan people and he has been to Siam and has an Isan girl friend.*

*Rogay's assistant is called Rosano. Later Rosano had one hand cut off by Saudi authorities because he walked out of a big store with goods he had not paid for. Then Rosano was sent back to Italy. Poor man. A bag of goodies for an arm.*

*There are bunk beds for four men to sleep in a room in our quarters. My room-mates are Kumsing and Noi from Napo and Daeng from Ban Jok. Each of us has a small steel cabinet to keep our belongings. The bedroom is tightly sealed to keep in the cool air that comes out from a humming machine.*

*At the time of writing, we are to rest for a day, our day off. We cannot go anywhere around here in the desert. I can save money to send to you so you can take care of our parents and children.*

*Finally, I pray to all holiness and the goodness of our parents and ancestors to protect you and everyone in our family.*

# A Wandering Monk

Pundit Piksu's trek could be seen as an act of renouncing his abode, a further attempt to detach the self from all possessions whether they were *his* monastery, *his* sleeping quarters or *his* bedding. The priest limited the necessities to a begging bowl, a bottle of drinking water and a *grod,* a large umbrella equipped with an insect screen and a wooden stake.

The wandering monk headed towards Sisurachwood where Kumjai and the band of outlaws had taken control.

After several hours of trekking, he came to a creek, where several women and some of their children were digging the cracked earth, foraging for tiny frogs.

When the diggers were aware of his presence, they fled.

Then the priest followed the fleeing folk.

Later he saw some thatched roofs and vegetation that bordered Soka.

At the edge of the hamlet, the disciple of Lord Buddha had found a suitable spot under a tall native gum tree. There, he staked the *grod* and set it up as a tent.

Then he sat outside in a lotus position, eyes closed.

After a long span, he opened his eyes and beheld two old men sitting a few paces away.

The laymen performed a *namuskara* gesture.

They were blessed by his presence, they said, since the monastery in Soka had been left a ruin after the last monk departed a decade ago.

"A community without a monastery is not a good place to live in. But what can we do? Many families have moved elsewhere and rumours of an impending battle between the troops and the outlaws in these parts make us sleep badly at night. We're most grateful to you to give us a chance to make merit by offering you breakfast tomorrow morning."

Eventually they left him in peace.

That night, he curled round the pole of the tent, listening to the wild.

Early in the morning the two doddery men returned with some rice and a hard-boiled egg.

46

After having consumed the meal, Pundit Piksu bestowed the blessings.

Then one of them asked:

"What place do you intend to reach?"

"I wish to enter Sisurachwood from the direction of Huaysai."

"Don't go into Sisurachwood. We've had so many bad tidings from that way. A number of people have fled from their villages near Sisurach. Their huts have been burned and the dwellers have been killed."

"Surely no harm could come to a monk anywhere."

"Then there won't be anyone to offer you alms, we fear."

They also feared for his life.

The priest eyed them with compassion, seeing their inherent goodness. However, in case there was an informer in Soka, the follower of the Lord wished it to be known that he intended to enter Sisurachwood to make contact with the partisans.

"I, a monk from Napo Monastery, want to talk with the outlaws to convince them to lay down their arms and give themselves up to the authorities."

When they left him, the monk thought: *News will travel quickly ahead of me, and so Kumjai and his men will move forward towards my approach.*

Then he progressed towards the wildwood.

That breakfast could be his last meal for a few days unless there was another village between Soka and the forest.

After a long trek across the wasteland, the wayfarer took to the shade of a gum tree.

The great expanse of the Plain of Nadhone was burnt brown by the summer sun. For centuries nothing grew except some hardy gnarled trees and perennial tussocks, surviving in the poverty of the rainless seasons.

Sitting still, in the lotus position, he saw Guru Kumjai walking from Wa Village, crossing the Plain of Napo, a singular man bearing his dreams which he wanted so much to share with the band of buffalo boys. Now, the little monk could fathom the depths of such loneliness, and enter deeper into his own and the stunted mind and the innocuous soul of a submissive child, taught to learn by rote and to fear the masters and the authorities.

One could hardly blame the teachers whether it was Guru Kumjai or those trained pedagogues at a city school. They were not aware that they had unwittingly allowed themselves to become mind-maiming instruments.

Compared to the mind of a talented European, the priest's remained undeveloped.

His longing for a taller and stronger physique also recurred.

During an unguarded moment, self-pity overwhelmed him, and the images of Wihelm Hagenbach, Lord Norbury, and Charles Tregonning loomed over him, seemingly taunting him with their fully developed bodies and minds.

"Granpa Tatip," the little monk addressed an image of the late seer of Napo. "I know now what you meant when you said I would wince, seeing some tall, good-looking white men. Being made aware of one's losses is certainly a form of retribution."

Towards sunset, he approached a wooded area that had some coconut trees, kapok trees, mango trees and bamboo groves, a sign of a habitable location on the plain. But then he saw the burnt stilts and charred remains of huts and scorched earth.

Sensing the vibes of violence and death, the wanderer stood still, attempting to quench his anger.

Before it would be completely dark, he chose a spot under a seared mango tree to stake the *grod*. From the bag, he produced a tightly rolled cotton yarn that Abbot Boon had given him.

Loosening the roll of the sacred thread, he took three steps and then let go the yarn to the ground, threading it around the tent, forming a perimeter so the string had become a circular shield.

Sitting in the lotus position inside the tent, he calmed himself with slow, steady breathing before chanting the *yatha* mantra to dispense compassion towards the souls of men and women and children who had been killed.

Dawn came silently since the last rooster had perished along with the inhabitants. Inspecting the burnt stumps, the monk guessed that there had been 14 huts. Whoever had atrociously destroyed Yang and slaughtered its people must ensure that nothing remained to tell a tale.

Pity, sorrow and anger rose in his heart once more, but the ordained one held these undesirable sentiments in check and then dismissed them.

Realising that there would not be a living soul to offer him alms, he hurriedly went into the woods.

48

Time passed while a desire for food and water could still be kept at bay. Once in a while he rested under some tall leafy trees. Then he forged ahead, deeper into the forest.

Later he heard a call.

The woods had become forebodingly dense, and his robe had been torn by brambles and briars. His right ankle was bleeding. The slanting sun warned him that darkness was only a short time away.

In the dark, the jungle could turn perilous. So then while there was sunlight he looked for a spot in a glade to stake the *grod*.

Tall trees towered over him. Birds and reptiles watched him as he exerted his strength till the earth yielded. Then he set up the little tent and lowered the insect screen.

Turning round to survey the surroundings, he paused at one point.

A moment later Sisurachwood reverberated a heart-rending cry.

"Buddho! Dhammo! Sanko! Napo!"

The loud call sounded as if the holy man had become incensed by sheer longings.

Then a response came from a long distance away.

Back to the tent, Pundit Piksu decided not to create the invisible sacred shield with the blessed cotton yarn so as to leave himself open to all forces. Thus, the man of the robe sat down, eyes closed.

Peace gently approached and enfolded him and then circled upward into the canopy of nearby trees. He remained absolutely still as if having been turned into a statue.

In the dusk, dark figures of some 20 outlaws appeared. Slowly and cautiously they approached the meditating monk.

When they came closer, the leader sat down a few paces away and performed a *namuskara*. Meanwhile the *K-Force* members crouched, deferentially submitting themselves. Some of them believed that they were witnessing a miracle, seeing a glow surrounding the holy.

When Pundit Piksu opened his eyes, Kumjai spoke.

The partisans tensely followed the conversation.

Some of them marked a few high-sounding words such as 'democracy', 'freedom', 'constitution', 'liberation' and 'ideologies'.

But Panya Palaraksa did not care much for such dialogue. He had been tired of the war game and the life of a fugitive in a malaria-infested forest of Isan. But, hearing his name being called, he became alert.

"Anu, Chanticha, Panya, and the rest of you, do you trust them? Do you think they will let us walk out of Sisurach as if nothing has happened? The fact that we are still alive today is because they allow us to survive for a reason. They can use us as an excuse to log Sisurachwood for timber and wood chips and for land until there is not a bush for us to hide in. They want the logs and the land first, then our lives later. As you can see, they have already had loggers and squatters in at certain parts of Sisurach in the same way they had done to Kaoko, in Petchaboon. If we walk out of the woods now, we'll be walking into a trap!"

Even with his normal eyes the priest perceived that the former teacher had become deeply embittered and totally consumed with hatred. Yet, the holy man hoped that he would be able to convince Kumjai and his supporters to follow him out of Sisurachwood and lay down their arms.

But then the *K-force* contingent disappeared into the darkness.

# The Party

To the party, the Pis invited the Prime Minister, members of the cabinet, generals, bankers, ambassadors and clan members of the richest families in the kingdom.

At the entrance of the Golden Hall of the Imperial Palace Hotel, floral arrangements were such that some on-lookers stood agape at the sight. Inside, the decoration was even more tantalizing.

Furthermore the art of ice carving greatly enhanced the event.

Two huge sculptured ice blocks, each in the form of a writhing dragon, towered over a table, laden with 230 gift-wrapped boxes. In each box, a 23-carat gold coin lay in wait for 230 guests.

One might wonder why 23 had been chosen.

Madame VP's astrologer had prescribed that it was an auspicious figure for her business enterprise. Thus the party in honour of her son and the thank-you party should be held on the 23rd December.

Suprapada Sukesan, Executive Secretary of The VP Group of Companies, manned this most precious table. She performed the *namuskara* welcome saying: *Sawasdi ka choen ka* before presenting the gifts of gold to the in-coming guests.

A pace away from Suprapada, stood the minister and the president of The VP Group and the heir. Farther down the line, the hotel's General Manager observed the Food and Beverage Manager supervise the waiters and waitresses.

Karl-Michael von Wittenberg also glanced at the stage sign that boldly inscribed in red and gold:

**Welcome**
**Dr Dhani Pilaskulkosol**
**&**
**Happy Christmas and Prosperous New Year**

The GM felt relieved to see no mistake in the spelling. But, the fear of disturbances still gnawed at him. However, his anxiety evaporated when he gazed on the much-decorated generals and their be-jewelled wives trooping in.

KW took it as a perk of the job to welcome royalties, international celebrities, statesmen, and billionaires. The throng of diamond-laden dowagers and glittering ladies also gave him much pleasure. This was definitely the finest gathering of divine people from the highest echelons of Siam. No wonder the capital was aptly named the City of Angels. But, why the expatriate community gave it an unlikely name of Bangkok, he had no idea.

When the GM moved closer, Dani said:

"Thank you for organizing the party."

"Thank you, Khun Dhani."

"Where's Heinz?"

"He's sick."

"What? Have a Krug ready for us in your suite. We'll have a quiet drink together when this is over."

"Yes, Khun Dhani."

Then the Prime Minister arrived.

Dozens of cameras flashed. The Golden Hall suddenly became the heavenly hall of blinding flashlights.

To the GM, it was a privilege to be in close contact with the super rich and the most powerful. Thus, he took charge of welcoming the rest of the guests after Minister Prakarn and Madame Vichitra and Dr Dhani had escorted the Prime Minister to the high table.

When all the guests had been seated, Karl zoomed in to say *sawasdi krap* to Suprapada.

"It's time for you to sit down. There's a table reserved for us."

"It's very kind of you. But I'm supposed to work."

At an appropriate time, Madame VP nudged her husband.

The mighty power broker waddled towards the lavishly decorated platform. At the podium, he spoke at length, ending with a request to have his son by his side.

Then Dr Dhani admirably addressed the Prime Minister.

Afterward a gentleman in the audience requested the presence of Madame Vichitra.

The formidable *Napoleona* strutted forward. It was indeed an opportune moment to show off to all at once the sensational diamond necklace that had a 28-carat diamond pendant, said to be, at one time, a treasure of an Arabian palace.

Then, the heir handed her the microphone.

"Please sing a song," another gentleman begged.

At first she fervently made an excuse.

Meanwhile the stage curtain went up, revealing the Bangkok Orchestra performing *Tonight* from *West Side Story*.

"Thank you for your request. This song is for our highly revered and beloved Prime Minister."

Embarrassed, Dani left the stage while his mother and father crooned. At the end of the third song, Madame VP invited the Prime Minister to sing, for he was also an excellent singer.

How mellifluous his voice resonated! How charming he looked in his shiny silk jacket! What a singer! What a Prime Minister! What a party!

When the last course was consumed, well-satisfied diners followed the Prime Minister and his entourage out of the Golden Hall.

Then relations and invited VIPs proceeded to the top floor.

"There's no way out now, Karl," Dani aired. "So, let's meet in the Emperor Suite."

There, the heir observed his mother separating the women from the men.

"The ladies retire to the Empress Suite," Madame V commanded.

Dani resorted to the balcony to get away from the clamouring men surrounding his father, who was presiding over one of the card tables.

Looking at the nocturnal view of the city, the visitor to the kingdom could not register anything for now, in his mind's eye, he saw himself strolling round the statue of King William III in St. James's Square.

*Charles said that in early May in the Square the tulips should be in bloom, that the Queen of the Night variety was his favourite... I do miss the old man and my noble friends...*

Also it was deplorable that he could not be with Reinhard von Regnitz over the festive season.

He had looked forward so much to showing his German brother the newly acquired properties.

"Counting your properties, are you?"

Taken by surprise, Dani scowled at the lawyer.

"I thought you were gloating," said Dr Prawit Witayakul. "Do you know that you own over 10 per cent of Bangkok? See, there, that tower, and that one, and that one. Look over this way, there is another one, and another one by the bridge, there."

At that instant the billionaire recalled having seen this little man with the team of business executives at the signing ceremony in his father's ministerial office.

"I'll invite you to my office when you have your feet firmly on the ground," said the ubiquitous lawyer.

Somehow the effeminacy amused the 44th richest man in the world.

*One does not have to be near him to see that he wears a wig and cosmetics.*

"You look quite different from other Siamese. What are you?"

"I'm not exactly a full-blooded Siamese. In fact I'm a mongrel. My Chinese father studied at the University of Edinburgh, and married a Celtic Jewish American in Scotland. I was born in Scotland. That made me a Chinese-Jewish-American-Scottish Siamese, in that order, if you please. So take me as I come."

"Very droll!"

Dani turned away from the city view to look inside the Suite.

"Must they gamble right away? I thought these admirable leaders would discuss politics, the economy or the well-being of the Siamese people when they are together."

"Ah, you aren't aware that your father has become the ultimate power broker. You don't know the ritual, the sacred rite of passage."

"You speak in riddles."

"The cabinet reshuffle will take place very soon. Mr NM who sits opposite your Papa wants Forestry which has a going rate of 300 million. Mr SK on the left wants Interior, or 'Home Office' to you Anglophile, which will be at 400 million. Mr WA is edging for Transport. At another table, your Papa's PPS, who is a bachelor to watch, is playing on the Eminence's behalf since your dear father cannot be at two tables at the same time. The biggest bidder at PPS Plaek's table is Mr MP, who is vying for Telecommunications, the second biggest is Mr SR who is going for Education. Tonight your dear Papa might make over a billion from both tables. Then another 200 million could be had if TC, the self-proclaimed *good man from Isan*, over there with those bulging bankers, could raise it by midday tomorrow. TC wants Agriculture. At this stage he is a bit short of cash, having spent 100 million in vote buying in the last election. As a result, he has not been invited to sit at any table. Look at him! He is salivating!"

"Are there any ministerial posts that can be given freely to able and deserving members of parliament?"

"One or two. The Foreign Office is not at all in high demand. Hardly any members of parliament want it since it requires policy-making abilities and diplomatic skills, decent or presentable appearances, excellent knowledge of international affairs and most of all a good command of English. Moreover, the position has hardly any opportunities from which one can profit unless appointments of ambassadors could be made lucrative. It's so rare these days that an ambassador could sell an embassy site and get away with it like the sale of the Siamese embassy land and building in Holland. That ambassador only had to change his name."

"And Education?"

"There are plenty. For an example, a stipulation that state schools, colleges and universities are to be provided with computers and software can bring five times more than an initial purchase of only 200 million. Go and ask the contracted supplier, if you don't believe me. Computer suppliers bang their heads, rushing in to be the sole supplier. You know what it takes to have a monopoly. Just look at the people who have control over telecommunications. Public Health can render nearly ten times more than 100 million from just one contract given to the supplier of medicine and medical equipment to state hospitals. Forestry easily bestows on you no less than 300 million to turn a blind eye to illegal logging and granting the so-called *degraded* forests and public land to eucalyptus planting companies and property development firms. Communications can trawl in 100 million just by granting a monopoly to a telecommunications corporation. England has certainly made you dull and unimaginative. In comparison, the British MPs seem whiter than white. They have very few aspects that might land them in jail...sex scandals, taking cash for asking questions in the House, not declaring interest free loans, a leak to the press that one accepted free accommodation and meals at a certain hotel, helping some aliens to obtain British passports, sleeping with prostitutes, the abuse of expense privileges or making excessive fraudulent expense claims. These are nothing in comparison to what goes on in our glorious land."

Just as Dani was enjoying the chat with the lawyer, his mother appeared.

"Ah, there you are, darling. I want you to go to the other side. The ladies are panting to meet you. Excuse us, Dr Prawit."

She speedily took him to the Empress Suite.

Once there, a gaggle of women of various ages surrounded him. At that instant, the adorable bachelor seemed to be oozing with charm, gliding suavely from one grand dame to another, answering smilingly their sweet questions with a noble air.

Eventually his future wife was revealed.

Sopinya Soponsakul appeared glamorously sophisticated, with a subtle hint of sheathed conceit. She was aware that theirs would be a contract marriage, wealth to wealth, and banking to diversified businesses.

At this juncture, Dani surmised that his Mama was watching him for she had hoped that it would be love at first sight. The heir gazed with sheer adoration, when he learnt that the lady was educated at a public school in England.

"As for me, I merely had a peek at Roedean from the road on my way from Seaford to Brighton," Dani declared.

He gave her his full attention and complimentary remarks before moving on to his aunt who had been one of the mistresses of General Nakawaki during the Second World War.

According to rumours, the General had enriched her and her family with immeasurable wealth as well as a collection of precious stones which included emerald and diamond necklaces and the legendary flawless 14 carat blue diamond ring.

Then the heir impulsively disengaged himself from the women.

Without bidding goodbye, he walked away, passing a line of security officers, and then into the lift to the floor on which the GM Suite was at the end of the corridor.

The general manager invited the hotel owner into the living room where Suprapada was imbibing wine that had obviously gone to both her head and heart.

"I say! Isn't that the bubbly I asked you to have ready for us, Karl-Michael?"

"Yes, Khun Dhani. You see, Supa and I were not invited to the private party, so we are consoling ourselves," said the very virile hotelier.

A moment later Suprapada took leave.

"Merry Christmas and Happy New Year!" Dani toasted after the GM handed him a glass of champagne.

Then the telephone rang.

"Merry Christmas to you too, Brown," Wittenberg responded.

Having ended the call, the GM explained:

"It's from one of the butlers in the Empress Suite. Your mother wants you to go back to the party."

"How did she know?"

"She knew and demanded your return, said Brown."

"Who is Brown?"

"Brown, Gregory Brown, is one of the butlers. The other is Timothy Dawson."

"Perhaps I should have moved in and had their daily service instead of living in that dashed ghastly imitation of Buck House, being served by grovelling cretins. I told them not to crawl and grovel in front of me. They must stand up as if they had spines or I'd fire them. Gormless creatures! Any day when the Emperor Suite is not occupied, I'd like to stay and be served by Brown and Dawson for a change."

"It will be my pleasure to arrange that, Khun Dhani."

"I'll leave your suite only when we finish the *champer* and only if you come with me."

Having emptied their glasses, both men left for the Emperor Suite. Once there, the duo met glances from the portfolio bidders who seemed to mistrust the presence of the foreigner in their midst.

"He's all right. He's the general manager of this hotel," the ultimate power broker assured them.

Meanwhile, Dani felt strengthened by the nearness of his new friend. The devine pair joined a group of bankers and a hopeful politician in the round of cognac and cigars.

"Which is Brown and which is Dawson?" Dani asked.

"Brown is the tall, fair, fatherly one."

"Cognac, sir?" Brown inquired.

"I don't like cognac. Do you have a vintage Krug?"

"Yes, sir. Krug 76."

"Good!"

"Very well, sir," said Dawson.

The lawyer, who had been most subdued in the company of heavyweight bankers and members of parliament, moved over to add strength to the gang of two.

"Me too, Dawson," Prawit said and then primly prattled away. "Do you know what Dawson sounds like in Siamese?"

"Pray tell," Dani said humorously.

Before speaking further, the jolly lawyer turned to look at the back of Dawson and sniggered:

"A short willie!"

"Tell Dawson that, and he'd say his is the opposite," the GM revealed.

"How did you know?" Dani perked up.

"I stood next to him in the *pissoir.*"

"Dear me! We'll have to change the subject," prurient Prawit deprecated, covering his chest with the palm of his right hand, pretending to blush.

Then Dawson deferentially presented the desired drink on the silver salver.

But, despite his deprecation, Prawit adhered to the topic of names.

"There was a professor at my old college called Rankin. Do you know what Rankin sounds like in Siamese? It sounds like *raengkin,* which means 'devoured by vultures!'"

Dani looked as if he was going to say in the manner of Queen Victoria: *We are not amused.* However, after scrutinizing the glass of sparkling wine held at eye-level, he said: "Very fine bubbles. Clear pale gold." And after he had tasted it: "A wonderful blend of fruit and vanilla, richly full-bodied with a long, complex and full finish. What would we do without such a superb bubbly?"

DP's comment became a soliloquy when none of the drinkers knew much about the wine.

Later The Honourable Taninsak Chinarongkul, MP (TC for short), the self-proclaimed *good man from Isan,* said that he would expose these well-sheltered bankers to the hard-cored professionals at the Caligula Club.

"Care to come with us, Khun Dhani?" the ingratiating MP inquired.

"Karl?" Dani turned to the GM.

It would be salubrious for the hotel-bound manager to leave the building for a good night out and particularly in the company of the hotel owner.

As for Dani von Regnitz, it was an excellent opportunity to get away from the gambling men and gossipy women, one of whom might, at this very moment, come to take him back to their party.

"Me too!" Prawit readily picked up his handbag.

Then it was a matter of who was to go with whom, and in whose cars.

"Danny and Karl come with me," said Prawit.

Prawit's BMW was the last to depart. In trying to catch up with the Mercedes ahead, it disobeyed the red light and almost hit another car.

"That was close," Karl-Michael remarked from the back seat. "A highly successful lawyer like you should have a chauffeur to do the dirty work."

"I have, but when I go out at night, I don't want my driver to know where I go, with whom, and for how long. It's all right for a hotel general manager to ask his F&B manager to pack caviar, *foie gras*, smoked salmon, lobster terrine, bread and wines to take out and have fun outside the hotel. But he doesn't know that he shares the love nest with a close colleague. Jonas didn't know that either till he found the picnic boxes bearing the name and logo of The Imperial Palace with some leftovers inside in his friend's fridge a day later. How did I know? I always keep tabs on my graduates."

Looking at the front seat passenger, Karl-Michael sounded genuinely concerned when he asked:

"Are you all right, there, Khun Dhani?"

Dani did not bother to answer. He was greatly annoyed by the devilish driving.

"Dash it! Slow down!"

In that instant the car sped past a crashed motorcycle with its wheels still spinning and a body lying a few yards away.

"An accident! Did you see the body lying there?"

"I didn't see. Must have been looking the other way," said the lawyer.

KW kept quiet, surmising that one of the cars ahead of them might have hit the motorcyclist. However, the accident seemed out of his mind when he went inside the Roman villa that boasted gigantic Ionic columns at the front. The advance party had been waiting for the trio at the main bar, where young and attractive waitresses in scanty togas were tending to the requirements of club members.

When the three men were inside, TC led them into a dimly lit lounge where a show was on. As soon as they sat down facing the performers, the good MP from Isan asked a waitress for a bottle of XO cognac.

"Khun Dhani, would you change to cognac or stick to champagne?" TC asked.

"Champagne."

By now, the billionaire did not care whether the sparkling wine was of a first rate brand or not.

"Prawit and Karl?"

"Same," said the lawyer and the GM at the same time.

So while waiting for their drinks, the newcomers watched the show.

*Well! I'm dashed!* Dani silently swore.

But he viewed them with the interest of a passer-by glancing at dogs coupling in the street. Then he looked disdainfully around at other customers who had paired themselves with female companions in intimate postures and covert activities.

It appeared that only his table was left without the service.

Presently the manager showed up, kneeling so as to be lower than the sitting VIPs and close enough to hear the badge numbers of the preferred women being mentioned. It so happened that two out of the chosen numbers had been preoccupied due to choices of earlier clients. That hardly posed any problems since there were over 100 numbers available.

Karl-Michael did not have to choose for now No. 99 zoomed in on him. She knew that the foreigner was not a member or a regular who might have a particular badge number in mind. She was not disappointed since Karl readily accepted her body as he would accept a cup of tea handed to him in a respectable home.

Dani and Prawit refused to touch the *gifts* given to them. Hence, the rejected presents were returned unopened.

Facing the performers, the Anglophile thought: *How disgusting!*

Instead he sneered:

"How boring!"

"Bring back the girls to entertain my two friends," the high-spirited MP ordered the manager. Then, turning to the hard-to-please guests, he expatiated: "Girls in this club are under twenty and most attractive and willing. Have a blow job while drinking, if you like. But, don't sit there, empty-armed, and say it's boring."

"Come on, Wit. Have a boy. We know you like boys. Plenty of sexy teens here," blabbered one of the obese bankers, nicknamed Sumo Piggy due to the fact that he had the build of a Sumo wrestler and his devotion to grilled piglets.

"I don't want a boy tonight, I've a headache," Prawit giggled.

All, except Dani, laughed.

How matey they felt towards each other now.

That was what TC wanted. The congeniality might ease a loan of 200 million from Krung Siam Bank.

After the chosen females had been with them for half an hour, the good Isan MP declared:

"I prefer the comfort of my own bed rather than the hard seats of this club. Let's take the girls to my place."

Calling for the bill and the fine for taking the ready women out of the premises before closing time, the portfolio-seeking politician acted as if money was no object, as if his speeding car had not hit a motorcyclist.

Soon, the perfect host served cognac and cigars in his penthouse. His Mongolian face brimmed with alcohol enhanced joy now that the pork devourer, Sumo Piggy, lustily-fondled No. 88's oozing breasts. Kinky Duck followed the example set by Sumo Piggy with No. 63, while Oily Indy had No. 12 on his lap to suckle.

Meanwhile KW displayed his prowess in love making.

Dani considered their unashamed foreplay disgusting and so focused his attention on what Prawit was saying:

"Bank of Siam may announce..."

"Screw the Bank of Siam," cried the hedonistic host. "Karl! You first!"

But the very virile K-M did not hear while No. 99 took all his attention.

"Karl! You first!" TC repeated.

KW carried his partner to the master's bedroom, followed by the host and the sex-seeking bankers, arm in arm with their playful dolls.

A moment later Dani heard through the door left ajar:

"Wow! Karl!"

Unable to resist the temptation, DP did a Peeping Tom act.

"Beast!"

Witty tugged at the billionaire, whispering:

"Shall we go?"

# Any Man's Anima

"What exactly is your ambition?" Madame VP vociferated, scowling at the general manager of The Imperial Palace Hotel.

"To make The Imperial Palace one of the top 10 best hotels in the world."

"When?"

"In five years."

Primly taking notes, Suprapada Sukesan had been inured to verbal abuse in the formidable office for so long that she had ceased to mind the growling *Napoleona* with invisible whip in hand.

Most males seemed to quail in front of Madame V, but this European was neither sheepish nor squeamish. Looking the vicious employer in the eye, the charming man confidently reiterated:

"Yes, one of the top 10 best hotels in the world,"

*When it becomes a reality, I'll put 'von' back on my business card,* Karl-Michael Maria von Wittenberg determined.

"You'd have made it in fewer years, if you hadn't spent too much time and energy being a stud. Where was Heinz? I didn't see him at the party."

The grand dame paused, heaving and fuming and foaming at the mouth.

"He had a heart attack."

"Supa, check with Dr Prawit concerning the contract and how much it would cost to get rid of him. And you, Karl, do you think you can handle Heinz's job?"

"Yes!"

"Good! But it wasn't pleasing to see some members of my staff entertaining one another at *my* party when they were supposed to work. You know how much the banquet last night cost per head. You pay for the pretty face you entertained at your table. Off you go!"

On returning to his office, the GM found that Khun Dhani had been awaiting him.

"I say, Karl. After your fantastic performance last night, I came by to see how you are," beamed Dani. "Your secretary rustled up a cup of coffee for me. The waiting room is full of people waiting to see you. Two are auditors from London. The other is an American, a computer consultant. My dear chap, you look so radiant? Are you in love? It wasn't ego-bashing after all, what?"

"Not quite. On the other hand, I may have to move out of here soon."

"Don't tell me she has sacked you again, has she?"

"No, Khun Dhani."

"You mean the 57 Varieties? Your secretary told me that he had a heart attack. It might be a good thing if I make myself useful by going to see him in the hospital as your messenger, bearing a bouquet. She said all you have to do is to sign this get-well card. I'll pop back in the evening at seven, and then we'll have dinner. Sign the card. Good! See you then. Bye."

In a private room of Bramindhira Hospital, the billionaire, who had become a member of the Young Billionaires Club based in the USA, adopted a caring mien, observing bedside manners.

Hermann wondered why he deserved the visit. Nevertheless, he said:

"It is very kind of you, Khun Dhani, to come to see me. I'm sorry to have missed the party."

"You deserve a better hospital than this. I was told that we have our hospital which is nearer to the hotel than this one."

Heinz was touched by the young man's concern and did not doubt the sincerity. But, if possible, he must be safely out of reach of *her* people, doctors and nurses included. Hence, he said:

"There's very little any doctor can do for me unless I have a by-pass operation."

"Then have it, Heinz. You have many years…"

"It would mean a great expense. It would mean going to Germany or Switzerland."

"I'll check with Zurich on this."

The patient sighed, knowing the basic truth.

*Your mother will not allow it* came to his mind.

At that point, Herman changed the subject.

"I heard that the party was a great success."

"Karl-Michael is holding the fort while things are falling on top of him. People are queuing up to see him -- the auditors, the computer consultant, the personnel manager, three hotel guests who had their cash and cheques stolen, and two policemen on the trail of a murder case. I sat in his office for 10 minutes, and they zoomed in while the poor man was being attacked by my mother in her office."

"Yes, I know the usual morning smacking rather well. You also saw me at the receiving end. I think she deliberately does that every morning to prop herself up for the day's work."

"I don't know how you have time for everything. I can see that the same old problems keep cropping up on top of new ones all the time."

"Problems we can cope with. There are problems everywhere, in any office, but it's the supervision after supervision, the follow-up after follow-up that is killing. You can't be sure that the staff would carry out the assignments according to plans and rules and schedules. You must constantly check, supervise, scold to ensure that there is no shoddiness or cheating or stealing. It seems that most of them are children who don't think and wouldn't exert themselves to excel in their work. Their ideal jobs should be 'easy and comfortable and well-paid'. It seems they have never been disciplined; they don't even know what discipline is. Perhaps that is why efficient hotel managers have to be German or Swiss slave-drivers. At the end of the day I get tired of thinking for them, seeing and doing things on their behalf. The only things you don't have to do for most of them are eating and having fun. Of course, some of them use their brains, but unfortunately not for the good of the hotel. There are cases of theft every week. Two English peers, Lord Norbury and Lord Bewly, and a gentleman by the name of Robin Compton had their travellers cheques and cash stolen. The travellers cheques were carefully torn off from every other leaf. As for the cash, the thieves were clever enough not to take the lot. So it took the guests some time to notice that they had been robbed. It took me months to catch the thieves. Then, every single day, one of your uncles came to the hotel, and sat in the lobby for hours. When he is not sitting, he goes round the outlets, ordering the staff to do this and that as if he were their boss. After eating a three-course meal, he refused to pay. Eventually I had to put my foot down. Your mother brought a ton of bricks down on me when she heard of it. Karl believes he could turn The Imperial Palace into one of the world's best hotels in a few years. Good luck to him. Indeed, one of the world's best hotels, with thieves on every floor, in every kitchen, in every outlet and in every department."

"He's a young man in a hurry."

"Lately he has become her pet. I wonder what he has done to turn her round just like that."

"I say, Heinz. Is Karl-Michael bisexual?"

"Well, it is not for me to say. His private life is his own affair. That's how it should be nowadays."

But then the envy of the younger, healthier and handsomer colleague spurred old Heinz who had not heard of Jung's concept of anima. Thus, he spoke plainly from his own point of view.

"But now that you have asked, I'd say he is half a womanizer and the other half is the other way, depending on the person and the situation, I suppose. When Baron Ahren von Kandern und Urach and his entourage are in house, Karl blends in so well with them, rendering personal services so well that you wonder. You'll see it for yourself in a matter of days. Karl has been busy organizing a fancy dress New Year party in such a style that would surpass all other parties organized for the Kandern set. The last one was the talk of the town for months. Can you imagine that a hundred fairies turned up in Louis XVI period costumes, sparkling with diamond tiaras and necklaces and earrings and blond wigs decorated with pearls and glittering gold dust. You'd never see anywhere else but at The Imperial Palace the gathering of gays to pay homage to the Baron. Of course, the hotel makes a great deal of money out of them. All the suites, including The Emperor and The Empress, were booked out for weeks. The income from the food and beverage they consumed in two weeks was more than a five-star hotel in Bangkok can make in a month. And the Baron comes every year to our Divine City of Angels and always to The Imperial Palace."

"Was Karl in the period costume too?"

"Of course! He dressed as Louis XVI to match the Baron, glamorously made up as the queen. I was told that *her* wig alone cost over one million. It would make Elton John burn with envy, I am sure. You should have seen the pair of them among the throng of fairies. The Hall could not pack them all in. Standing room only!"

"Did Mama say anything about this, when our hotel is overrun by gays?"

"No. Not a word while we were raking in the money."

"Talking about Mama, I meant to ask you one thing. That morning when I first met you in the waiting room at her office, you saw me reading a piece of news. Then you looked at me as if you knew something."

Hermann remembered that encounter well. But he would not expatiate. Instead he shifted, turning to look round the room as if to check whether a nurse was quietly standing behind the screen.

Dani noticed the change in Heinz and so said:

"I have the right to know. That schoolteacher was murdered and my mother's name was mentioned, and not a single person would elucidate me."

"Who would dare? I'm merely a slave-driver. I shouldn't be concerned with the socio-economic and political issues of this country. You'll have to find out by yourself."

"How? At least you can tell me how!"

"At the Krungtep Post, I believe back copies are kept in its library. Go there and read back a year or two or talk to the journalists who filed those reports. Some of them seemed daring enough. They dared to put her name in the report, and that is a good start. As for me, I know just by reading the English language newspapers. Occasionally I can link companies, which are owned by or are subsidiaries of The VP Group. Some of them hold functions or meetings in the hotel and demand special discounts. I didn't know that you owned a soft toy factory till the fire razed it to the ground and killed nearly 200 workers and injured more than 400 slaves because of the blocked fire exits and locked doors. On the other hand, two months ago there was a piece of news about the murder of a doctor. He made a campaign against blending melamine with soy sauce and milk, and against mixing antibiotics banned by the EU and formalin and dyestuff with animal feed. The doctor claimed that consumers, who ate meat, fish, prawns and eggs from the animals fed with such feed, could develop cancer. On the other hand, anaemic workers, who relied on their strength to cope with heavy work and long hours, could not possibly last unless they took amphetamine tablets. According to the doctor, a vast majority of labourers, factory workers, farm hands, truck drivers and bus drivers had been on the drug for a long while. The outspoken doctor did not live long. A few days after he went on air, an assassin gunned him down in front of the hospital. Then there is another report on the disappearance without trace of a labour leader who led a strike at one of your factories..."

"How about drug trafficking. Is there any link, any allegation?" Dani interrupted.

"It's not for me to say, Khun Dhani. It's a very serious allegation."

"It's very damaging! I must know why I was not permitted to enter the United States. At the beginning of this month I flew from London to New York, and was refused entry with no apparent reason at all."

"Have you confronted your parents with the question?"

"Yes. But the explanation didn't seem to hold."

"Then I can't help you there. Please don't tell anyone that we talked. Now I'm sorry for what I've just said. I apologize. It's like vomiting all over you, Khun Dhani. I've never spoken to anyone like this before. Then suddenly it all came out. I'm sorry."

Dani Pi sighed, rising to his feet.

"I'm glad you talked to me, Heinz. I'll see that you have a by-pass operation. I promise. *Auf Wiedersehen.*"

But the young man did not see old Heinz again.

On the 27th December, when The VP Group Executive Vice President – Hotels & Resorts, returned to work, a team of able policemen arrested him. He was charged with *employing aliens without work permits.* The aliens were two British auditors, who had entered the kingdom on tourist visas.

Dani knew of the arrest from the Post's headline: **German hotel manager arrested**. Then a telephone conversation with Wittenberg revealed that Hermann had died of heart failure in jail.

# The New Year Party

In the departmental head meeting, Karl Wittenberg focused on Johannes Schultz, Food and Beverage Manager.

"Jonas, include in the Kandern account the cost of the two-day closure of the Hall to turn it into the State Ballroom of Schonbrunn, and another day of closure to dismantle the set when the party is over, at the rate of a superior reception for 1,000 persons. As for the New Year's Eve Party, you keep the food cost well below 40 per cent but step up the price per person 1,000 baht more from the figure you previously quoted. It's peanuts to them and a lot of it was made from slave labour during the war. Last year we went for quantity and that was why it was standing room only. This year we will go for quality, a dinner-theatre style, with ample room for 60 couples to waltz at any one time. The period costumes for the members of the Orchestra must be ready by four o'clock on December 30th, and go over Mozart's concerti and the Viennese waltzes with the conductor, and let me see the list by midday tomorrow. The pianist, who will be Mozart, must come to the rehearsal tomorrow evening at seven. Housekeeping! The period costumes for one hundred waiters must also be ready on 30th December. Their white gloves must be spotless. Jonas! Pick good-looking boys for the job. All of them must be made up to look as if they were pages at Schonbrunn. Make sure they put on proper shoes. Their fake Nikes will clash with the Habsburg garb! Take two most handsome boys from The Bordeaux Grill to serve at the Baron's table. He likes them muscular and well-tanned.

"The sound system must not go awry especially while the Baron impersonates the Queen of the Night and mimes an aria from Mozart's Magic Flute. And I'll do Tamino's.

*Dies Bildnis ist bezaubernd schon,*
*Wie noch kein Auge je geseh!*

"Housekeeping! Has my wig been set, sprayed and decorated? Deliver it to my suite by tomorrow evening for the dress rehearsal. The Baron wants to rehearse the scene when Mozart performed at Schonbrunn and when she mimes the chosen arias."

Due to this hectic time, KW completely forgot to attend HGH's funeral.

Having received an invitation to the Viennese Night & New Year's Eve Party, Dani Pi accepted with two conditions. Firstly, for him, it would have to be white tie instead of dressing up as a courtier. Secondly, he would not be in the Golden Hall the whole time since he had a few guests of his own to entertain in The Bordeaux Grill.

It was obvious that the heir was indifferent to the bride-to-be. On the other hand the chosen one did not care much for the fiancé either. But in any case, love had nothing to do with an arranged marriage. It was a matter of tying the pivotal knot that would take the Pis into finance and banking, a sector in which The VP Group's tentacles had not yet reached.

To Minister P and Madame V, the marriage, if it produced a male offspring, would be in keeping with the tradition of reproducing the dragon's seed in undiluted continuity. Their grandson must be carefully reared, then sent at an early age to China for education.

Madame V had checked Sopinya's bloodline and found to her satisfaction that the dragon's blood had been kept uncontaminated.

But there were two stumbling blocks.

One: Dani neither showed interest in the forthcoming marriage nor in the fiancée.

Two: Sopinya had been heard chiding their name as being heinous. In some circles, 'sinister' had been applied, claiming that the Pis had become immensely rich through opium trading in the forties and the fifties before Field Marshal Sarit Dhanarat banned the drug.

Regardless of the gossip, Madame V was pleased with the planned courtship of the two lovers. The tryst took place in The Bordeaux Grill. Each side brought his and her own chaperon. Sopinya had her close friend, Sowarop, nicknamed Di. Dani invited Prawit, nicknamed Ewit in gay circles.

Prawit had at first refused, saying that he would be Maria Teresa's Lady-in-Waiting at the other party.

Dani had to put his foot down.

"Dash it! You've dressed up as a dashed silly drag queen countless times. This is work! Bring your stopwatch with you if you like."

Пира Судхам

Over dinner, Prawit had to hasten the tempo of the charade for he had little time left to apply more cosmetics and dress as a glamorous lady-in-waiting.

"It's in vogue these days for a married couple to live separately, in the same house, but in different parts. My wife and I have been doing just that. She lives in her own wing and I have the other. We rarely see one another."

"You're married!"

"Of course, I am. I've been married for years. And from day one, we made such an arrangement. She has her friend or friends, and I have mine. It's rare that we are seen out together. What happiness there is, we have it."

After the dessert, Dani addresses his fiancée: "May I invite you and your friend to join Mama. She wants to see my new flat and a country house I have recently bought in England. Witty, you and VVK are also invited."

"Who is VVK?" Sopinya asked.

"He's Visually Virile Karl, the hotel general manager" Prawit giggled.

"What a wonderful idea," Di said. "We've been thinking of going to St. Moritz. Anyway, Soppy, we may go to London first."

"Of course you may," Dani agreed. "I'd like to go to Switzerland too. It would be fun. I say! Arosa might be better than St. Moritz. St. Moritz is full of gawping tourists. Prince Charles has been to Arosa. There, we can have wonderful meals and superb wines at Hotel Anita. The wine list alone is tantalizing."

"He knows his Switzerland. What do you think guys?" Ewit asked.

"London and Arosa then," Sopinya said. "Now, Di and I must go to another party, a hen party at Di's. We don't want to keep the girls waiting. Do we, Di? Thank you, Khun Dhani, for dinner and for the invitation to London and to Arosa. We accept."

"With pleasure," Di punctuated, rising to her feet.

The two gentlemen stood up.

While on his feet, Prawit said:

"Now I must go to the GM's suite to put on my costume. Must run! Otherwise the German queen shall be waiting for the lady-in-waiting. And that would be outrageous. See you at the ball."

After the lawyer had gone, Dani sat down. Soon boredom claimed him. To overcome it, he left the dining room, passing artificial plants and trees in the lobby. Inside the Golden Hall, gays in period

70

costumes took no notice of him for now they were being mesmerized by the Baron in the fantastic form of Maria Teresa on stage, miming the Konigin der Nacht aria:

*A vengeful hell burns in my heart*
*Death and despair rage all around me!*

At the end of the aria, the Queen of the Night stood erect, with her diamond tiara-adorned head haughtily tilted upward against the thundering applause, wild shrieking, sharp whistles and cat-calls from hundreds of hysterical drag queens.

The alluring Lady-in-Waiting forced her way towards Dani.

"Danny! Come! I'll introduce you to the Queen of the Night."

"I'd rather not!" Dani pouted, walking out of the ballroom.

Ewit ran fervently after him, holding on to her wig.

"At least you should see VVK doing Tamino!"

She determined to pull him back to the party.

"Dash it! Let go of me. You dashed silly drag queen! You don't have to tear at me!"

The billionaire followed the glittering Grand Lady of the Viennese Court into the ballroom in time to see and hear VVK, in a magnificent princely outfit, mime:

*O help me! Help me now! Or I'd be killed*
*by this vile serpent for victim be taken!*

Then Tamino fainted.

Three fairies appeared; each was heavily rouged, dressed in flowing pink chiffon, holding a silvery spear. They stood near the burly body of Wittenberg.

Facing the audience, the Three Fairies sang:

*Go, monster, by our power!*

They stabbed the air where the monster was supposed to be with their spears. One of them dropped her weapon, screaming and stomping and jumping out of the line to fetch it. Then she minced back to her former place.

The well-wined audience screamed and shrieked.

After a few seconds of overt coyness, the Three Fairies continued:

*Triumph! Triumph! It's done!*

Squatting to give Karl a kiss of life, the First Fairy hollered:

*A beautiful youth, how sweet, how fair!*

Because she took the opportunity to kiss her man a moment too long, 200 fairies screeched and guffawed.

When the uproar died down, the Second Fairy bellowed:

*So lovely as I have never seen!*

And she knelt to resuscitate Tamino.

The Third Fairy tried to pull the Second Fairy away from the fallen prince by the wig which came off at a yank.

Everyone, including the Three Fairies themselves, screamed and hollered while the two Fairies fought like  hysterical women. The First Fairy attempted to stop the fracas and dragged them back to the line. The Second Fairy was erratically putting on her wig. The Third Fairy frantically readjusted the heavily padded breasts, squawking at the roaring audience:

"Quiet! Quiet! Now it's my turn! Quiet!"

When the audience calmed down, she sang:

*Yes! Yes! He is as lovely as a painted picture!*

Then she sat on her heels; her free hand lifted up the lower part of Karl's robe, and groped Karl's groin. The groping caused VVK to come back to life, trying to get away from the Fairy's active hand.

She bawled, forcing him to lie down again and keep still so that the groping could be repeated. Then she rose, lifting the modern-day underwear for all to see. And that seemed to have brought the house down.

Dani too laughed so much that his eyes watered; his ears ached from the pandemonium. Wiping his eyes with a handkerchief, he said to no one in particular:

"Would Mozart be amused?"

Then he left the thundering hall before some fairies could see that he had enjoyed the show.

In the lobby the hotel owner mingled with the partygoers for a short while before going inside The Bordeaux Grill.

"We're fully booked tonight," the *maitre d'hotel* Alain Grenadier informed him.

"Set up another table for me then!"

When the table was ready, DP immediately claimed it, and ordered the sommelier to pop the cork of another vintage Krug.

*How people strive to be happy on the eve of a new year,* the billionaire observed.

Every outlet of the hotel was full that night, and a section of the lobby had been turned into a celebrating area as well.

"So many wrong notes!" Dani griped at the quartet performing J S Bach's *Air* in the lobby.

"A gentleman asked whether he could sit at your table. He's on his own, sir," the headwaiter delivered the request.

At first Dani thought: *Who would want to share the dining table with a stranger?* But, when he saw the be-suited, foreigner standing at the entrance of the restaurant, he surmised that the poor man, being alone on this festive night, should deserve his sympathy.

The man approached and thanked the hotel owner and introduced himself as Dick Fuller. All of a sudden, the 44th richest man in the world seemed to be oozing with charm as well as generosity.

"Champagne?"

"Thank you."

"I'm afraid you have no choice but the New Year's Eve Six-Course Menu."

"Then I'll have it and the same," Fuller indicated the bottle in the silver chiller. "Yes, another bottle of the same."

"It's a vintage Krug."

"Well, tonight, it'll be worth it," said Fuller, who was dining out on an unlimited expense account. "My wife went back to the US, and I'm at a loose end."

"You should have been in the ballroom where the Viennese Night is in full swing. I've never seen anything as hilarious as the burlesque they're putting on. I've never laughed so much in my life."

"Actually I'm having a writer's block. Perhaps an evening of fun might do the trick."

"A writer! Well, well, well."

"I dabble in ... er ... short stories."

Pira Sudham

The two men held a pleasant conversation until 11 o'clock.

"I must go back to my house and wait for a phone call from my wife at midnight. But before I go, I'd like to pass on a message from a colleague whom you've recently contacted -- that *you go ahead*. Here's a phone number. Don't make telephone contact unnecessarily, and don't phone from your residence or from this hotel. Goodbye."

"You don't mean... Thanks for the message. Goodbye."

Dani had previously contacted the Drug Enforcement Agency of the US Embassy. However, the covert way in which the meeting was organized made it difficult to expatiate. Furthermore, an informer could not provide the gist of the conversation that had taken place between the *persona non grata* and the DEA. Therefore, it was considered best to wait for the event to take its course.

Leaving the dining room, Dani asked Housekeeping to open the GM's suite for him to use the facilities. Once there, he went into one of the bedrooms.

Lying on the bed, he thought: *I can proceed. But where should I start?*

At two o'clock in the morning, Prawit and his young friend found Dani asleep in their bed.

"Wake up! Wake up, you brute!" Prawit shook the sleeper until Dani woke up, rubbing his eyes.

"Where am I?"

His aching head throbbed with the potency of alcohol.

"You're in heaven with us, dearie!" Ewit quipped.

"Am I dead?"

"Pinch yourself!"

"Egad!"

"No, my darling, not god but just two lovely fairies. Now get out of my bed and go to sleep in the other room."

"And we need it quickly. This girdle is killing me," the writhing young thing mimicked.

Dani made a move, shaking his head up and down, left and right, to tear away from drowsiness. Rising, he staggered. Then the two fairies took him to the other room.

When the general manager returned to his suite, it was a surprise to find the hotel owner asleep in his bed.

When Dani woke up, it took him some time to realise in whose bed he had slept. Suffering from a terrific headache, he staggered into the bathroom.

It was a relief that Wittenberg had already left for the day's work. Having dressed, Dani went in search of Ewit.

"Witty! Get up!"

"Why? Is the hotel on fire?"

"No, but you will be if you won't take me out of here in 10 minutes."

"What's the hurry? It's a holiday. Happy New Year! You weren't with us at midnight. We sorely missed you!"

"Lying bitch! You didn't think of me at all."

"It's your own fault. You were chasing that fat *farang* in The Bordeaux Grill instead of being with us."

"You knew?"

"Of course! I have my spies everywhere. What happened to him?"

"He left me for his wife."

"You should find someone young, slim, good looking and unattached instead of barking up the wrong tree."

"Actually he was the right tree. Only he had to go home to wait for his wife to phone from the US at midnight."

"O my God!" Prawit Witayakul, a Yale graduate, mimicked a Southern American drawl.

"Get up! Dash it! I'll wait outside. I'd box your bally ears if you don't come out in ten minutes."

In the evening of January 4th, Dani and Prawit had dinner with Karl-Michael in The Bordeaux Grill to plan the London-Arosa tour which included their stay at The Ritz and at Wealdshire Park.

"It will be my first stay at The Ritz," said the general manager. "It has been one of my ambitions to stay at The Ritz in London and in Paris, and some day, manage one of them."

"Perhaps you shall. Mama wants to negotiate a management contract with the London Ritz on this trip. And presto, Karl-Michael, your wish may come true. You know who owns the Paris Ritz, don't you? No, he isn't British. There have been several failed attempts to obtain a British passport. Regardless of how hugely rich he is, he has to keep on trying. I greatly sympathize with him. I can see him being a champion of the rejected British passport seekers as well as our benefactor, a concessionaire, exploring for oil in the Gulf of Siam."

"What makes it so desirable to be British?" Witty prettily perked up. "I've a British passport and that's from the good fortune of having been born in Scotland and having Scottish ancestors."

"Lucky you!" said Karl. "You don't have to subject yourself to the rigorous visa application at the British Embassy and join a long queue at Immigration at Heathrow among hundreds of *The Others*."

"It makes you wonder why both Conservative and Labour Governments turned down *his* application for a British passport time and again."

"To indicate that they're truly superior, perhaps," surmised Karl-Michael.

"Perhaps it's a curse, particularly if it's an Egyptian curse, or retribution for some unmentionable dark deeds and a certain secret scheme, or simply the wheeling dealings that any man is capable of doing," offered Witty without any compunction.

"Should you ever find out, would you still want to be part of it? Would you still work for us if you had known that our fortune is *filthy lucre*?" Dani challenged.

"We'd better keep our dear, dear Karl in total ignorance then, shouldn't we?" Witty sneered.

Their dinner meeting ended on a good note with: "Karl-Michael, I must apologize on behalf of the buggers for making a mess in your suite," Dani mentioned. "Send me the bill for cleaning the dirty linen. By the way, I meant to tell you that I helped check the English text of the press release on your new appointment when I was in Mama's office this afternoon. You look great in the photo. Witty, close your gaping mouth. It's true about the dirty linen, is it not?"

"I'll rape you one of these days," Witty made a jocular threat in the car while driving away from The Imperial Palace Hotel.

"For telling Karl about the dirty linen?"

"Yes, and I am taking you to my house to do it."

Prawit's Palladian place was spread out in two semi-circular wings, between which a kidney-shaped swimming pool sparkled under spotlights.

The main living room was an enormous atrium, aptly called the Garden of Eden. Guests could hear the sound of water trickling away in small streams flowing into a clear rocky pool in which fish swarmed under the foliage of ferns, cycads, flowering orchids, palms, and well-trimmed banyan trees.

"Thank goodness you didn't make an arrangement to entertain me with some of those numbered bodies from the Caligula Club," said Dani, sitting on a sofa in Prawit's Garden of Eden.

"You'll be surprised, what I have in store for you. These are not numbered."

"Well! I'll be dashed!"

"The boys and the same old me and Dom Perignon."

"Let's limit ourselves to Dom Perignon, shall we?"

"At your service," said Witty, making a curtsy.

Some time later, the jolly lawyer returned dressed in a full-length gold-embroidered black silk kaftan.

"Tranz! Tranz!" he trumpeted to announce the arrival of the Queen of Sheba.

Ewit swirled histrionically.

"Well! I'm dashed! Now I know why we call you a *screaming queen with gay abandon*. You scream a lot and don't give a hoot. Where is Dom Perignon?"

Three handsome houseboys dressed as sailors trooped in. The first carried a silver tray that bore a distinctive bottle of the sparkling wine in a silver chiller. The second took care of two Waterford crystal flutes on a silver salver. The third, the most winsome, bore a white napkin on his arm.

It was he who would uncork the bottle and pour the wine.

While the loveliest lad was popping the cork, Dani observed:

"Do we require three people for this simple job?"

"They come cheap. Besides, they have nothing to do in Isan. So I handpicked them to render delectable services."

"It's such a dashed abominable attitude that brought down the Tsar and the Shah."

"It won't bring us down in Siam. These boys believe it is divine to slave day and night in my marble mansion. They're most obliging, and grateful. I've saved them from unemployment and starvation."

"It's *noblesse oblige*, is it?"

"Of course, it is. You saw three of my 12 boys. Then there are two adopted sons."

"I didn't know you keep a harem."

"I prefer to call it a five-star youth hostel. When these boys first came to me, or to be precise, when I took them in, they were zombies. They had useless brains and useless eyes. I had to teach them everything. You know why? It's the authoritarian education system; it's the way they are taught in school. They learnt by rote and by being taught to fear the authorities. They were taught nothing that would help them think and be independent. On top of that they learnt at a very young age to be hangers-on, to look for hosts. And we make them so to keep them meek, mindless and totally obedient so that we can have cheap slaves at home and in the factories and sweatshops; and plenty of bodies in brothels, massage parlours and whoring beer gardens. You have to give me credit. I send mine to learn English, computer science, catering and hair styling. So they can get jobs when they reach their sell-by-date of 21. In a few cases, I have been known to stretch to 22. Then I get younger ones to replace the ones I farm out to hotels, restaurants and gay bars. Look at those pretty boys in The Bordeaux Grill. Most of them are known as Prawit's graduates."

"You're absolutely outrageous, Witty. Does your wife know about this?"

"She can walk in here any time and see for herself. I will tell you this much. She left me once but returned shortly after. And now we live happily under the same roof forever more. Take off your jacket and tie. Relax."

"It's quite cool in here. Surely, it must cost a fortune to air-condition the whole house, including this enormous atrium."

"I work for your family."

"You're a very rich man then."

"Not as rich as you are."

"Would I be much richer on paper if some of the black or grey areas of the enterprise and activities were officially accounted for?"

"Oh yes, much richer. If *Fortitude*, *Forbes* or *Fortune* had all the figures, you'll probably be the fifth richest man in the world."

"I don't care much for such listings. But I do want to know all concerning the companies in which my name has been used. It's been alleged that some of my ships have been used to smuggle drugs and petrol. I have the right to know. I should know also why some of my subsidiaries in the agrarian sector use the cancer-causing chemicals and antibiotics banned in Europe; and dyestuff in poultry and aquatic farming; and formalin in food and drink. Chickens and ducks, fish and prawns and eggs from our farms and fish sauce and beer contain high levels of these toxic substances. Even our soy sauce has melamine in it. It has also been alleged that our animal feed contains dyestuff to make meat reddish. Isn't there Food and Drug Administration in this country? The FDA of the US has reportedly halted the import of our chickens and prawns and soy sauce and eggs due to the use of these cancer-causing additives. If you are as good as you seem to be, Witty, you'd better come clean with me for I've had information from a highly reliable source on this. Isn't it strange that it's the CIA that goes after us instead of the FDA? And you can correct me, Witty. I personally feel responsible for the murders of idealistic schoolteachers, labour leaders and environmental activists. Tell me. How and to whom did I pay for these killings? Is it true that a secret scheme code-named DDT (Damage Destroy Take-over) is at work?"

"Of course, you can, in due course, in the fullness of time. But I cannot put them all down in writing. You'll have to come to my office for that."

"Now, about Papa's PPS. Is he a threat as Mama made him out to be?"

"You don't have to worry about PPS P. Your Mama only sees one side of the whole affair. She thinks that your Papa has become too dependent on his PPS. People see them together. Some say they are like father and son and that son is being groomed for a leading role in the Party, but he is too young yet to be Deputy Leader. And Madame doesn't like it when she is aware that your Papa's favourite has also been nibbling at the cake. She is afraid that His Eminence might give him a big piece since the unrivalled Portfolio Broker worries that you will never get married and produce an heir. Your Mama does have ways and means of doing things to people whom she wants to get out of the way. Look at the Hermann case. Rest assured. Blood is always thicker...."

"By the way, I meant to ask you this. Why have there been attempts on Papa's life?"

"Don't you know that these days every great man has his life on the line? And your father is no exception. But he's not afraid of opponents and the syndicates that have moved into petrol smuggling and gambling inside the country and at the fringes of the Burmese and Cambodian borders. You couldn't expect other Godfathers to bow out willingly."

"Another thing, my dear Witty. Did the good MP from Isan get a bank loan?"

"Of course he did. Why should he have difficulties in grabbing a loan of mere 300 million? The President of the Bank and Vice Presidents can give loans to certain politicians of higher risk and mostly without collateral. Why, bank executives rush in, their heads banging against one another, trying to give loans, when they have just a slight whiff of a potential borrower. You may wonder why. Well, each of them may enjoy a cut of five per cent minimum."

"But I thought our good MP from Isan wanted to borrow only 200 million. Why did it go up to 300 million?"

"My dear chap! How naïve you are!"

"Dash it, Witty! Tell me why!"

"Oh dear! Oh Dear!"

"Stop oh dearing!"

"You need 200 million, no more and no less for a portfolio, okay? So you borrow at least 300 million so that after, say 20 per cent cut for the four who help facilitate the loan, you'd barely have enough to spare. You'd want one or two latest top of the range Mercedes to go with your new position. You'd want to keep one or two mistresses. There you are."

"Still it's hard to believe that one can yank 300 million off a bank, just like that."

The lawyer laughed: "Your Papa didn't have to yank though one of the bank's financial advisers had to flee to Canada as a result. But look at the property developers. They merely have to snap their fingers and the bank presidents and vice presidents offer them loans on silver platters. That's why condominiums, office towers, golf courses, housing projects, gigantic shopping complexes, high-rise hotels, and shop-houses pop up everywhere. And then some prominent family members who are major shareholders have that nasty habit of siphoning funds from their banks. You may wonder whether it can go on like this. The day will come when the inflated economy cannot stand it any longer. It will crash. Empty banks will crash, and bad loans will fester and the pus will run and the Bank of Siam might not be able any longer to put up the reserves to defend the weakening baht. The Bank of Siam has already spent 28 billion US dollars to prop the baht up. How long that will last? When the crash eventually occurs, the taxpayers will have to pick up the pieces, and people in certain quarters will blame that currency trader, George Soros. Oh dear! Oh dear! My poor country! My heart bleeds. It's like *a tree, rotten to the core, falls of its own accord.* I'm sitting tight, watching and waiting. I'll play my fiddle when the fall finally happens. You are safe when the baht tumbles. Your money is in pounds and francs."

"And did the good MP from Isan get a portfolio?"

"No."

"Why not?"

"Why are you interested in him? He's just a petty provincial godfather from a poverty stricken Isan constituency. Anyway, your good man had to go whimpering to your Papa to save his skin. A hit and run MP has no place to hide in but many palms to grease, especially when the unfortunate man died, and there are witnesses. To keep his seat in the House and avoid jail, your dear friend had to sell his soul to the devil. So your beloved Papa sent him to little me to confess. Yes, many a time I have been Father Confessor as well as Mother Superior. If he refused to confess, he wouldn't be saved. With a signed confession in hand, the man is fit for a stratagem. He has become one of our wraiths, a tiny chick in our hand. We can squeeze it dead when we like."

"Dash it, Witty! I wish you hadn't used 'we' and 'our' like that. You made it sound as if I had a role in the dashed dirty work."

"Oh dear me! You have taken it to heart. It's only a manner of speaking."

"So has the hit and run MP been saved?"

"Of course! Back in the House as if nothing had happened. Think of what one can do with 240 million from Krung Siam Bank."

"How about the dead man's wife and children? How about the witnesses?"

"You're behaving like a Samaritan. It's not becoming of you. You've kept me talking for so long. The bottle is empty, I presume."

Once more the ebullient host clapped his hands, and the prettiest houseboy appeared.

"Another bottle of the same, Nid. And put more ice-cubes in the chiller."

The master eyed Nid's retreat.

Then, turning to Dani, Ewit said: "Nid can give a very good massage. Want to have a go? It will relax you."

"No thanks. I don't want him to touch me. I don't mind being touched by you though. At least you've a Celtic brush."

"Wow! It's a good start. You may sleep here tonight."

"Don't get excited. Should I spend the night here, it's only for a good sleep."

"You can sleep here anytime. I'll put it down as client relations, or perhaps it should be PR, pubic relations."

"Dash it, Witty! Why do you have to be frightfully prurient?"

"It's fun. That's why."

Thus, time passed pleasantly.

# A Parley in the Woods

In July Kum Surin died.

Had there been a doctor in the area, the death might have been certified as a case of untreated tuberculosis.

A day after the cremation had taken place, Piang and Poon resumed rice planting. Silently they toil while their children played under a gum tree.

In the afternoon, just before Piang would halt the planting for the day, she suddenly felt a pull at the heart. The woman shuddered, telling the sister-in-law to gather the children and follow her home at their own pace.

For now she had to run.

At home, Boonliang was kindling a fire. When the old mother saw the daughter staring at her, she asked:

"What is the matter? Where are the little ones?"

But Piang did not answer. Instead, she turned back. Half-way she met Poon's party. Taking her youngest child up to her hip, the mother turned back and took the lead, heading for home.

Meanwhile, in Napo Monastery, Pundit Piksu welcomed the new priest.

*This might mean that it would be tenable for me to disrobe, now that there is a priest to assist the abbot.*

Yet, the little monk delayed his plan, being wary of danger lurking outside the monastery.

Chief Singhon had an excellent reason to be exalted. For now electricity could be had in Napo. Furthermore the completion of the Muang – Napo tar-sealed road called for a celebration.

To celebrate the progress, the headman organized a feast. Old Chinaman Ching gleefully rubbed his bare paunch, having sold all the rice wine.

On this joyous event, a television set was placed on a table as an exhibition of development. The people ate and drank and danced to taped music.

But, the Surins were not among the revellers.

According to the headman's wife, the said family had been in mourning since sad news had reached Napo.

Piang's husband had died in an explosion in Saudi Arabia.

In the hut of the Surins, the grief-stricken women were weeping. The presence of Pundit Piksu failed to comfort them. After a while, the monk went away. But, instead of returning directly to the sanctuary, he headed for Chief Singhon's house.

"Have you done anything to rebuild the school?"

Sorrow brought about by the loss of his father and brother-in-law, and the pitiful sight of his suffering folk, affected him to an extent that his outburst sounded as if it was an accusation, causing the village chief to bark.

"Heavens! Give me time! Education is not as important as transport and electricity. Now let the people enjoy the celebration!"

The priest became sadder, as a result.

One day in November, four fully-armed military men arrived at the monastery, asking for Pundit Piksu. The holy one received them in the *sala*.

Major Ayumongkol Mongkolkulthorn knelt in front of the priest and deferentially performed the supplication.

"We learned that Your Venerable has contacted the members of the *K-Force* in Sisurachwood. May we beg you to lead us there to announce the amnesty."

There was power and polished manliness in the voice, against which the monk's gentle reciprocation sounded such a contrast that some peasants could tell the difference. The elderly folk present heard the positive answer. Therefore, they praised the priest who would assist the military to bring back to the fold the wayward men of Napo.

On the appointed day, 30 vanguard members of the special task force, fully equipped with modern war weapons, arrived and stood at ease in the precinct of Napo Monastery, waiting for the monks to finish their luncheon.

It was quite a sight when the armed men followed the little monk along the lane into the surrounding fields.

Pundit Piksu remembered the route well.

He quickened his footsteps so that he would not delay the trained killers.

At dusk they arrived in Soka or the remains of it, following the massacre and the conflagration.

Pundit Piksu kept what he had known of Soka to himself and decided to make them rest there for the night. Major Ayumongkol knew he had no choice but to order his soldiers to bivouac.

The monk calmly sat under a tree, observing the men gathering dead wood to make a bonfire.

While the subordinates were busily occupied, Major Ayumongkol sauntered towards charred stumps. The little priest allowed anger to expand while looking at the back of the army officer.

Being aware that he was departing from the Right Eightfold Path as prescribed by Lord Buddha, the holy one subdued his temper, chanting a mantra to impart compassion to the dead.

The next day, after breakfast, the monk and the men trooped off towards the old site of Yang Village which had met its destruction earlier than Soka. When they reached the devastated location, the rangers took to the shade of surviving trees.

The priest moved farther to the edge of a bare patch that had been a hut, with the major catching up on him.

Should the ordained one have said: *Now, Major, you may piss on the dead earth*, he would have broken one of the five precepts. A snide or cynical remark such as this was improper coming from a priest.

Silently Pundit Piksu contemplated the scorched soil, while Major Ayumongkol shouted an order at his men to go ahead.

They knew the way to Hauysai.

Hauysai, a small sandy creek that flowed only in rainy seasons, was probably the best place to camp, since it was too late to enter the forest. At nightfall, a bonfire was lit, sending up flames into the darkened sky.

To keep peace within, the monk meditated deep into the night, while most of the warriors were asleep and owls hooted and wild dogs howled.

In the morning Major Ayumongkol, on his knees, offered the monk a bowl of instant noodle boiled together with powdered eggs. After the monk had accepted the alms, the army officer made the *namuskara*, bowing his head to touch the top of his fingers that pressed upon the earth. After lifting his head once again to face the monk, he reversed on his knees to a suitable distance before standing up.

All the laymen waited while the monk consumed his repast. As soon as the holy one emptied the bowl and rinsed his mouth, the fighters began to relish theirs.

When they were ready to enter Sisurach, the monk recommended that only Major Ayumongkol and Captain Udom and eight rangers should follow him. The rest should remain at the camp, a reason being common sense – if the insurgents were outnumbered by an armed contingent, it would be difficult to convince them of the amnesty.

The major agreed.

"One of you can take the first aid kit, but no guns and grenades, not even a pistol," the monk advised.

"With respect, Honourable Brother, you don't expect us to go into the forest empty handed?"

"Yes, I do. Lord Buddha's holiness and his teaching, the *dhama*, and my yellow robe may protect all of you, I am sure. You go to them unarmed, and they will give their arms to you."

The chosen men divested themselves of their weapons before picking their way, following the priest into Srisurachwood.

Several hours passed.

The major halted his men and looked at his wrist watch, while the priest bent down to pick a thorn out of his bare foot.

"Not long to go now," Pundit Piksu addressed the earth.

The party progressed deeper and higher until they reached a knoll.

"We'll make smoke here," the monk mentioned.

Hence, the soldiers gathered leaves and dead wood.

In a few minutes, smoke rose.

After a moment of waiting, Pundit Piksu made a layman-like roar.

"Buddho! Dhamo! Sanko! Napo...o...o...o..."

A minute later a cry from a long distance was faintly audible.

The Captain ordered one of his men to extinguish the fire.

Standing close to the priest, the officer took a good look at the little monk, asking:

"Are you an Isaner?"

"I'm Napo born and bred."

*The major has not done his homework or the military has no file on me.*

"And you, Major. You look rather different from your men."

"I was born in the City of Angels, one of the 12 millions who inhale dust and fume and other pollutants 24 hours a day. I've come to appreciate clean fresh country air so much now."

But he did not mention that he was the son of a formidable General whose father and forefathers had been Generals.

The time and place were not suitable to talk of his sojourn in England and reveal that he had led his troops to vanquish the insurgents' strongholds in Puparn, Sakolnakorn, and Pakam, Southern Burirum. The only task left for him to finish was to disarm the members of *K-Force* and bring to an end the protracted guerilla warfare and get the amnesty over quickly, so that he could go back to the  capital where promotion awaited him.

Had Major Ayumongkol expatiated on his training at Sandhurst, the priest might have discovered that they had a mutual friend named Dani.

Meanwhile, a cry came from a nearby thicket.

"Guru Kumjai! Brother Kiang! Tongdum! Panya!" Pundit Piksu responded. "I'm with 10 military men.  They are unarmed. Yes, unarmed!"

When there was no response, the major shouted: "Show up and be pardoned! Come out. Give up your arms and accept the amnesty!"

"It's not a trap!" Pundit Piksu assured. "I guarantee your safety with my life. This is your only chance to return alive to Napo."

"Soldiers! Walk slowly down the knoll to the east!"

The priest led the way down the gentle slope to a glade.

Kumjai alone emerged, looking like a scarecrow, aiming his gun at Mayor Ayumonkol while pacing carefully forward. Halting a few feet away, he gave his gun to the military leader before approaching his former pupil. Then the leader of the insurgents knelt, performing the *numaskara* on the ground near the monk's feet.

When he rose, facing the major, Kumjai asked:

"Under what conditions?"

"The conditions are few. Firstly, the pardoned shall be imprisoned or put under house arrest for six months. Secondly, the pardoned must not be politically active all their lives. Thirdly, they must inform the District Office of their new domicile after having been released from prison or house   arrest. And here is the State Pardon Notice."

The Major stretched his hand towards the Captain who produced a document.

"Read it, and if in agreement, then sign. Each of the pardoned has to come forward and sign."

Kumjai carefully examined the content.

"I'll sign," said he and asked for a pen.

"How about the others?" Major Ayumonkol questioned.

"Chanticha, Sawitri, Anucha, Kiang, Tongdum, Panya, Nopadol, Chakkrit, Arnuparp, Dan, Khen, Saishon, Sisalai, Denchai, Sungwian and comrades! Come out now! It's safe. We will go to Napo today with Venerable Brother Prem."

Sungwian Suwanapumi was the first to appear, a pitiable husk of the former monk of Wat Borombopit, followed closely by Kiang Surin, another scarecrow, and then scraggy Panya Palaraksa, with Tongdum Tinthaisong by his side, and the rest, cautiously appeared. All wore black tatty clothes. The weary skeletons of the starving champions of the oppressed moved towards the monk to whom they paid homage by kneeling to do the *namuskara* on the ground.

When Kumjai realised that the comrades, a splinter group of *Chin Haws*, the Chinese brigands, who had escaped from the massacre at Kaoko in the seventies, had not turned up, he looked towards their hiding places. Turning back, the leader searched Kiang's face for an explanation, but Kiang kept his mouth shut.

So Kumjai read aloud the State Pardon Declaration. At the end, he told them that he had signed.

Tears welled up in Panya's eyes.

Kiang had not yet heard that his father had died.

In his mind Tongdum had already reached Napo, walking fast towards his hut where Toon and his children were awaiting him.

So now they handed their weapons to Captain Udom.

At that instant, guns were fired.

Sisalai, Saishon, and Dan fell almost at the same time.

Kumjai spun to face the assailants, shouting:

"Stop! Stop shooting! Comrades! Stop!"

Then he fell. The wary warriors were fast enough to take hold of their guns once more to combat their former brothers in arms, the *Chin Haws*.

They fired indiscriminately while the military men ducked for cover. The monk alone remained standing as if to shield the men.

The fighting ceased when the *Chin Haws* abandoned their covers and escaped into the depths of the woods. Dan and Saishon died instantly. Sisalai was wincing and quivering, holding his bleeding stomach. But then he died a moment later.

Calling for the first-aid kit, Major Ayumongkol tore the shirt off Kumjai and treated the wound.

"You're very lucky. The bullet missed your heart," said Ayumongkol.

Meanwhile, the monk went over and lowered himself to hold Kumjai's hand.

"You will live. You will see Napo again," he promised, gripping Kumjai's bony fingers so as to pass on his inner force and healing power.

A moment later the priest rose to his feet and moved away so that the members of the K-Force could gather around Kumjai.

The soldiers were gathering boughs and creepers to make stretchers.

"Captain Udom," Major Ayumongkol commanded. "Go quickly to the camp and radio for a helicopter to fly the wounded to Sarakarm Hospital."

Captain Udom accepted the order with a salute and rushed off.

Major Ayumongkol ordered one of his men to unload the surrendered weapons and bundle them with vines. Then several members of the *K-Force* lifted their leader and the dead onto the stretchers in readiness for the journey to Hauysai.

Thus arranged, the military leader suggested that the bearers should go ahead in haste, leaving the monk to follow at his own pace.

When they arrived at the Huaysai base, a helicopter was waiting in a field. Later, Kumjai was admitted to the Emergency Ward of the provincial hospital of Sarakarm.

# The Pardoned

Out of Sarakarm Hospital, Kumjai joined the former *K-Force* members in Napo where the pardoned awaited the official surrendering ceremony.

Meanwhile a soul-beckoning rite was organized. The surviving members of the Sisurach contingent of guerrillas, including Nopadol Jitwisuth, Chakkrit Intrachart, Anucha Rajapakdi, Arnuparp Tantiprakara, Khen Nasong, Denchai Podhikam, Sungwian Suwanapumi, and the Dhamasart University lecturers Chanticha Satayadhama and Sawitri Somwang, were invited to participate.

The first four former insurgents had studied at Dhamasart University, from where they had escaped together and women, were now sitting on the floor, facing a large ceremonial copper tray that bore flowers, three burning candles and incense sticks.

At the centre of this solemn gathering sat a white-haired sage, chanting a mantra that pertained to wandering souls.

Wisely, the soul-binder made several readjustments to the text, optingfor appropriate words which denoted battles, woods, hills, ravines and plains. Now and then the old man chanted a reprise of a heart-rending plea.

*Come! O souls. Cease your wandering. Your homes are here now.*

The ritual ended when the elders had finished binding the former insurgents' wrists with blessed cotton yarns.

The village folk and the pardoned convened inside the precinct of Wat Napo. There, Lieutenant Colonel Ayumongkol, together with Major Udom, led 100 fully armed Tiger Men from a special insurgent suppression division to take their positions in front of a committee, comprising senior government officials from the provincial town hall.

Soon the turbulence in the air and swirling dust caused some civilians to scream. The young cried, clinging to their elders.

The helicopter landed on the bare patch that was once the playground of The Napo Primary School. A minute later General Ekarach, followed by his adjutant, walked towards Wat Napo, allowing several half-naked boys to run up to the helicopter. There, the curious urchins gawped at the *gigantic iron dragonfly* that they had seen in propaganda films and on the headman's television screen.

90

By the time the boys dashed back to the monastery, the much-decorated General had already been saluted by the platoon. Exuding a wealth of power, the representative of the Siamese might stood before the congregation of submissive villagers.

In contrast to the upright, awesome soldiers, Pundit Piksu sat composedly on a stool as if he had been turned into a golden statue, while the Napo headman and two assistants gathered the *K-Force's* weapons, and presented them to the awe-inspiring General.

The Lieutenant Colonel commanded his former enemies to appear before him. One by one the partisans came away from the Napotians to stand in line as directed.

Then General Eckarach spoke.

Photographers and cameramen were in the throes of recording the historic event.

At the end of General Eckarach's impressive speech, Lt. Col. Ayumongkol ordered the former insurgents to enter a nearby tent so as to be photographed and fingerprinted and to register their domicile so that their new identity cards could be prepared and later distributed to them.

While such activities were going on, General Ekarach proclaimed the State Pardon Declaration.

After the pardoned had returned, taking their positions in front of the commander, Lt. Col. Ayumongkol cited a vow of allegiance, phrase by phrase, so that the former fighters could repeat after him.

When the vow had been made, the ceremony ended.

The military departed, taking with them Chanticha, Sawitri, Nopadol, Chakkrit and Arnuparp who would serve their six-month's sentence in city jails.

The arms, which had once belonged to the insurgents, would become exhibited items in a military museum in the capital.

Life in Napo resumed its natural course.

Then Kumjai planned the priorities.

As for Anucha, who had no wish to finish his studies at the Faculty of Political Science at Dhamasart University, opted for terms of house arrest in Napo so as to help Kumjai rebuild the school and teach the children of the poor.

Prem the priest welcomed this decision as much as that of Kumjai's bonded friend Sungwian. The former monk of Wat

Pira Sudham

Borombopit re-entered the priesthood, residing at Napo Monastery. Thus, his ordination raised the number of the ordained to four.

Due to such an increase, Pundit Piksu decided to return to the world of laymen so that he could help Kumjai build The Napo Withayakom School.

Meanwhile Dani Pi and Elizabeth Durham arrived in a chauffeur-driven limousine with a bodyguard.

The arrival of the angels from the City of Angels with a gorgeous female foreigner created some excitement.

A throng of villagers milled round the automobile while waiting to feast their eyes on the *maeying falang.*

Most Napotians had seen a white man, the late CIA agent, who had accompanied the military propaganda unit many moons ago, but this was the very first time a white woman had turned up.

At a deferential distance the bodyguard and the driver sat, keenly observing the monk to whom their master and his Public Relations Consultant had come to pay homage.

Could this be the monk who had attracted rich men and women and powerful politicians, seeking his blessings and sacred talismans? Was this the famous monk who could ward off bad luck and bestow good luck and great fortune on those who came to pay homage and made donations? Could he be the one who had predicted accurately time and again the winning lottery numbers?

"I've recently come across an old friend who's now a colonel," said Dani. "On his return from a campaign in Isan, he told me of a meeting with an extraordinary priest in Napo Village. You know there are three villages of this name in Isan? But my friend pointed yours out to me on a military map."

"That old friend of yours must be Colonel Ayumongkol. Now, please elucidate me how you could make this Yorkshire lass leave her beloved London for the kingdom in conflict."

"We literally bumped into each other in front of Hatchard's, didn't we, Liz? I made an offer that she could not refuse. So she left her PR firm in London to help me with my PR activities in Bangkok. Liz is now an expert in Siamese, having taken a course at The School of Oriental Studies. I'm pleased to say that she didn't play hard to get. But I suspected that it might have been you for whom she decided to leave London. She only made use of me to come to see you."

"Your PR activities?"

92

"Well, it's my intention to enhance the image of my family. I've established the Pi Foundation to carry out community services as well as providing funds to deserving organizations or individuals who have been helping the less fortunate. By the way, Charles Tregonning sends greetings."

"Thank you. How was he?"

"The old gentleman looked healthier, having given up smoking."

"How are Reiner and Wilhelm?"

"I don't know. Reiner was supposed to come and stay with me for a few days before I left for Siam, but he had to cancel the flight at the last minute. Since then I haven't heard from him. I rarely hear from Willie. Of course, as always, he has a hectic schedule. Not long ago I told him that I'd sponsor the Philharmonic to perform in Bangkok. But, as you know, he flies from one city to another in Europe and around the world, with no time to reply to my proposal."

During a pause, the boss turned his attention towards his PR Consultant.

"Dash it, Liz! Don't just sit glumly there. Say something!"

"We've come hopefully to ask you, Venerable Brother, to go to Bangkok with us and help me with some PR activities. I can't do press statements in Siamese though I've been working hard on the written words. But now we know for sure that you ..."

"There's Plan B," Dani decisively stated. "Let's see what we can do to help the penurious people in Isan. Perhaps you, Honourable Brother, can advise us. What is the very first thing we can do to help the poor in your area."

"Build a school! The old one was demolished a long time ago. Make it bigger for two or three teachers to teach the children of Napo and from outlying villages. Come! I'll take you to see where it should be built."

The monk rose to his feet and led the visitors out of the monastery.

"Once, there was a little shack called The Napo Primary School on this spot. If you would be so generous as to give sufficient funds towards the construction, I'll be most grateful. There are two volunteers to teach here. They are, at this very moment, in the provincial town, trying to obtain the official appointments, or re-appointment in the case of the former leader of the *K-Force* who previously taught here."

"With respect, Honourable Brother, would you be so grateful that you'd disrobe, leave your home village, and come with Liz and me to Bangkok and help us administer the funds? You can be the go-between of the Foundation and the people of Isan. I can't speak your language, and you know your people."

The monk stood still, head down, contemplating the ground.

"Yes."

"Yes?"

"Yes," confirmed the monk slightly louder.

"Well, then, I'll be delighted to donate 10 million baht."

Some villagers gasped.

Then Pundit Piksu took the visitors, with the day-dreamers trailing behind, to tour the village.

They arrived at Ching's shop which boasted not only a television set but also the very first refrigerator ever installed in Napo. Elizabeth Durham approached the Chinaman and asked for a *Cola*.

"Okay! Okay!" Ching croaked.

How quickly foreign words such as *Cola, okay,* and *dollar* had become household words even in such a remote impoverished community!

Within a week of having a television set, the prosperous shopkeeper had also adopted more foreign words, one of which old Ching happily used on this occasion. Thus, the cash-conscious Chinaman sniffed the air and smelled big money. Already a good whiff of it came to his keen sense for cash as the female *falang* handed a crisp 20 baht bank note to him in exchange for a Cola.

But when he came back to the shop front with several coins in his hand, the white woman had gone without waiting for the change.

Old Ching grinned and sucked his teeth with pleasure. The shopkeeper remained stooping there, gloating. The grin still remained fixed on his wrinkled face while looking up, gazing at the parade that raised clouds of dust into the sweltering air.

Along the path, this curious confluence of angels and earthlings moved forward, gathering more and more excited followers until the monk halted in front of a thatched hut that was the home of the Surins.

Grandmother Boonliang seemed stunned, facing the crowd. But she managed to pull herself together, asking Piang to fetch mats and Poon to offer drinking water.

Having no time to put on a shirt, Kiang used an unfinished bamboo basket, which he had been weaving, to hide his naked torso.

Dani seemed reluctant to accept the hospitality.

*Not on a bally bug-ridden bulrush-mat! Besides, I have never sat on my haunch on the ground in all my life.*

If the little monk could miraculously materialize a Chippendale chair out of thin air, the princely person might condescend to lower his bottom onto it.

Standing with both hands in the pockets of his trousers, the 39th richest man in the world addressed his former flatmate:

"I didn't know you had lived in a hovel such as this!"

At that instance, a jolly bumpkin bawled:

"Grandma Liang, water is not good enough for the master who has just made a donation of 10 million baht to build the school. Give us beer! Icy cold beer from Jek Ching's!"

"Beer! Beer! Beer!"

The chorus rose in unison. The dream drink had been advertised daily on the radio and television and in the newspaper that Chief Singhon brought from Muang, making most men in Napo long for it. But those thirsty criers did not think how the poor old woman could afford such a luxury, when not a single baht could be found in her hut.

But then Elizabeth asked the priest:

"May I buy them beer?"

The holy man could not say yes or no. But he translated her question into Lao so that the expectant Napotians could understand.

On hearing the translation, the men roared with joy. Thus, they sat down on the bare earth in readiness for a drinking bout.

Elizabeth emptied her purse of all the cash which she gave to several adults who volunteered to fetch Beer Sing.

Pundit Piksu told his mother that he would take leave of his priesthood. He had decided to go to the City of Angels to work for the donor of 10 million baht.

"I promise to send some money from my salary to you so you can feed and clothe everyone in the family," he concluded.

Somehow, the priest's vow touched the big brother, making him move closer to the quivering crone. Lording over her, he announced magnanimously:

"Your son lived with me in London for several years, and we've become brothers. You have a very good son, an excellent man. Due to him, I shall build you a new house and provide sufficient funds so that you and your family may live comfortably."

Turning towards his little brother, Dani made a confirmation.

"Apart from 10 million baht towards the construction of the school, I'll give three million baht to your mother."

Old Mrs Surin became dumb. But the crowd exclaimed:

"O, so wonderful! So truly wonderful!"

After bidding farewell to his people, the *piksu* led the visitors away from the party to which bottles of Beer Sing were duly delivered.

Inside the *gutti,* Pundit Piksu knelt, making a plea to the panel of monks.

"May I return to the world and all men regard me as one of them."

Hence, Pundit Piksu left the priesthood.

With foresight, Elizabeth Durham had brought trousers, shirts, briefs, socks and a pair of shoes in a suitcase.

Behind the closed door, Little Prem disrobed. The clothes which ED brought perfectly fitted him.

*Thank goodness! She remembers the sizes still.*

Shortly afterward, he sat between his two friends, in the back seat of the limousine, on the way to the City of Angels.

Hearing that millions of baht were coming to the Surins, the headman came to investigate.

Refusing to join the party, Chief Singhon snarled:

"So it's true! I don't like city people coming here, making a deal over my head with you lot. Not over my head! You hear? Kiang! You are a wounded dog, just out of the woods!"

The former insurgent did not dare to retaliate.

The fearful folk gaped, eyeing Mr Ten Percent who made a parting shot with:

"Watch out, the lot of you!"

# A Tarnished Image

A day after the former monk of Napo Monastery had been housed at VP Place, Dani Pi and his Public Relations Executives convened in the Blue Room, their headquarters.

"I took my mother and my former fiancée and the entourage to England and Switzerland. Everything went well and we had a great time, but on returning to Bangkok, the engagement was off. If the image of my family is truly tarnished then I want to do something to correct the tainted image. Firstly, I want to look into several issues. This is what both of you can do. Go to the library of the Post and read the newspaper back three years. Look for reports on the firms and subsidiary companies and individuals on these lists.

"Secondly, I will give each of you three million baht to open a current account with a leading bank that provides credit cards so that you'd have easy access to the money at any time to pay for anything you require in carrying out your PR duties, including entertaining the bureaucrats, policemen and members of the media.

"Primo, you also open an instant access savings account with an initial sum of 15 million baht with a major bank that has a branch near your village. The money should cover the cost of building the school, the teachers' houses and your family house. See that the school has durable tables and chairs, educational equipment, and amenities including toilets and water tanks. Also, see to it that your new house is suitably furnished so that Elizabeth would be comfortable in it. I want you to write to the man who will be the headmaster of the school and ask him to come with two or three villagers to see me as soon as possible. When they are here, you take them to your bank and open an account under the teacher's name with three million baht which should be a reserve in case of emergencies. Give him a camera to take photos of the construction and make a progress report to me once a fortnight until the school is ready to open. Liz, come up with a PR action plan to publicize the construction and the opening of the school and the hand-over ceremony when we donate the building to the local authority. When the project is completed, both of you go to the village to make preparations for the opening and interview the headmaster, the village chief, and some senior officials concerned. It shouldn't be difficult to churn out PR materials for the media. Work with Khun

Pensi, PR Director of VP Group. Ask her to compile a list of journalists and television crews to cover the opening. Hire an air-conditioned coach and load it with food and drink. Both of you get on it and take the invited media people to the village. By the way, Primo, I meant to tell you that our old flat in Hyde Park Square is rent-free to Liz. So now she has a place to leave her things and to where she can go back when she is tired of being with us in the kingdom. I'm sure she will let you stay there when you go to London one of these days. If not, you can make my apartment in St. James's your base. Probably you haven't heard that I also own a country house in Sussex. I have also become the lord of the manor! Now you may say *Yes, my lord. Very well my lord* to me!"

"Yes, my lord," Little Primo obediently responded.

"That's a good start," sniggered Elizabeth. "How about the concert? When can we slot that in?"

"I don't know yet. I may have to fly back to London to make inquiries. From here, it seems I talk to the Europeans from the end of the world. We shall have to see which orchestra would perform here. I haven't given up on Willie. But it can also be the Halle or the Berlin State Orchestra or the London Philharmonic."

The billionaire believed he could throw money at anyone and get the desired result. But he meant well, and was perhaps on the right track in using some of the proceeds from the *filthy lucre* to benefit the poor.

Having heard of the scheme to bring a renowned orchestra to perform in Bangkok, the Executive Vice President Karl-Michael von Wittenberg perceived that it was a challenging public relations exercise. Hence, he welcomed the plan that might lead to a series of musical performances by world-class orchestras. He speculated that such a PR activity would become a rewarding annual event that could eventually turn The Imperial Palace Hotel into a cultural centre of Siam.

To start this promising PR project rolling, Karl proposed a luncheon meeting to discuss the scheme. Incidentally Dani had planned to give a birthday party for Prem as well as a celebration to mark the promotion of Ayumongkol that very day. Therefore, the working lunch and the auspicious party conveniently coincided in The Bordeaux Grill.

Among the guests of honour were Colonel Ayumongkol Mongkolkulthorn in a bespoke suit, Elizabeth Durham in a tied-dyed silk dress, The Hon. Taninsak Chinarongkul MP (TC to good friends) in lounge suit, Suprapada Sukesan in a Chanel dress, Dani Pi in black-tie and Dr Prawit Witayakul in a cream-coloured suit that put him in the camp of Noel Coward.

"I say, Witty! You'll have to behave for at least three hours. No camping. You're sitting next to a mighty gay basher," Dani warned.

Witty pretentiously gaped in shock, glancing at Colonel Ayumongkol.

"I hope it would be the Berlin State Orchestra," the host was saying. "I know Christian Ehwald, the conductor."

"Really! Then we have a hope," Dani beamed.

"So you and Prem were classmates," mentioned Colonel Ayumongkol, or Ayu to close friends.

"Yes, Colonel," Elizabeth answered.

The former monk of Wat Napo became aware of his tonsure just then while seemingly concentrating on the menu. Then he gently ran the fingers of his left hand over his shorn head as if to check whether the stubble had grown a little more.

"Prem, what do you remember most vividly of England?" Ayu asked.

Having taken a few seconds to recall, the former hippy revealed:

"A walk on Haworth Moor with Elizabeth in search of Wuthering Heights."

"In search of what?"

"Wuthering Heights, the old farmhouse in which Heathcliff lived," Prem grinned impishly at the military might, obviously pleased with a subject the future Supreme Commander had no inkling.

"You like stay in Siam, Khun Lisabet?" TC asked.

"Very much! Bangkok is more modern than I thought. Though I didn't expect BKK to be as pristine as *The King and I* suggested, you know, elephants mingling with people in the streets and tigers roaming the jungles and rich men wallowing among beautiful women in their harems, that sort of thing. I was amazed that it is so cosmopolitan."

"No more jungle, Khun Lisabet," TC interpolated. "We cut down tree. You see elephant in street in Bangkok. Isan people bring elephant here to make money but no harem now. We have *mianoy*, kept women, in house, condo or apartment, and ready women in massage parlour, club and bar."

"And then I thought that once you left Bangkok, you'd enter the forest. But it's not so. There are factories after factories and shop-houses after shop-houses almost all the way to the hills. Yes, you're right. There are hardly any trees left standing on either side of the motorway. And from Korat, it's a desolate semi-desert country," Elizabeth pertly prattled.

"Ah, you go Isan! Very good, Khun Lisabet. Bangkok people no want go Isan. My constituency is in Isan. So now I push for airport there," TC proudly proclaimed.

It was widely known that TC's family and business partners had already garnered vast tracts of land not far from the site of the planned domestic aerodrome. There, a colossal commercial development and a casino project would materialize so as to create another Las Vegas should the parliament pass a bill to legalize gambling.

Fortunately, TC had the family's resources which included construction companies and quarries to exploit in order to make the airport and the proposed *Las Vegas of Siam* a reality. In the House, he raised the issues of employment, taxation and tourism whereby the Casino Scheme would benefit the impoverished Isan Region and the country as a whole.

Now, feeding his eyes on the pretty English crumpet, the people's representative from Isan, who seemed unable to resist his desire to taste an exotic dish, salaciously said:

"Khun Lisabet, I want to know you gooder. We eat rice together when I come back from New York. Okay?"

"Khun Suprapada, I'm glad you could come," Wittenberg was saying.

"For Khun Dhani, I'll do anything."

"And for me?" the hotelier asked expectantly.

"You are my superior."

In that instant that superior thought of his very own superior, who had been lavishing some considerable degree of generosity upon him during and after the European tour. The promotion followed, causing the Vice President – Hotels & Resorts to move out of the office in The Imperial Palace Hotel to be nearer to the boss, with quick access to Suprapada Sukesan, who acted as his executive secretary as well.

"I go next night to London and from there I fly Concorde to New York," TC revealed his flight plan to Prawit.

"Was it easy to obtain a US visa?" the lawyer asked.

"More easy than peel banana and put in mouth!"

Prawit glanced quizzically at Dani Pi. The two men's eyes met for a second. Then DP spoke:

"Dear friends. Yes, you are, all of you, my dear friends, old and new. The oldest is Ayu. He, at Sandhurst and I at Oxford, met in London. Remember our first meeting, Ayu? The newest is The Honourable Taninsak who has just joined the family. By the way, he has become a trusted member of my father's inner circle. Anyone who is trusted by my father is also my trusted friend. I'm pleased to say that it is a wonderful occasion that all of my close friends are here to celebrate, not only Primo's birthday, but also to congratulate Ayu for his recent rise in rank. Happy birthday, Primo! Congratulations, Ayu!"

*I did not like champagne then,* the birthday boy recalled the night of a harrowing blizzard, the 22nd of December in which he drank a finest wine with Helmut von Regnitz in Bavaria before the composer passed away. *And I do not like it now. A bottle of this brand costs more than an Isan rice farmer could earn in 100 years from selling his produce."*

Every time the freak lifted a glass of wine, he saw in his mind's eye an undernourished child drink muddy water from a bog in summer while his buffaloes looked on.

He was unaware that the most expensive wine on the wine list cost only a minute fraction of the billions made from drugs and smuggled petrol.

"Khun Taninsak," Dani said. "I'm delighted to hear that you'll fly to London tomorrow night. What airline?"

"Siam International first class," the MP spoke, while chewing a mouthful.

"In that case, Liz. You should upgrade yourself and go first class too to keep Khun Taninsak company," Dani glared commandingly at Elizabeth who scowled in perplexity.

She had not known beforehand that she was to fly back to London.

"Khun Taninsak, Elizabeth has been terribly homesick. Incidentally she is booked to fly to London tomorrow as well," Dani explained.

Then to Suprapada, the lord and master commanded:

"Supa, when you go back to the office, make certain that Liz is on Siam International's First Class. Keep her return flight open. And arrange an airport pass for me and Primo. We want to have farewell drinks in the VIP Lounge and wave Elizabeth off at the departure gate. Do join us in VIP Lounge, Khun Taninsak. You are travelling alone. Yes? Perhaps you would like Liz to sit next to you. Yes? Supa, see to it that they sit next to each other."

Having thus said, Dani started savouring his first course of Smoked Salmon and Beluga Caviar. A few minutes later the billionaire mentioned to the host:

"Since Elizabeth is leaving, I think we'd better talk about the proposed concert when she's back."

"Yes, Khun Dhani."

But Elizabeth Durham could hardly say 'Yes, Khun Dhani' in the same manner as the ingratiating hotelier. In fact, she was furious. One day she would dare to refer to the domineering employer as being *sinisterly rich*.

*Just you wait,* she mentally added.

For now she wanted to say, just as any liberated, forthright European woman would say: *No I haven't planned to go to London tomorrow, and I don't want to go anywhere tomorrow!* But she refrained from such utterance for the sake of her friend and his people and the Napo Development Project.

Silently she partook of *Roast Rack of Lamb*, leaving the rest of her share of *Chateau Latour 1975* untouched. Meanwhile she allowed her aversion rise higher as the sinisterly rich man's voice abrasively vibrated in her ears while he name-dropped, showing off his expertise in wine appreciation to the Colonel.

"This is one of the best recent vintages, and what a massive classic wine, very rich in oak and tannin," Dani von Regnitz was glowing. "I tasted *Chateau Latour 1975* en primeur with Michael Broadbent in September 1976. I dare say it has superbly matured since, but it is still rather early to drink now. Broadbent said 1985 onward should be just about right. Primo here had imbibed *Chateau Latour 1961*, which is the vintage of the century. It was in Germany, with the late Helmut von Regnitz, famous composer, and later in London at Claridge's with Wilhelm Hagenbach, our famous conductor. For an Isan buffalo boy, our prim and proper Primo has been a darling of certain celebrities and aristocrats who had gone to some extraordinary lengths to make him drop his trousers."

The former priest blushed.

If the choice of the claret and the caustic remark were intentional to remind the meek little man of his painful experiences in Europe, then Dani succeeded. But, for having been a Buddhist monk, the tormented man remained outwardly affable and calm while praying silently for time to transmute the sharp pang into dull pain.

Nonetheless, in his tortured mind, the images of Lord Bewly, Lord Norbury and Charles Tregonning in their stately homes merged with those of Helmut von Regnitz and Wilhelm Hagenbach.

Suddenly, the word *'Tod'* escaped from his mouth, and so he tried to cover himself by taking a mouthful of *coq au vin*.

"What is it now?" Elizabeth asked, having heard a peculiar utterance.

"Nothing! I merely talked to myself. A bad habit of mine."

*Danny does not spare me even on my birthday. Now I know why he wants me near him. To him, I am a boxer's punching bag. It cannot hit back. He does not know yet that I have a way of hitting back not only at him but also at all the men here. I can make use of them as extra characters in my book. I can make them talk and behave the way I want them to for I am their creator, controlling their destiny.*

*Danny's reference to the aristocrats has given me an idea. The first chapter should be set in Lord Norbury's Kennington Hall where the recluse moves from one magnificent state room to another, passing a collection of pictures and original period furniture and the collection of Indian artefacts. In a following scene, he is seen gazing at the expanse of a delightful landscaped garden. The aristocrat's white hair caught the sunlight as he rode on his favourite horse in the manner which Grandpa Tatip Henkai, the unsung seer of Napo, had seen during a trance.*

*In the following sequence the recluse was laid to rest. His soul underwent torture in hellish fire for a long time before being implanted in the womb of the poorest of the poor in Isan. In later years, not only his body but also his mind would undergo further deprivation and torture by poverty, bullies, brutal men and the authoritarian education system that enforced rote learning on the young.*

*In the succeeding chapters, the birth of the baby boy and his deprived and torturous childhood should be easy to put into words for they would pour out of my heart…*

"Danny told me that he is helping you build a school in Napo," Ayu was addressing the Napotian. "I've been thinking of sending 100 recruits from the Korat regiment to help dig a water reservoir. I noticed how dry the village was the last time we were there. What do you think? Would the villagers like that?"

"Oh, yes, please," Little Primo quivered, emerging from the glorious garden of Kennington Hall.

"I would also like to go back to Isan to see how Kumjai and Panya and the rest of the pardoned men are doing," Ayu ventured further.

"Oh, yes, please."

"Let's drink to that," the colonel raised his glass.

"Khun Prem, you know who your MP is?" TC interrupted.

"No I don't," the little man from a constituency in Burirum foundered.

"You see, people not know their MP. They vote man who pay bigger money for vote," pontificated TC, one of whose vote canvassers had stashed 12 million in 100 baht bank notes in a van, enabling TC to gain a landslide victory in the previous election.

"I say, Primo!" Dani intervened. "Khun Prawit is one of Siam's most prominent lawyers. I've asked him to draw up The Prem Surin Trust which we shall support."

The Isaner acquiescently accepted the offer.

When the party came to an end, Dani decided to remain at the table with the pair of lackeys.

"Liz, I can read you like an open book. You have to bear with me for making you fly off with TC. It has to be spontaneous; otherwise, it would not ring true. I want you to be with him, particularly in London, and find out what he does there, whom he sees, and if possible, find a reason to go with him to New York to do exactly the same there. Have you flown Concorde? No? Well, it'll be an experience. But don't let him fool you. Your good MP can be perfectly devious and deadly dangerous. And so is Witty Wit, by the way. Don't be taken in by Wit's glib, pert talk and affected mannerisms. Like many lawyers, the man is Machiavelli incarnate. As for TC, I suspect that he might bring some disgrace to me, to my family, one way or the other. While in London, go to my apartment in St. James's and see whether everything is all right."

"Yes, my lord."

# International Networks and High Power

"Primo, I meant to ask you about your priesthood," Dani mentioned during the morning meeting. "Which of the 227 tenets did you break or find most difficult to observe during your holy time in the monastery?"

"It's *Do not urinate on grass and leaves.* You have to find a bare spot to pee when you go walkabout. Another one is to avoid taking lives. You are likely to step on unseen ants and insects."

"Didn't you kill a mosquito?"

"No."

"Would you kill one now?"

"No."

"If I were a Buddhist monk, I'd break too many tenets. The one that says: *Do not make the semen move* must be almost impossible to observe, is it not?"

"Not having meals after midday until the following morning helps."

"But how can a young man like you avoid having sexual desire when the libido is at its peak? When the brimming cup runneth over, what? You must have had plenty of erections, surely. You must have tossed yourself off, naturally."

"Steady on, Danny!"

Seeking an escape, the former priest left the table for the windows.

"Dash it, Primo! We're grown men now. And there are only two of us here. But, if Liz could be with us at this moment, she'd have found the subject most interesting, would she not?"

Looking at the forecourt below, the little man sighed.

"There were some salacious thoughts but I didn't masturbate. There were erections, of course. But I turned my attention elsewhere. Besides, meditation always attenuated it."

"What a dashed awful waste. A lot of men would do anything to have your erectile power. I'm sorry for interrupting. Go on."

"Later I consumed less and less food. But, when that failed, I went to the outhouse that had no flushing toilet and contemplated the sh... excrement and inhaled the stench. That usually worked."

"So you merely suppressed your libido."

"I don't know what li ... libido is."

"Naturally, you must have thought of your Lizzie and your Willie in your fantasy."

"Danny, you're being absolutely absurd. For a start, I don't have any fantasy."

"Do you miss your Lizzie now?"

It took a while for the punching bag to bounce.

"I'm sure you miss your Reiner more so than I miss …"

"Not now. I'm inured to our long separation. Now that I can't reach him and he won't get in touch, I've weaned myself away from him."

The punching bag dared once more to bounce back.

"There's Karl now."

"Don't be daft. How can one replace an old friend known in childhood with a passing ship?"

"I know you well enough. My third eye sees your other 'von' more than a passing cruiser. After all he's perfectly Germanic and with that burly build and the golden hair, the blue eyes, he's right up your street. He reminds you of your Reiner, I'm sure. And my sixth sense…"

"Dash it, Primo! Don't give me your dashed silly third eye and your bally sixth sense! What I don't like about you is that you make things up about yourself as you go along!"

"I dare say the super liner named Wittenberg is superbly anchored in your heavenly haven."

"You should turn your penchant for poetry to better use. Write more poems from now on. I should have sent you to Germany to entice your hunky Hagenbach to come here with the orchestra."

"It wouldn't work."

"It worked when Liz went to Napo."

"How little you know me."

"I know you well enough to see that you've abandoned the holiness of priesthood and returned to the sinful world of men *with your eyes wide open*, as I overheard you say to Liz. Now you gladly put on the clothes and shoes that you would have thrown into the fire. You've given up absolute abstinence for utter indulgence, forsaking your frugal Isan life for urban affluence. Don't tell me that you do all these just for me."

"Do you think I have a hidden agenda?"

"I wish I had known. Unlike Liz, you're a closed book. I realised since our London years that I couldn't penetrate the maze of your twisted mind. There are too many bally blockages and dashed dead ends. But I would be hugely flattered, if it's entirely your devotion to me."

"If I say because of you I gave up the priesthood, came away from my home village to carry out whatever you ask me to do, would you believe me? *Ah, my hidden agenda! I must start resurrecting 'The Monsoon People' before going down in the whirlpool of sins.*"

"Yes, I would. Say it! Go on! Say it! Assure me that I can trust you. In my world, I'd give half of my fortune to the one I can trust."

"I don't want half of your fortune. I've already been deeply in debt to you for your good intention to build the school and modern houses for the teachers and for my family. Your accursed *filthy lucre* has already caused havoc to my people."

"What?"

"I've just received a letter from my brother. Alas, for a mere mention that you would give them 10 million to build the school and three million to build our house, both Guru Kumjai and my brother Kiang have been under pressure from certain people in authority. They want their share of the spoils in the form of donations to some charities, and for this and that though the school and the houses aren't built as yet."

"Well! I'm dashed! Let them have some! Spend the bally money! It's not worth losing sleep over it, not to mention one's life!"

"You haven't given us the money yet."

"Ah! The money! The bally money! You'd better send for the teacher and your brother to come with two or three villagers as witnesses then. And we'll get the money matter over with. Come, brother. Come and sit down and give me a report on yesterday's reading at the Post."

Back to his chair, Little Primo cleared his throat.

"I read a very interesting book, *Pulping the South* by Larry Lohmann and Ricardo Carrere. One of your pulp and paper companies was assisted by a Canadian consultancy firm financed by a Canadian aid organization. It also stated that your company received 95 million pounds allocated as 'foreign aid' from one of Britain's development agencies a year after your Chief Executive Officer had been arrested for illegal logging and encroaching upon forest reserves in preparation for expanding eucalyptus plantations. Despite the Company's notoriety for land grabbing, encroaching on national parks, strong-arm tactics, and environmental irresponsibility, the UK

Corporation doled out 95 million pounds towards eucalyptus planting and the construction of a sawmill in an environmentally-sensitive watershed area where land speculation and forced eviction of small-holders had been on the increase. In some areas the forced evictions were exceedingly violent."

When Dani stood up and went to the windows, Little Primo paused.

"Dash it! Why was the fountain turned off? Go and tell the chief gardener to turn it back on."

"Now?"

"Now!"

"There're more…"

"Let's stop for a while. While you go down, I'll have our aperitif ready."

Venturing into the well-tended garden was a delight. But, the Chief of Security deterred the Napotian from venturing further, saying that the fountain would be spouting again soon.

"Should I not walk anywhere around your place, Danny?" Little Prem, having returned to the HQ, asked his employer, who was scolding Tanong Komkam, the servile manservant, for spilling the champagne.

"A drop of that is worth more than his day's wage! Dash it! How many times do I have to show the spineless cretin how to pour champagne? Damn it! I'm surrounded by idiots!"

"Does that include me as well?"

Dani slumped onto his chair.

But then he suddenly leaned forward, picked up a crystal paperweight and threw it at the servant.

Apologetically grinning, Tanong concentrated on mopping up the wine with a white napkin while Dani poured his own drink.

"Go away!" the lord and master growled.

Tanong knelt at the feet of his master and made a *namuskara* on the floor before crawling a few yards, then slowly rose to his feet and slunk away.

"Should I not walk anywhere around your place, Danny?" Mr Prim Proper Primo repeated, hoping that he could lessen Danny's anger by creating a diversion.

"No, you shouldn't. I meant to tell you that you aren't supposed to walk around unescorted. Papa and Mama are very security conscious. Zum Wohl!"

"I wonder whether I'd become accustomed to drinking at 10 o'clock in the morning," the little man beamed at the lord of the manor while committing to memory that somehow he must make up to Tanong, the battered servant.

"If you stick around here long enough, you will. Come to think of it, I know now why Papa went to London that year…the year your passport expired. I asked him to sign as your guarantor so that the Embassy would issue a new one. You and I went to meet him at The Ritz, remember? I always wanted to know the real reason why he was in London. He did not go there just to see us! He went to clinch the deal and get 95 million of British tax payers' money! Why did the CDC make such a huge donation? Siam has never been colonized and hasn't become a member of the Commonwealth to qualify for aid. What is the catch? Can you make that out?"

"No. I read English. You did International Relations at SOAS, Political Economy at LSE and Mathematics at Oxford. You work that out."

Dani tried to think of any plausible reasons why such an organization sponsored by ODA, Britain's official bilateral aid agency, accountable to Parliament, bestowed 95 million to a notorious foreign company that had already schemed to trawl in huge investment from China as well.

*Is my rapacious and shrewd father, who is also very generous with kickbacks, playing one against another?*

"Perhaps it may help if I read further from the note," the PR man contributed. "The CDC has been making investments in Africa, Asia and the Pacific. In Swaziland, it owns a forestry company that runs vast eucalyptus and pine plantations, and is a joint owner of a pulp company. It enters areas where private UK investors could not. In the case of Shell's failure to establish the proposed eucalyptus plantation project in Chantabury Province, one of the most fertile areas of Siam, CDC has to make sure that it has a foot in the door."

"I see. You're rather clever for a student of English. Go on."

"CDC seems to have competitors of the same nature, including Finland's FINNIDA, Sweden's SIDA, Canada's CIDA, and Japan's JICA. These are bilateral agencies. The book points out that Britain benefits less than Japan, Canada and Finland, when it comes to sales of machinery, consultation with the pulp and paper industry and the import of wood chips and pulp.

"And another thing, one of the articles claims that over five million people in Isan have been evicted from areas designated for eucalyptus planting. The fast-growing eucalyptus has been chosen to provide wood chips and pulp to the paper industry in Japan and China as well as to pulp and paper manufacturing plants in Siam. The trees greedily deplete water in the soil and moisture in the air, and thus they eventually caused less rainfall. After a few years of their growth, grass and other plants cannot survive underneath, due to the desiccation and acidity deposited in the soil by their fallen leaves, a self-protecting and generating way so that only eucalyptus can generate and grow. Wildlife avoids the trees; wild mushrooms, which are a source of food for local dwellers, cannot be found where the eucalyptus trees are grown. Soil experts claimed that it could take 30 years or more to improve the soil where eucalyptus trees have grown, if we want to get rid of the acidity and the poverty of the soil to give the land back to other trees. You and I sit here drinking one of the world's most expensive wines while the native trees in the remaining forests are being logged, slashed and burnt. We make pigs of ourselves eating and drinking while some environmentalists are being murdered by hired gunmen, and while millions of people are being brutally evicted to make way for the damaging eucalyptus. Now I understand why Nero played his fiddle while Rome was burning."

"Morbid."

"After your parents' visit to Finland and Sweden, an agreement was signed to assign FINNIDA to fund Siam's forestry master plan. But, because Siam's per capita GNP was too high to qualify for aid, Finland's aid money under FINNIDA's scheme had to be diverted to UNDP which subsequently chose Finland's biggest forestry consulting corporation as the master plan consultant. Later a Finnish firm was contracted to build a gigantic pulp and paper plant in Chachuengsao. Nobel was also cited for having a major slice in the gigantic pulp and paper project."

"Take care! Don't mention Nobel or use words such as 'damaging' or 'destructive' in your report or in your book. I plan to nominate you for the Nobel Prize for Literature."

"My book? I haven't written a book!"

"I know there's a book in you."

"Oh!"

"At our Hyde Park Square flat, I read *The Monsoon People*."

"It's most improper to read someone's private notes."

"You don't tell me what is proper or improper. I've the right to know what's going on under my roof!"

"It's not nice..."

"I knew that you burnt the manuscript. So it's only a matter of rewriting it. But, for now, you continue with the report."

"In Stockholm, your parents had a grand reception, but the reports did not indicate what the couple had achieved there. However, I made a list of major companies that stand to benefit from the pulp and paper enterprise and from turning Siam's arable land, forest reserves and parts of national parks into eucalyptus plantations. There's a mention that a labour leader, who led a strike at one of your manufacturing plants, has disappeared without a trace. I have his name here in case you want to know. I didn't know until now that only a minor sector of the public is aware of the pressure to have greater areas to grow eucalyptus. The populace at large is kept in ignorance of the danger from water and air pollution the colossal pulp and paper mills have been causing. You know, Danny, if you hadn't asked me to go to the Post's library to read these publications, I would never have had an inkling of all this. I am from the region that has been turned into eucalyptus plantations but would not have known the harm eucalyptus planting and pulp and paper manufacturing can do to the land, the soil, the air, the rivers, and the people in the area. I wonder why the authorities and the investors single-mindedly choose eucalyptus over other kinds of trees. And why investors spent less than three per cent instead of the required five per cent of the investment on the pollution control measures? Have you any idea?"

"Eucalyptus is the fastest growing tree variety. It can be harvested within five years, and that brings about quicker returns."

"At the expense of millions of human beings and the ecology?"

"Who cares about the underclass human beings and the ecology?

"Prince Charles does."

"Now I'll have to dash or I'll be late for luncheon with Karl. Are there more?"

"Few short passages only."

"Shoot!"

"Both foreign and domestic eucalyptus planting concerns have been associated with political parties in power. Yours, for example, has had a former Minister of Forestry and Agriculture as the board chairman.

"Here's a penultimate item: when an Australian aid organization proposed to supply iodized salt to every household in Isan to raise the level of intelligence, your father turned it down. He was quoted as follows: *There is no need to make the Isan people intelligent. Cheap and no-problem workers are what we want.* I didn't know that iodized salt improves IQ in people. But, apparently it has been scientifically proven that iodine intake during pregnancy has much to do with high IQ in later life.

"Lastly, an MP from the opposition pointed out that your father shouldn't parade along life's thoroughfare wearing the cap of an honorary doctorate degree. It was reportedly said also that even for a Master's Degree, your Papa hired an academic to write the thesis."

"Poppycock!"

# A Dollar Carrier

The morning after the public relations consultant had returned to the kingdom, the trio held a meeting.

"Why didn't you fly back with TC?" Dani asked.

"I went to Eastbourne to see Mum and Dad."

"They live in Bradford, don't they?"

"Bradford is so crime-ridden now."

"It's also one of the Asians' strongholds, is it not?"

"Mum and Dad aren't racists at all. They're very fond of you, aren't they, Primo? Eastbourne is much safer and has more hours of sunshine per year than anywhere else in all England."

"By the way, while you were in London, did you, by any chance, have a look at my flat?"

"Yes, but it was the last thing that I did. I also took Nin to Speakers' Corner."

"Nin?"

"I mean Taninsak."

"To speak! Good Lord!"

Little Primo's quip failed to amuse the lord and master.

"No. His English isn't good enough," ED quibbled.

"Thank goodness for that!" Dani sneered.

"From the Oxford Circus branch of Bank of Credit and Finance International, we tottered along Oxford Street. London in March was still awfully cold. In Bangkok, he said, he would not be seen walking anywhere. But we continued from Marble Arch to Speakers' Corner..."

"What did he do at BCFI?" Dani interrupted.

"He deposited a million."

"Cash?"

"Yes."

"And then?"

Elizabeth yawned.

"Sorry, it's jet lag."

Looking at her wristwatch, she exclaimed:

"Gosh! It's 3 a.m. in London!"

Imploringly she looked at her lover.

But the little man seemed unwilling to intervene.

"Dash it, Liz! Get on with it!"

"Over lunch, sorry, luncheon at Cafe Royal, he asked me to go with him to New York. He wouldn't enjoy New York on his own, he said. So after luncheon, we went to Travel Bag at Piccadilly Circus before going to your flat in St. James's. I played a tune or two on your Steinway. Taninsak was much impressed with the pictures, the furniture and the colour scheme."

"Well! I'm dashed! He knows about art and colour schemes!"

"Though his English is *snake snake fish fish*, as he himself said, your good man from Isan seemed to know quite a lot. He knew exactly whom to see at BCFI."

"Were you with him when he made the deposit?"

"Yes. He asked me to go everywhere with him because of his poor English. He even asked me to help carry his case to get through Heathrow."

"Dashed silly girl! You shouldn't carry anything for anyone going through international airports!"

"I did it because he trusted me. You see, he let me see the contents of the case."

"Dash it! There's no trust among thieves!"

"I'm not a thief! I'm just a pretty face, a dumb blond from Yorkshire, a Bradford butcher's daughter. You said so yourself. I just wanted to feast my eyes on that amount of cash. There was a sense of intrigue and some degree of risk and excitement involved."

Lovely Liz giggled and made faces at her friend.

But Dani was not amused, shaking his head in dismay.

"I'm amazed, Liz. With all the education you've had, you could..."

"She read English not Economics," the little man defended his love.

"No doubt! Both of you, students of English -- one firmly believes in reincarnation so that he'd walk into an English country house to reclaim the stately home that he believed to be the family seat, and the other practices promiscuity -- would carry anything for anybody through customs. I bet he told you the bank account number as well."

"He didn't have too. I was with him all the time in the bank, and put the documents in the case for him at the end of the transaction. Regardless of what you said about him, your good man from an Isan constituency was extremely generous. He bought me this gorgeous ring at Tiffany's when we finished the business in New York."

The beautiful blond stretched her left hand forward to exhibit the sparkling diamond.

"What business?"

"We opened a bank account."

"Did he do anything else?"

"We dropped in on a real estate agent on Fifth Avenue. He wanted to check on property prices."

"What did he want to buy?"

"A hotel and an apartment."

"A hotel?"

"Yes. The Winsor Plaza."

"If he can afford The Winsor Plaza, our man must be richer than I."

"Well, after all he's one of your father's trusted men."

"Did he see anybody?"

"Yes, a Singaporean and an American."

"What about?"

"Buying crude oil from Iraq."

"What?" Dani suddenly stood up, glaring.

"Buying crude oil from Iraq."

"Can he do that?"

"The American said it could be done. The Singaporean assured that the crude could be refined in Singapore or in Malaysia. Then, the petrol or 'gas', as the American said, could be smuggled into the kingdom and Burma."

Now Dani was agitatedly pacing the floor. Obviously such information bothered him. Turning swiftly, he growled at Mr Prim and Proper Primo.

"Have you been to the Post Library lately?"

Caught off guard while mentally wandering in Hyde Park, the little chap was jolted back to the table with the images of daffodils still vivid in his mind.

Elizabeth saved him.

"While in London I read in a newspaper that Wilhelm Hagenbach would be conducting at Royal Festival Hall next week."

"In that case I'd fly to London while Willie is there and ask him to bring the Philharmonic to Bangkok any time that suits him. I'll make another offer that he could hardly refuse or better still our little fellow here may want to convince his old friend on my behalf. You know, Liz, they knew each other quite well. Our Mr Pee may have a bigger clout than I. So, quickly Primo! Have you got anything for me today?"

"Oh yes!" said the Isaner, glad that the subject on his relationship with Hagenbach was expurgated. "Firstly, the headline: **200,000 acres needed to grow eucalyptus** – a colossal China-Siam pulp and paper venture could be in jeopardy because the authority involved could not secure for Siam Progressive Agrarian Development Corporation enough land to grow eucalyptus. The Corporation, being one of Siam's largest pulp and paper manufacturers, asked the government to assure China of raw material supplies for the mill in order to keep the 100 billion baht project here. On the other hand, a government spokesman, Sakawit Puechpolcharoen, claimed that a further five million people might have to be evicted from their properties or a vast number of forest reserves might have to be sacrificed to provide the firm that much land to grow eucalyptus. Meanwhile, Babin Suntharaksakarn, CEO of SPADC, said authorities should think twice before China changed its mind and switched the venture to Malaysia. He described the 60 billion baht pulp mill and 40 billion baht eucalyptus project as world-class ventures. Though China might consider Malaysia, it still saw Siam as having a better infrastructure and without any stringent environmental measures. According to a source at the Ministry of Agriculture, the Prime Minister is expected to inform Chinese officials concerned when he visits China next month that the government could secure 200,000 acres in Isan for SPADC.

"Secondly, apart from the alleged petrol smuggling activities, a suspect had done a deal with a Burmese army colonel based in Shan State to move a massive amount of smuggled petrol across the border. But the deal is in direct competition with the Puma Group headed by a godfather who is also in control of an illegal logging enterprise. Incidentally there was a report of an attempt on your father's life in the same week.

"Thirdly, a politician is in the process of relocating an illegal casino operation in the Golden Triangle to a location some kilometers from Siamese soil on the Cambodian side. Another politician is heavily promoting a casino at the Burmese border, following the inauguration of an airport close to it. The names of these men are on the "A" List.

"Fourthly, your father is alleged to have received a gift cheque of 100 million for granting a monopoly in telecommunications to a tycoon."

"Peanuts!" Dani snapped.

"Fifthly, another politician, also on the "A" list is suing Reuters and the European News Network and a Siamese vernacular, Kaosod Daily, for damages following their reports pertaining that he was refused a US visa due to drug trafficking."

"Stop there! Give me the name of that politician. Liz! Get in touch with the bureau chief of Reuters and find out about the case. Would it be beyond your ability to dig into the source? What is the date of that news report, Primo? What? Almost two years ago! And not any mention of the case since? No? Then it's likely to be an out-of-court settlement. Find that out, Liz."

The conversation was interrupted by the Chief of Security.

"There are several Isan men to see you, sir."

Having heard such, the Isaner exclaimed:

"They are here!"

"Bring them here," said the lord and master.

"Here, sir?"

"Yes! Where else? From now on, every time Isan men arrive, bring them here right away."

"Yes, sir!"

It took almost fifteen minutes for the escorted visitors to reach the Blue Room.

Kiang, Tongdum, Panya and Chief Singhon stood rigidly behind Kumjai, dumb in amazement at the sight of the glittering crystal, rich fabric and gilded decoration in the heavenly hall.

*They have brought a throng of Napotians with them,* Little Prem's buffalo's eyes perceived.

*They are the damned of the earth in the splendour of the sinisterly rich,* the cynical blond seized the irony.

*A bunch of scarecrows, and they stink,* Dani put on a charming front as soon as he had a whiff of the rustic scent of the country folk when each of them approached and performed the *namuskara.*

He also endured the sight of their unkempt appearances. Nevertheless, the magnanimous billionaire invited the visitors to sit at the long table.

"How was the journey? The night bus must be rather tiresome. Tanong! Tell the housekeeper to put my friends up on this floor. They will be here for two or three nights."

After the servant and the CoS had left, Dani turned to the Napotians.

"I trust Khun Kumjai has been re-appointed."

"Not yet, sir."

"It's sticky, is it? Is there someone helping you?"

"No, sir."

"When it seems almost impossible to get something done in the land of the nicest people money can buy, it may indicate that the machine is clogged and so it needs some lubrication. So why don't we lubricate it? The village chief should be the one to be entrusted with the grease."

"But, sir, we have no grease at all," Singhon whined.

There's plenty of grease for clogged-up machines. Khun Prem will give you a good supply of it. He will take all of you to a bank so that there will be no more problems."

Addressing his public relations executive, the boss exuded his princely charm.

"I say, Khun Prem! I want to set the Napo Project rolling as soon as our friends here put their things in their rooms. Let's start with setting up bank accounts as we discussed previously. Later, you present 10,000 baht in cash to each of our guests so as to cover the cost of clothes and shoes and other things they may want to buy. Then have luncheon at the coffee shop of The Imperial Palace. I shall catch up with you there later. Khun Elizabeth may wish to accompany you on this venture."

"Yes, tannai, kobprakhun mak mak ka," the PR Consultant purportedly grovelled.

"But before you go, my dear Lisabet. Call Karl-Michael. Tell him to meet me at The Bordeaux Grill at half past twelve. Ask him to have the hotel photographer ready to take photos of me presenting a cheque to the Napo people. Later you can do a press release on that. Chop! Chop!"

# Operation Norma

To wed, Panya Palaraksa had good looks on his side but his penury posed a problem. To make the situation worse, the workers, who had returned from slaving abroad, had become hugely prosperous in contrast. Furthermore, most nubile women had left for the capital or some lucrative seaside resorts where foreign visitors thronged.

Then Little Prem made it possible for the spunky bachelor to pay off the family's debts, regain the land title-deeds from the usurer and connect electricity to the house.

Soon the former outlaw sported a gold necklace, a wristwatch, and smart new clothes. He made an extension to the old house so that he had a room of his own and equipped it with new furniture. For the family, he afforded a television set and a refrigerator. He also bought one more buffalo, and kept an ox and a cow for calves.

The scheme worked wonderfully, for now the new-rich could announce his forthcoming marriage.

All went well.

So the project manager penned a note to the billionaire.

*Dear Danny,*

*Kumjai and Anucha have been officially appointed.*

*Chief Singhon is organizing a party to celebrate the new school. As for the hand-over ceremony, he will leave it to you to fix the date. Obviously he delights in taking the credit for everything new and progressive, including the water reservoir, which 100 soldiers from a Korat regiment have dug for us.*

*I'll make a separate report to Col. Ayu and thank him on behalf of our people for the reservoir which should hold water throughout the year.*

*With gratitude,*

*Prem*

If the effervescent blond had been with him, she would have been following him like his shadow as he went from site to site.

Now the little fellow wondered how she was getting on with the boss in Bangkok.

*You must not mind Danny's hubris and contentious nature,* the project manager wrote another letter. *Deep down, believe me, he is a decent human being. To me, he is like a brother. I can feel our brotherhood deep in my heart.*

At that very moment the University of London graduate was having a discussion with her employer in the headquarters.

"Nin said *let's fly together again like our trip to London and New York.*"

"Didn't he tell you where he was going?"

"No."

The employer and the employee scowled at one another.

"All right! You may go with him. It's no fun staying around here with me, is it?"

The Hon. Taninsak MP used the same case and the same suitcase that he had on the Bangkok-London-New York route.

Lovely Liz sniggered when her Randy Nin said she could open the case and see the content.

"Just like old times!"

Opening the case, her eyes dilated.

She could not resist the temptation, fervently caressing the bank notes.

Having landed at Chiangrai Airport, a chauffeur-driven limousine took them to Chiangsaen and finally to a hotel on the bank of Mekong River.

Here, the lively lass stood beside the Isan MP, holding a glass of sparkling wine on the balcony of their hotel room, overlooking the oozing river.

"There Lao," TC pointed to the right. "This side Golden Triangle. Over there in Burma a casino complex."

"So this is the notorious Golden Triangle! I never thought I'd live to see it. What a view! What are you going to do with those dollar notes?

The dollar-carrier silenced her with a kiss, and then led her into the bedroom.

In the evening they dined alfresco, on the extended terrace of the hotel dining room which looked onto the river below. How peaceful and unhurried the great river seemed to be at that hour.

The enviable lovers remained at their table long after other diners had left. Elizabeth had been drinking red wine, and still had a glass to finish, while her lover had progressed to his favourite XO cognac.

Under the stars, the lascivious lass professed that she had been happy, absentmindedly caressing the diamond ring.

"Dani told me that you're married and keep a mistress as well, is that true?"

"True. No big secret. Many Siamese men keep mistresses."

"O Nin. I wish you could speak English so well that we'd talk seriously."

"No need. Speak English no need for MP. One former Prime Minister cannot say 'thank you' in English but can do thesis for a degree, quote English book and French book. Siamese people bow and *wai* him, lick foot. No need speak English. Action gooder than talk."

"You see, when you try, you can speak English."

"Why try. English people no try Siamese."

"But when you travel abroad, you need to speak English."

"I travel you travel. Ha! Ha! Ha!"

In their suite, Elizabeth found that the bed had been turned down and the room had a peculiar smell. She quickly checked the dressing table and the wardrobe.

*What a strange scent*, she wondered.

A thought flashed.

"Nin! You'd better check the case."

"Money safe here."

"You shouldn't have left it there!'"

"No one think one million dollar in there."

"Why did you have to bring so much money here?"

"I make it same same like we go London New York. It make me happy."

"Really! You're incredibly sentimental!"

"I love you, Lisabet."

"I don't believe you, a married man who also keeps a *mianoy*. It's sweet-talking."

"No sweet mouth. I show one more time."

While TC and his Lisabeth were blissfully together at the borders of three countries, PS sat on the floor of his unfurnished new house, with a piece of paper in front of him. The light from a candle was sufficient to jot down the objectives of The Napo Project.

*In modern Siam, tens of thousands of remote villages in Isan are impoverished and suffering greatly from poverty, drought, disease and ignorance.*

*Recently the Napo Project has been established to provide assistance to the poor, the needy, the disabled, the aged and the sick.*

## The objectives of the Napo Project

*To improve living conditions in any way possible, including improvement of health, soil and water supply;*

*To help the helpless, who are disabled or retarded, and widows with several children to fend for, as well as those who are over 65 years old by providing financial support, food, clothes, and medicine;*

*To provide scholarships to the children of the destitute;*

*To minimize migration from rural to urban areas by providing arable land for the landless and instill in their minds pride of being Isaners instead of feeling ashamed of having been born in Isan.*

He reread the draft once more.

*My English is far from perfection but still the wording sounds as if I am reaching for a star. How much can I achieve?*

The little chap stayed awake, imagining and reflecting, unaware of the humming of mosquitoes.

The morning sun had already increased the temperature. So the project manager perspired profusely while helping the builders clear the scaffolds and discarded planks. Despite the strenuous physical exertion, his mind had been preoccupied with the thoughts of the community development scheme.

Fed by dreams, the dreamer forgot to partake of luncheon.

In the afternoon, he went to a furniture shop in Muang in a hired pick-up, a vehicle that had become fashionable among the new-rich in Isan villages.

He thought of buying a car. It would be convenient to be able to drive back and forth between Napo and Bangkok, Napo and Muang, and transport the sick to and from the hospital some 60 miles away.

At present, the very poor, who were ill or had accidents, could not afford the transport so they suffered at home, waiting to recover or to die.

On the other hand, it would make the journeys more pleasant and enjoyable as opposed to travelling by bus. Many a time one had put one's life in the hands of those daredevil drivers. It was scary to read frequently the reports in newspapers of gruesome accidents in which most passengers did not survive.

*But Lizzie does not mind, having to travel by bus.*

Thinking of his love, Little Prem wondered: *What is she doing now?*

At that very moment, Lovely Liz was telling her boss about her 'flight of fancy' with The Hon. Taninsak MP.

"When we landed at Bangkok Airport, he told me to make myself scarce. His driver and a bodyguard would be meeting him, he said. So I stood farther from him at the carousel. When he picked his case up, it seemed rather heavy. You can tell how heavy it could be for he had to lift it with both hands. I noticed too that at the hotel the bellboy found it too heavy to lift with one hand when we checked out. But on our way up to the Golden Triangle, it was lighter in comparison."

"Did he meet anyone in Chiangrai?"

"No. I was with him the whole time, except when he or I were in the bathroom."

"Get in touch with Little Primo. Ask him to come back. I have a surprise for him. Now, let's go down to the gardens. I want you to see some rare orchids."

Far from all ears in the formal garden, the boss gave an instruction.

"At six, we'll go to The Imperial Palace. While I'm with Karl, you dash to the nearest shopping centre. Use a public telephone to call this number. Ask for Dick Fuller. Say you're Norma. He'll tell you where to meet him. Tell him everything concerning your trips with TC to London and New York and Chiangrai. By 'everything' I don't mean you'd include the bed-talk and the romps. Give him the names of the banks and account numbers. Describe all the contacts he's made. By the way, never telephone DF from here or from the hotel, or mention his name to me or to Mr Pee while we're inside."

"Where are the rare orchids?"

"Not in this garden."

# A Drop in the Ocean

"Have you a driving license, Primo?" Dani inquired, sitting down at the head of the table in the headquarters.

"Yes. But I daren't drive in Bangkok. The way people drive here is mortifying."

"Drive like everybody else then. Forget all the rules that you might have observed in the U.K. Here, most drivers don't stop for pedestrians who were waiting for a chance to dash across the *zebra path*. And there's no 'give way to the right'. Most drivers don't observe the solid yellow lines or double yellow lines for that matter. You can whimsically change lanes, or overtake from the left. Everybody does, including our chauffeurs."

"Is that why there're so many accidents? On the way from the airport yesterday, I saw a gruesome accident at an intersection," said Lovely Liz who had accompanied Taninsak on a flight of fancy to Hong Kong. "The worst traffic offenders are Mercedes drivers, and the policemen seem blind when a Mercedes jump the traffic lights."

"That's why our Mr Pee is going to drive one of them," Dani revealed. "It's waiting in the garage. Liz! You have yet to tell me about the visit to Hong Kong. After that you check the responses from the members of the media invited to cover the opening and the hand-over of the school. Then, get in touch with Jonas. Tell him the total number of the invited media so he can arrange food and drink accordingly. Primo, I want the media people in Napo at noon. Co-ordinate with the headmaster and ask him to let us know the number of high-ranking officials from the provincial town to attend the hand-over ceremony. Warn him that a catering van will arrive before noon that day. The catering staff members need help to set up a marquee and the tables and chairs. How many television camera crews are going?"

"Eight."

"The English language newspapers?"

"Two."

"National newspapers?"

"Six."

"Chinese vernacular?"

"Three."

"The weeklies and monthlies?"

"10."

"Karl-Michael?"

"Confirmed."

"Witty Wit?"

"Confirmed."

"And Ayu?"

"Confirmed."

"In that case Karl and I will go in my Rolls. We can't have too many Mercedes in a tiny village. I know Ayu has a Benz, and Wit will show off his new Benz. By the way, Primo, I don't want any of your upstart MPs or their vote canvassers to muscle in on this to get publicity. Now, Liz, your dashed fancy flight to Hong Kong."

"Once again Taninsak let me open the case to have a peep, and it was full to the brim with tightly bound one hundred dollar notes."

"Did he ask you to carry the case to get through Kai Tak?"

"No."

"Then?"

"Then to the hotel. What a sumptuous suite! If it had not been for that towering office block that has hundreds of round windows, you know, the building said to be the tower of a thousand .... holes, we would have had a panoramic view of the Fragrant Harbour. I don't know why they call it Fragrant Harbour. It stinks. You could smell it even in the cabin the moment the aircraft landed."

"Dash it, Liz! Cut out the dashed stinking crap!"

"Sorry! TC did not waste much time. We went to the BCFI branch and emptied the case there. A chunk of it was consequently transferred to New York. By four o'clock we were back at the hotel. He felt much at home in Hong Kong. He speaks Chinese, too."

"He's a *Chink*. Third generation," the boss croaked as if he was not one himself. "His only thing that's straight is the hair on his head."

"Gosh! Is that original? I would like to say it to his face!"

"Get on with it, Liz!"

"After breakfast, we caught a ferry to an outlying island and we had a meal at a seafood restaurant near the pier. It was fabulous and, being a working day, it wasn't full. After a leisurely lunch, sorry, luncheon, we took the ferry back, but instead of going to the hotel, we went straight to the bank, and repeated the same procedure. I wondered why he took the risk, carrying that case full to the brim with 100 dollar notes all the way to the island and back. We could have gone to the bank after breakfast to get rid of the cash before catching the ferry. That would have been logical and with hardly any risk."

"Did he see or talk to anyone on the ferry or in the restaurant?"

"No. I was with him all the time except when he went into the ferry toilet just before landing on the way back. His case seemed heavier after that. He didn't let me carry it, but I could tell that it was heavy the way he handled it."

"The same case, Liz?"

"Obviously."

"What is it?"

"Samsonite."

"How long was the blighter in the toilet?"

"About five minutes."

"The switch could have been made in the ferry toilet. I think we are on the right track. What a tangled web! Bangkok - Golden Triangle – London - New York - Hong Kong."

"There could be more. Lower Burma and Shan State for instance," the creep contributed.

But the ring leader did not acknowledge the little man's remark. He was writing on a piece of paper that read: *Use a public phone to call DF. Tell him exactly what you have just told me. If you did manage to jot down the MP's HK bank account number, give that to him as well.*

Nonchalantly, Dani handed the note to Elizabeth.

After she had read it, he put his hand out to retrieve the paper, and then quickly tore it up in tiny bits.

"Now, Primo, it's your turn."

"There's only one précis today."

"I say! You've been lazy!"

Ignoring the remark, the public relations manager read: "Under the headline: Bank Financial Adviser fights extradition, Krung Siam Bank financial adviser Rajkit Senaskul, who was fighting against extradition in Canada, claimed that should he return to Siam he would immediately be liquidated. It has been alleged that your father has squeezed a large amount of bank money from Mr Rajkit who had to leave the country in a hurry as a result. The … "

"Primo!" Dani interrupted. "Since we are going to have our hands full in the coming week, you may stop your reading at the Post Library. Liz, you concentrate on the Reuters and ENN case and talk to Reuters Bureau Chief again."

"I don't want to be a bore, Danny," Little Prem mentioned. "But, please elucidate me as to why your father, who's already become exceedingly rich, had to squeeze more millions out of bankers."

"It's sheer greed! Look at his hideous monkey face and large pointed ears. His satanic eyes gleam greedily. His mouth salivates at the sight of cash. People like that can't bear to see indigenous trees left standing. They must be logged. They can't bear to see forest reserves and public land unclaimed, believing also that the entire indigenous people are a great source of cheap manpower. Mama, the power behind the man, spurs him on, taking advantage of his supreme position and political clout. Between the two of them, they have to take the largest chunk of everything, controlling the most lucrative sectors of commerce. They can't bear to see a prime site without wanting to put up a hotel or a towering apartment block or a condominium; a lucrative location without wanting to open a supermarket or a convenience store or a restaurant. They must make use of a space on the pavement to set up food stalls for one of their ant-like army of minions to sell the so-called Diamond Roast Chickens. It's a money-grubbing Chinese shopkeeper's mentality which regrettably I've inherited and can't expunge! I can't tear it out of me! Damn it! I can't!"

Dani shifted agitatedly, scattering the papers on the table. Grabbing a crystal paperweight, the furious Siamese of Chinese extraction threw it seemingly at the source of his anger.

"Look where it's landed you! Now you're the 28th richest man in the world! Surely your father isn't that odious. It's not the Oedipus complex, is it? I'd like to know him..."

"Dash it, Liz! Don't be a dashed bally moth attracted to the flame!"

Dani stood up suddenly, toppling the chair, and walked the floor back and forth and then to the window and back to the toppled Chippendale.

Seeing great pain in the benefactor, the freak rose and put the chair back to its previous position, thinking of a cure.

*Oh, I know. Wine usually does the trick!*

"It's aperitif time, Danny. Dom Perignon is coming!"

The freak gaily glided out of the room.

Ten minutes later the jolly jackal reappeared with Waterford crystal glasses, followed by Tanong, carrying a silver wine cooler.

"You haven't learned to say *Dom Peri-yong*. I've told you so many times, Primo. You don't want Karl to sneer at you, do you?"

"No, I don't. *Dom peri-yong*. How's that?"

The self-appointed valet popped the cork and poured the liquid into the glasses while instructing the servant:

"Tanong, I'll serve. You may go now and tell Maid Samorn to come and collect the shattered paperweight over there. Tanong, I didn't break it. Your lord and master did."

The servant bowed and left.

"To the Napo Project," the former monk toasted.

Soon the sparkling wine worked wonderfully on the bibulous billionaire. DP condescended to smile after ED had told an imbecilic joke about an Australian jackaroo from an outback station near Laverton, out on Kalgoolie town for the first time with a prostitute in Hay Street. It had a punch line of: "If it's like a kangaroo, I'd need all the room I can have."

"Your Mr Pee here revealed to me why he went into the priesthood. He wanted to have a pure heart and to be kind and compassionate in this life so as to deserve a rebirth in old England and regain his family seat. Have you ever heard anything so absurd and as puerile as that?"

"No, my lord."

"Do you know he truly believes that in his previous life he was a British military commander doing a stint in India?"

"He told me that too, my lord."

"You believe him?"

"Yes, my lord."

"Your chap also believes that he can walk into a stately home in England, and claim: 'It's mine! It was, in the past-life, at any rate.' Listen to this! When he and I visited Lord Norbury at Kennington Hall, your Mr Triple Ps dashed here and there, examining the furniture, pictures by old masters, sculptures, tapestries, the chandeliers, and then muttered: 'No, definitely Kennington Hall isn't.' He also firmly believes that being pure in the heart, doing good deeds and carrying out charitable activities to benefit the less fortunate, he would be rewarded with a rebirth in old England as well as recovering the family seat. Ha! Ha! Ha!"

*Just as well he didn't know that in childhood, I was called the freak, the creep, the wimp, said to be no better than a lump of excrement.*

Dani's derision rang throughout the marble hall while his alcohol-enhanced mirth furled and swirled above the head of a meek little maid who was carefully collecting every shard.

On schedule, a catering coach from The Imperial Palace Hotel reached The Napo Primary School half an hour before Dani and Karl arrived in a chauffeur-driven Rolls-Royce. The students were excited at the arrival of vehicles and men from the capital. The sight of the uniform-wearing hotel staff members and the elegant man and an enormous white man made them truly believe that these were the angels from the City of Angels.

Hence these bewildered children, who had been told to put on their best clothes for the day, stood ramrod in their classrooms. The desks had been moved out to serve as food tables in the huge tent that was being set up on the lawn between the school building and the water reservoir, dug months ago by 100 army men from Korat.

Kumjai had told his pupils that a great number of masters and dignitaries were coming to visit them. So then he ordered them to stand still, cup their hands at their chests and pray to the Divine Lord to prevent the imminent event from being dampened by the rain.

Kumjai supplicated along with them, his first batch of children, deprived of education during the years he had struggled for survival in the woods.

At times the headmaster could feel vigorously young. He had been revitalized by the children's eagerness to learn and by the sight of the substantial building that had toilets and water tanks. Many a time he had experienced a sudden joy. Despite the bloody battles, he had returned to Napo alive.

Emerging from prayer, the headmaster was startled to see two dignified visitors at the door.

Guru Kumjai welcomed the patrons to his class.

"Usually at this time, we pray for rain, but today we have just made a plea to Divinity not to cause a downpour," the teacher explained.

Then the class sang a song to welcome the visitors.

"Excellent!" complimented Dani.

Then the divine pair went towards the marquee. There, realising that the undersized chairs would not be suitable for the bureaucrats and the media people, the billionaire vented his displeasure.

"I'll get Primo for this! He should have known!"

"He can't think of everything."

"He doesn't think! Like the rest of *them*, he just doesn't think!"

"Well, all of us big boys can be little children for an hour or so. We can stand or move about; it'll do the bureaucrats the world of good," the charming hotelier made an excuse on behalf of the country lad who had not yet become a threat, a subject of petty jealousy. "Besides, there'll be plenty of food and drink. I'm sure they have never had smoked salmon, baked ham, lobster terrine, liver pate and wines before. Let's see. These little chairs might be sturdy enough even for my big backside."

Wittenberg lowered himself down on one of them to prove his point.

"Don't sit on it too long. Your 17 stone might break it."

"In a God-forsaken place such as this, a sweet little poet was born," Karl mused.

The sweet innocent sound of the choir could be heard.

"You mean our puny Primo?"

"Ja! Ja! He's the only gorgeous young man I know who isn't aware of his enormous potential."

"Unlike us, hm? We know we're charming and good-looking and our potentials are enormous. If we think otherwise, it's false modesty, is it not?"

Looking at his diamond-encrusted Rolex, Dani suggested: "I say! Let's have our aperitifs before the hordes come. I wonder what Jonas put in the Eskies for us."

The lord and master opened one of the large iceboxes. His eyes gleamed when he saw several bottles of sparkling wine.

"Yes, in what you call a God-forsaken place such as this dump, Pommery will do nicely. I'm ..."

"That's for the peasants," the versatile hotelier interrupted.

From another ice-box, Karl revealed Taittinger *Compte de Champagne* 1976.

"Jonas wants you to taste *Le Compte,* a sample bottle from an importer. He wants to know whether it should be on The Bordeaux Grill wine list."

"Those squalid shanties are full of beady-eyed gits. This isn't a proper place in which to taste one of the finest champagnes. What shall we do with the gawping nits?"

"Let them eat cakes!"

One of the waiters brought two sparkling wine glasses in time to receive the over-flowing liquid gold.

*How kind of you to come*, the little children sang from the school.

Their merry song caused Dani's to respond:

"How kind of you to let me come."

Performing the rite of wine tasting, the billionaire lifted the bubbling glass to eye level, proclaiming: "Clear pale straw. Fine bubbles." Then he tenderly brought the wine to his lips. Having taken half a mouthful, he gently swirled it round and round in his mouth, making a soft sucking sound at the same time to take in some outside air to blend with the wine inside.

"A fine full body, a perfect balance of fruit and acidity," Dani declared. "*Le Compte* certainly has finesse. Is it Blanc de Blancs?"

Scrutinizing the label, KW confirmed:

"Yes, it is."

"To us!"

At that moment Boonliang, Piang, Poon and Toon led a throng of old men and women, and the swarming children, to join the other village folk who had already been gawking at the burly, blue-eyed foreigner.

"Talking about nits and gits, here come some more."

Dani sounded as if he did not recognize the bent and wobbly Mrs Surin and her clan whom he had seen at their squalid hovel the first time he came to Napo.

The hotelier was quick to notice that he, not the hotel owner, had become the centre of attention. His golden hair, big nose and huge body fascinated the scraggy, skinny little people, young and old.

"These mangy crones and their ragged brats aren't invited to eat and drink, are they?"

"Of course not! They can feast their beady eyes on you instead. Try to be socially correct, Mick. Take care not to use those offensive words when Mr Pee is within earshot. He's frightfully sensitive when it comes to his people."

"What shall I use then?"

"Try *hygienically-challenged elders* for mangy crones and *sartorially-challenged cherubim* for ragged brats."

"My English is not good enough for that. In my line of work, I have always been politically and socially correct. But in the land of nits and gits, I can relax just a little, can't I? Are these dumb things looking blankly at me or are they thinking some curious thoughts?"

131

Pira Sudham

"Have you ever wondered whether animals think? When we stopped on the way here for you to take photos of buffaloes, the beasts looked at you just the way these good people are devouring you with their eyes. When you have never been taught to think all your bally life, can you or would you think on your own? I say, Mick, stare back at them and see what thoughts would come to your well-developed mind. Go on! Stare at them!"

In less than a minute, after having followed Dani's suggestion, Karl responded:

"I wonder why this lot has only the very young and the very old, and there is nothing in between."

"Young men and women have left to look for work elsewhere; many mothers too, leaving their brats with their parents. That's why 90 per cent of taxi drivers in Bangers are Isaners. That's why factories, sweatshops, brothels, bars, beer gardens, and hideous bordellos like the Caligula Club are over-supplied with obliging young workers."

"I also wonder whether among these hungry, half-naked children there is another Little Primo."

"Don't start that! Otherwise, you'll be competing with Witty, that cradle-snatcher, who specializes in innocent but cocky Isan teenagers."

"No, I don't mean that. I mean an uncut diamond."

"I prefer exquisitely-cut diamonds."

Meanwhile Dr Prawit arrived.

"Well! I'm dashed! Look at him! Who does he think he is, Noel Coward?"

The billionaire's heart sank at the sight of the dapper lawyer who had emerged from his Mercedes with three comely lads.

"Dash it, Witty! Must you have your slaves with you whenever you travel?"

"My dear Danny, to be fair, you should allow me a sip of champagne first before you'd launch an attack. These boys came from a neighbouring district. After the party is over, I'll take them to their villages."

"This is not a dashed jolly party! This is work!"

"If it's work, why do you have a glass of champagne in your hand?"

"Do me a favour! Make your boys less conspicuous. They can sit under a tree over there. The government officials, the media and Ayu will be here any minute now."

Meanwhile, Kumjai led Anucha, Chief Singhon, Kiang, Tongdum and Panya, into the marquee to pay respect to the patrons.

All performed the *namuskara* gesture first to Tannai Dhani and then to Khun Prawit and lastly to the big white man.

Kumjai deplored the sight of wet shirts on his team workers who had exerted themselves, putting up the marquee. There would not be time for them to change. For now the vans, carrying the provincial bureaucrats and civil servants of the province, pulled in at the edge of the playground, followed by Colonel Ayumongkol's shining Mercedes and then the coach that carried the members of the media.

"Am I to speak too, Danny?" Prawit inquired.

"No! This is my show. Besides, the moment you open your prim little mouth, everyone, including the peasants, will know. Where's your bally handbag?"

"In my car."

"Thank goodness for that!"

"Dear me, Danny! You're so bitchy today."

"Shut up!"

Dani graciously welcomed the provincial chief.

From that moment onward the 28th richest men in the world was all out to be charming, *sawasdi krapping* and *namuskara-ing* while photographers snapped pictures, and while the video cameras recorded.

"Sawasdi krap Colonel Ayumongkol," Dhani made a welcome greeting.

Later when they were not being filmed, Dani lowered his voice:

"My word! You look utterly smart in your uniform, medals and all, what? Every time we are to meet from now on, I forbid you to wear civilian clothes."

Then it was Guru Kumjai's turn to lead Anucha to do the *sawasdi krapping* and the *namuskara-ing* to the Governor and the civil servants.

Meanwhile Prem and Elizabeth approached their boss and made a report.

"All went well on the way. Liz did the briefing in English and I in Siamese. As you might have already noticed, we have with us an

American journalist from *Business in Siam*, and an Australian, who's the editor of *The Management*.

"How about Ayu?"

"He's been well-briefed by yours truly, and he has a copy of the programme."

"Very good, Primo. In twenty minutes, you can take the stage. Not that there's any, but you know what I mean. What is the name of the Chief again?"

"Khun Petch Nakararungsi."

When Dani had a chance, he whispered to Karl: "Let's ply them with drinks now."

From then on VVK took on the role of a catering supervisor.

The popping of the corks made an exciting salvo for those who had never heard them pop before. Several female officials and the crowding natives exclaimed in surprise.

Kumjai shied away from the drink being offered and went back to his students in the school building.

Elizabeth begged a waiter, who was serving a platter of smoked salmon sandwiches, for a full tray, which she swiftly carried off to the school.

After the food and drink were had sufficiently by all in the marquee, the Master of Ceremonies commenced. Having made a brief mention of the Napo Project, the project manager invited Dr. Dhani to speak.

The adorable billionaire assumed an elegant posture.

"The sheer necessity of education convinced me that a school must be built. Then again, it was also one of the headmaster's hopes and dreams to have a school in which he could continue teaching."

Then the MC invited the Governor of the Province to accept the school building and the teachers' houses.

On this auspicious occasion, the important man proclaimed:

"As a servant of the people, I am greatly humbled by the magnanimity shown by the compassionate son of the very revered Minister. How could a person in so high a place, living in luxury in the City of Angels, the highly centralized capital, 400 kilometres away, pinpoint our dire needs and thus condescend to alleviate hardship? Napo is indeed fortunate to have the care and kindness from such an influential, dignified person as Dr Dhani."

At the mention of his name, Dani stepped close to the Governor so as to present a large golden key, the key to the school.

Then the Napo Project Manager spoke of another admirable deed and gave the honour to Colonel Ayumongkol Mongkolkulthorn to present the Mongkol Pond to the Napotians' representative, Headman Singhon Homhaul.

Being a man of few words, the Colonel's speech was brief.

Now Singhon had the chance to gain face and impress his superiors and the dwellers of Napo. He did not fail to speak of the expediency by which the road and electricity and telephone lines had been brought to Napo during his short stint as the village chief.

"Not so long ago vehicles could not reach the village in monsoon seasons but now the Napotians have a chance to admire these grand cars," said Singhon.

Meanwhile, Elizabeth carefully carried to the Colonel a large silver bowl filled with water, symbolizing the water supply that Napo was now fortunate enough to have.

Colonel Ayumongkol handed over the silver bowl of water to the headman to receive it on behalf of the inhabitants.

Then little girls and boys emerged from the school building to form two rows several yards away from the marquee. They sang the well-rehearsed song of appreciation and gratitude.

*How touching!* Dani thought.

*I wonder whether I would come across some of these little children in a few years time in brothels, bars and nightclubs in Bangkok,* Prawit pondered.

*Oh, my dear little ones, how lovely!* Elizabeth's heart went out to every choir member.

*I could see myself as a nine-year-old among them,* Little Prem reflected.

The beautiful blond approached the members of the choir.

"*Deemakmak ka,*" she remarked. "Very good indeed. Now, let's sing in English. *Happy Birthday to you! Happy birthday to you! Happy birthday! Happy birthday Krooyai Kumjai! Happy birthday to you.* All together now!"

So the children sang along with the pretty *farang* woman, gingerly at first but boisterously when they repeated the second time.

What a surprise for the headmaster whose birthday would have passed uncelebrated. Then his former pupil presented a birthday cake baked specially for the occasion by the pastry chef of the Imperial Palace Hotel.

"I know now why you two schemers told me to pick today for the hand-over," said the lord and master.

"It's coincidental, isn't it Lizzie?"

But lovely Liz was concentrating on telling the headmaster that he should make a wish and blow out the candles.

Kumjai did as suggested.

"I'm a Cancer, a *poo*, too," Elizabeth told the head teacher as he blinked his eyes for not understanding the meaning.

Little Prem explained: "Your zodiac sign - birthday between June and July. Cancer is *poo* crab. I'm *pla* fish. Elizabeth is a crab like you." Then he switched to English. "But she's crabbier than any crab I know. She can be very loyal and doesn't let go of a friend once she has dug her claws in. She would rather lose a claw than let go."

"You're the fishiest of all the fish I know. A slippery survivor you are, and very quick to get out of sticky situations. Like an eel, you can wriggle out and away."

"Dash it, children!" Dani growled.

After the officials had departed, Dani looked at his watch and said to Ayumonkol:

"According to the programme, you should be taking the media people to tour the village in five minutes. This is one of your conquered villages. Let them have a field day interviewing the former insurgents, the pardoned men. I have two foreign journalists wanting to talk to me here."

"Right!" the Colonel responded.

"Remember what your mama said about talking to journalists," Karl reminded his friend.

"Don't worry. They know that I'd sue them for libel or issue a contract killing. You stay away from them. Once bitten, what? But first, fill up our glasses." Dani paused and turned to look for the Colonel. "See you back soon, Ayu!"

The billionaire gave a lengthy interview to the two editors, one of whom complimented him on his command of the English language. They could see that he was more English than a lot of the English, but they did not know that he was a lord of the manor in England until the lord himself talked of the purchase of Wealdshire Park and the manorial right. Then he went on to say that one of his ambitions was to own an English premier league football club.

"It has to be in the premier league, preferably Manchester United!"

When Colonel Ayumongkol and the members of the media came back from the tour of Napo, it was time to leave.

Back in Bangkok, Colonel Ayumongkol became the host in the Emperor Suite where he would stay the night. The pair of public relations executives occupied the other bedroom to be pampered by the butlers.

Since they did not arrive at the hotel until eight o'clock that evening, the supper was scheduled for 9 p.m. in the dining room of the Emperor Suite.

In the Executive Vice President's suite Dani, immaculately dressed in black-tie, was checking his appearance in the looking glass while Karl put on his dinner jacket. Then they were on their way to join the trio, who were gathering in the lounge, imbibing cocktails that Dawson had concocted.

Answering the door, Brown announced:

"Dr Dhani Pilaskulkosol and Mr. Karl-Michael von Wittenberg."

"No need to announce us, Brown," said Karl.

"Dash it, Mick! Let him do his job properly," the lord of the manor huffed.

The Napotian stared in amazement at the pair in grand attire as if they were peers of the realm dressed for dinner in old England.

"You toffs really make peasants out of us. We didn't even put on jackets."

"Have you been looking after my friends well, Dawson?" the lord and master inquired

"Yes, my lord," said Dawson.

"If you have Krug 76 ready, Brown, we'll have it right away."

"Yes, my lord," said Brown.

"Very well, my lord," said Dawson.

The two butlers, who always did things together, withdrew and disappeared into the pantry.

"How's all?" Dani intended to sound compassionate, sitting beside Karl.

Ayumongkol said: "Fine".

Elizabeth ventured to add: "The whole day went like a dream. We should find another Isan village and do the same again."

"Why not?" Dani sneered. "You still have some millions left in your bank account, I gather."

"There are thousands of Isan communities just like or even worse off than Napo," said the Isaner. "And there are some dead places too that need to be revived."

He was thinking of vanquished Soka and Yang on the way to Sisurachwood.

"Perhaps we can do something about the blasted road that links your village with that little town we passed through. You know, Ayu, Liz and I went to Napo, looking for our little chap here not long after you were there. The road has just been completed. Now it is in need of repair. The tar broke away. There are countless bumps and potholes. It's appalling. I don't know about your Mercedes, but my Rolls just couldn't cope with the bumps. What can we do, Primo?"

"There's hardly anything you and I can do, Danny, unless we attack it at the roots. The roots are winning bids by bribing and giving kickbacks. All in all it's sheer venality. You see there is one construction company that wins bids most times, and when it doesn't win, those committee members, who are against its bidding, have to perish. There are hardly any standards or quality control. If there are, it's likely that money makes the surveyors and the quality controllers blind. The road is not up to standard. The tar is thinly used. Every single piece of construction material has been subject of graft. And when the road has to be repaired then the merry-go-round of kickback grabbing and buying materials at highly inflated prices happens all over again."

"It's not only the substandard roads, the overweight vehicles are to blame," Ayumongkol expounded.

"Oh yes!" Little Prem exclaimed. "Truck and trailer operators and loggers overload their vehicles far beyond the limit, and they can magically make the authorities turn a blind eye. Then on top of that, according to the Post, they have lobbied the Ministry of Transport to increase the limit. And the very illustrious Minister came out in their favour!"

"My word, Primo! A few years back in Isan has certainly made a radical man out of you! When exactly did you say goodbye to the meek old you?"

"It's not only the roads," the excitable little man persisted. "It's everything. Look at the construction of Maehongson Domestic Airport runway extension. I read in the back issues of the Post that after it was constructed, aircraft bigger than the Boeing 737 still could not land because the extended runway cracked and subsided. It was reported that the construction company that won the bid belonged to the father-in-law of a certain minister."

"So we can forget about the road then. Ah! Here comes our Krug."

"Crook?" Ayu sounded perplexed.

Dani smiled; his eyes glistened with delight at the sight of his favourite beverage.

"Zum Wohl!" the billionaire toasted. "To us! We won't wait for Witty. I'm certain that his Mercedes got bogged down in Isan. He took his houseboys back to their homes after the hand-over ceremony was over."

"At this time, when the rainfall is late, it's likely to get stuck in a sand pit," said the Napotian.

"Serves him right," said Lovely Liz.

"Dinner is served," Brown announced.

"What did The Bordeaux Grill sent up to us, Brown?" Karl aske.

"Lobster Bisque and roast beef, sir. Philippe knows Khun Dhani is partial to roast beef."

"Behind my back he says *rosbif pour moi Anglaisphile boss*. One day I'll catch him saying it. Then the penalty will be a bottle of Latour 75. Tell him that, Brown."

"Yes, my lord."

"I wonder what the poor people in Napo had for dinner tonight," Elizabeth thought aloud.

"Smoked wild salmon, Beluga caviar, coq au vin, and then blueberry cheese cake," Dani retorted.

"You asked for it!" Prim Proper Primo said to the Yorkshire lass.

In the dining room, over lobster bisque, Dani mentioned to Ayumongkol:

"In Napo, I saw you talk with a handsome young man. Who's he?"

"That's young Panya, Panya Palaraksa, my former foe, one of Kumjai's *K-Force* insurgents. Now I want him to come out of the bog to be with us in Bangkok."

"Oh?"

"It's a long story, but I can make it short."

"Please don't. Tell us in all the glorious details," said Karl, whose blue eyes sparkled with interest.

"Please do. Let's have the full story," seconded Elizabeth who was keen on everything Isan.

Pira Sudham

"I didn't have time even to say 'sawasdi' to Panya," the wimp admitted.

"You've discovered another Primo," Karl surmised.

"There couldn't be!" Elizabeth quibbled.

"Dash it, Liz! Let Ayu tell his story," growled Dani "Go on, Ayu."

The Colonel finished his soup, touching his lips with the napkin.

"During the fighting years, we set up a listening post in Boraba, at the edge of Sisurachwood. Thanks to the Vietnam War, the CIA had developed a compact and easy to install a listening device so good that we could hear the voices of the guerillas. Occasionally we'd hear a peculiar musical sound. The tunes occurred sometimes in the night. One of my Tiger Men, who manned the listening gadget, believed that it was a sound of divinity, protecting and soothing the fighters. Of course, he could believe what he liked. My curiosity forbade me to storm those insurgents the way we did in Kaoko, in Petchaboon, in Pupan of Sakonnakorn and Pakam of Burirum. After Prem, who was then a monk, led us to the *K-Force* in Srisurachwood, we were not shocked at the sight of their appearances. They looked as if they had not eaten for weeks, as if they had no change of clothes for months. We knew they had been out of supplies for a long while since we had burned most of the outlying villages to force the last batch of guerrillas out of the woods. As you know, the parley was successful, though three lives were lost. On our way back to Napo with the surrendering insurgents, the same sound was heard. And it was Panya who was making music with a leaf in his mouth."

"He often did that and sometimes in the classroom," Prem contributed. "Guru Kumjai did cane him for it."

"Apparently he tends to snatch a leaf from a bough or a sapling as he goes along and puts it between his lips and produces a delightful tune. When I talked to Kumjai about this, the teacher confirmed that the boy was musically gifted. He can play a *kaen* very well, and can pick up any musical instrument and it does not take long for him to play it, without any training."

"Unlike someone I know, who has spent a fortune on piano lessons and still can't play properly," chirped the creep whose tongue had been loosened by alcohol.

"Someone we know?" Elizabeth quipped.

"Yes."

Dani scowled, saying: "That's because the flat at Hyde Park Square is too small to house a grand piano. And I hated going to the

140

teacher's studio in Brixton. Wait until you hear me play my Steinway in my new flat in St. James's."

"Bad dancers blame the music!" Prem sneered and was surprised that he had sneered.

As a devout Buddhist, he should never sneer! Naughty boy!

Dani was not amused.

It seemed Mr Triple Ps had provoked a sting.

"Not long ago I knew a young poet who burnt his books of poems and the manuscript of a novel, along with his suites, shirts and shoes."

"Anyone we know?" Karl joined in.

"Yes."

"Don't let them derail you, Colonel," plodded Elizabeth.

"In Napo today," continued Ayumongkol. "I suggested to Panya that he should come with us to Bangkok and take a course at Siam Music School. I would be delighted to support him. But he said he was a happily married man now."

"Women always get in the way," Dani sneered.

"Not this woman! Prem can do what he likes," stressed the future Lady Archisson who would be embarking on a campaign to ensure that Lord Archisson should be allowed to keep the title after having fallen from grace.

"You're not yet married to him. Wait till you are," Karl-Michael bitched.

"Prem," Ayu said seriously. "Do you think you can convince Pan to leave Napo and come here to attend a course at Siam Music School? I'll look after him. He doesn't have to worry about the expenses. Regardless of how musically gifted one is, some proper coaching can help develop the skill and technique. He may try his hand on piano or violin. It would be a great pity if his talent goes to waste."

"The world is full of people who let their talents go to waste," pontificated Karl.

"He can bring his wife too, can't he, Khun Ayu?" the freak tried to be helpful.

"But not the whole clan, I hope," said Karl who was familiar with tales of expatriates married to local women with their extended families living off the *farangs*, their meal tickets, their total providers.

"I'll see what I can do," the freak assured.

After the main course, a cake was brought with one lighted candle.

"What's this, Brown?" Dani asked.

"Khun Prem's order, sir."

"Egad! You took order from an Isan buffalo boy?"

"A chocolate cake for Lizzie," the little fellow explained. "She's not only crabby but also a chocoholic. Since her departure from her beloved London, she hasn't had a perfect chocolate cake. Besides, it was her birthday the other day. But we were too busy to celebrate. Happy belated birthday, Lizzie."

"Then Dawson should uncork another bottle of Krug," commanded the billionaire.

Soon the champagne flowed again.

"To Miss Elizabeth Durham of Hyde Park Square. Happy belated birthday," Tannai Dhani raised his glass.

"It'd be marvellous to be a young lover all over again," said Ayumongkol. "Danny, do you remember that night when we staggered around Trefalgar Square so drunk that we couldn't walk. Two bobbies questioned us, but when I told them that we had lost our way to Belgravia, they called a taxi for us?"

"Yes, Ayu. I remember that night well. How about the time you fell from a horse at Sandhurst and fractured your hip?"

"How about you! You were caught with your trousers down with a blond boy at Oxford!"

"There was nothing of the sort!"

"It's no big deal for Oxford," said the birthday girl.

"Thank you all for making today," Dani consulted his diamond-studded Piaget. "Yesterday, a great success. How time flies. Bedtime, I think. Ayu, if you want a good massage to put you to sleep, just ask Dawson. He can arrange."

In bed, Little Prem muttered:

"I should have been inured to Dani's idiosyncrasies by now, but his lexicon is still daunting. Dash this and dash that—bally this and bally that – I say this and I say that—my word this and my word that --egad this and egad that. Somehow, it seems odd for a ..."

"He's a snob!"

"I've never heard Lord Norbury use the *d* word and the *b* word."

"That's because he's a perfect gentleman, a real aristocrat. Besides, 'bally' and 'dash' and 'egad' and 'pray tell' have gone out of fashion ages ago. No one except a pompous snob uses them now."

"What's in fashion then?"

"Oi! Cor! Blimey! Bleeding! Bloody! Strewth! And you can always fall back on the *s* word and the *f* word."

"Be serious, Lizzie."

"I'm serious! If you like, I'll introduce you to Gordon Ramsay."

"Do you know him?"

"Of course, I do. Every time I dine at his restaurant, he always comes for a chat."

"Perhaps he thought you were a film star or a celebrity."

But then the little fellow felt compelled to change the subject: "Lizzie I worry about Danny. He drinks a great deal these days. Did you smell alcohol on him when he and VVK came in? He must have had at least a bottle of his favourite wine with his Mick before joining us. My inner eye could see through his outward charm. He's being tortured inside. There are some dark thoughts he is hiding from the world, I know."

"Let's confront him with my theory, shall we?"

"He would deny everything outright."

"Oh, well, it could be boredom. Sinisterly rich people tend to bend on destroying themselves anyway. If it's not alcohol, it's sex, drugs, adultery, gambling, family feud or suicide. Even some diseases seem to decimate a lot of them, though it isn't quick enough."

"How could you say that, Lizzie? It's so unkind. You've no compassion at all. You, of all the people, can be *la belle dame sans merci*."

"I save my compassion for the poor, the downtrodden, the exploited, the cheated, the salt of the earth, especially your people in Isan."

"You're such a pain. Why I love you, I have no idea. By the way, did Danny tell you that his applications for German and Australian visas have been turned down?"

"No."

"It must have been while you were in Hong Kong. His old passport expired, and when the new one was issued he applied for a UK visa and for the Australian and the German. The Australian Embassy and German Embassy rejected him with no explanation. He didn't intend to go to Australia, but he applied to see whether the Land of Oz was off limits to him or not. But Germany was for real. You know what that means don't you. It means he can't go to see his friend Reiner."

"Well, he has his Mick now. It seems that's all he wants."

"That's it! He's totally dependent on VVK now. There's a danger."

"You're not jealous, are you?"

"Don't be daft. Can't you see? To Danny, Mick is a sort of drug. When Danny has to wed, then what will he do?"

"Then it'll be a threesome! Anyway, that's for the future. For now let's enjoy ourselves. Are you happy?"

"Yes, very."

"I'm overflowing with happiness. My heart may not bear it any longer. I'm so happy for Headmaster Kumjai and Anucha and for all the people in Napo, but most of all, for you. Can't you see that we've now put you high on a pedestal in the eye of the government officials and the Napotians?"

"My darling girl, are you sure it isn't the wine talking? I don't actually like it high on a pedestal. There's always danger lurking below, especially when everyone knows now that I have millions available. Try to sleep, Liz, or I won't sleep. I need it. Why don't you have a headache like some other women?"

"Let's go back to Napo tomorrow. I mean today, after breakfast. Danny would let us go, wouldn't he?"

"How about checking the publications to count the column inches of publicity generated from the Napo Project? Who will monitor the television? Don't be so impulsive."

"To hell with column inches! To hell with television! I want to go to Napo!"

Turning away from her, the creep closed his eyes.

# Wild Winds of Fortune

"Good news!" Dani Pi announced, entering the GM Suite. "The Munich Philharmonic will definitely perform here. Meanwhile Mama wants to gobble up a five-star London hotel. Here's the other news. Supa will wed Papa's PPS next month."

"I haven't heard of the engagement. I spoke to her in the office just before I left, and she didn't say anything."

"Supa has very little to do with the marriage. It's been arranged. Mama has her hand in it. She believes that the poor girl is in love with me. But, alas, she isn't Mama's choice. Supa is a true-blue Siamese. Though she's a descendent of a noble man, it's the money. Her parents aren't rich enough for us and for that matter not in banking. I'm to wed a true-blue Chinese, a banker's daughter. At this very moment she is busily looking for another candidate, having previously made a failed attempt."

"I thought arranged marriages had disappeared from Siam."

"Arranged marriages, like rote learning, are alive and well in Siam. You can't deny that PPS P is definitely the best for her. He's very rich, very handsome and very high up in the government as well as in my father's political party. But, according to Witty, marrying Supa would ruin his candidacy of another kind. It's Mama's scheme to lower his chance so as to leave mine unchallenged. You see, by marrying Supa, his bloodline will no longer be 100 per cent Chinese. As for you, your boss has found a girl to marry you. She's from noble stock. Old money! The Nagarungsiths."

"Petra?"

"Yes! Mama thinks I'm too fond of you. We've become too close for her comfort. It's up to you, of course. Now you make up your mind whether we'll celebrate or not. If not, it'll be Le Montrachet to start with."

"Le Montrachet."

"Good! Brown and Dawson can wait on us in here. By the way, after we've taken over that London hotel, Brown and Dawson should be transferred there."

"They might not want to return to London."

"They've no choice!"

Karl shook his handsome head while making a telephone call.

"Hello Brown. Come to my suite with Le Montrachet and Romanee-Conti. We'll dine here."

When DP emerged from the bathroom, KW griped:

"If she hasn't already set the date of our departure for London, let's make it just before Supa's wedding. I don't want to have any part in it."

"London in October should be salubrious. Oscar Wilde's *An Ideal Husband* is still on at The Royal Theatre Haymarket, I think. It would be splendid to share the pleasure with you. Then we'll go to Wealdshire Park for a couple of days. Mick, let's take Little Primo with us. The blighter would love to go back, I'm sure. I want to show the Isan peasant St. James's and Wealdshire Park. At present the blithering idiot doesn't have much to do."

"Actually your slaves have been quite busy. That Durham female told me that they had been running back and forth between Bangkok and Isan and other places. The Napo Project seems to be going at full steam. Then I heard that they had just come back from the North, looking for the wife of that murdered schoolteacher. Did they find her?"

"Yes, but she wouldn't talk. Apparently there is the so-called *Dark Force* that puts fear in her heart. I want to do something for her and her children. But it seems there's hardly anything I can do for her now. Come to think of it, any form of assistance might prove an admission of guilt on my part."

"You could be right. But if you are so concerned, why don't you dole out compensation to the families of 188 workers, mostly women, who were burnt to death, and the 400 injured, in the fire at one of your factories? I read in the Post that the relations of the dead and the injured are making petitions with the authorities. The court case has been dragging on for several years now due to a series of obstructions from you. Of all the billions you are making, you can let go just a little to give to the poor people who have lost their rice winners. A few million baht would not hurt you in any way. Besides, it appeared bloody awful when the factory had over 3,000 workers, and there were no fire escapes or alarms and all exits were locked to prevent the slaves from stealing. How cheap and mean can you be?"

"I? I wasn't in Bangers when the blasted factory caught fire. But, thanks for mentioning it. You know, for a hotel manager, you're not dull and unimaginative at all. It's you who said that *the world is full of people who let their talents go to waste,* remember? Our Mr Pee is one of them. When we lived together in London, he wrote prizewinning poems. I found in his room a bundle of poems and a manuscript, a Nobel Prize for Literature stuff. Willie has one or two poems set to music too. One has become a hit, high up on the charts. Then the silly boy burnt them all. Can you imagine that! Liz said he was ashamed for having to go down on his knees to ask Willie to be his Beethoven. You know Beethoven turned Schiller's *Ode to Joy* into the *Choral* of Symphony No. 9. The little blighter considered that he was no better than a harlot in order to be published and sung."

"I'd love to see him on his knees!" Karl decried, committing to memory the innuendo to harm to the 'grabbing goblin', his competitor against whom he had begun to harbour animosity.

"He wanted to be Mr Nobody, reliving his Isan peasant life. But we must not let him. Let's pluck him out of the morass and put him back in old England and make him creatively active again."

"Do you think that's wise? What has he done to deserve your generosity? I wouldn't waste a baht on him, if I were you."

In an unguarded moment, Karl let loose his pugnacity, known among many victims and long-suffering colleagues, who had been at the receiving end of his bitchiness.

To KW, it was deplorable that, for dubious reasons, DP enjoyed the company of the greedy pair who could grab a bigger share of the spoils.

"While Ayu has his Pan with him in Bangers," Dani Pi expatiated, "I want to have our potential literary prizewinner with us in London and make him a pen-pusher again. Besides, he should finish his studies. You know he was sent down, back to Isan."

"What did he do to deserve that?" Karl sounded as if he cared while mentally damning: *And that's exactly the place where he should remain, the crawling creature, the sneaky imp.*

"He didn't study, didn't attend classes, and became a hippy, living in Earl's Court with Liz."

"I know he's a nasty piece of work, but she's worse. You shouldn't go overboard with this terrible pair. They're out for what they can get. You've already spoilt them."

"I haven't spoilt them. I know they're good eggs -- too good for this selfish, corrupt and violent world of ours. I can trust my Little Primo. Apart from him, there is hardly anyone I can trust."

For not having been considered trustworthy, Wittenberg was sorely disappointed.

"Don't you trust Salika and Peter Clifton?" KW asked, hoping that he might be included along with the couple.

"No I don't. I don't even want to see them. They're all out to beg me for my money now that they cannot borrow from banks. It's perfectly clear. Their real estate development scheme and their restaurant businesses are their downfall. They owe three billion baht and creditors are knocking at their door. When their latest restaurant was inaugurated, they wouldn't show their faces at the opening for fear of being pounced upon. Money! Money! Bally money! What is money to you, Mick? If I'd given you half of my fortune, what would you do?"

"Buy a hotel," Karl voiced resolutely; his eyes glowed with the thought of having such a fortune.

Seeing the naked greed in the eyes of his soul mate, Dani mused:

"I said *if* not *when*. My dear Mick! This country is stuffed with people who, as soon as they become exceedingly rich, buy or build hotels! And you want to be one of them. This city is littered with empty hotels, and many have to be sold and then resold. Some newly built hotels are laid waste. A luxurious hotel in Burirum, where Primo came from, had to cease its operation, while another one has been left unfinished. Here, look at that 500-room hotel across the Chaopraya River. It has been standing there empty for years. You'd go broke in no time. Then what would you do when I'm not around?"

"I'd buy a hotel in London."

"That's where we are going, with Liz and Primo."

"That would be fun. Your little PR man can show me his old haunts," Karl changed his tune for he realised that obvious enmity would not produce the desired result.

"But don't tell him yet. There's a surprise in store for our little fellow. Ah, here come Brown and Dawson."

"Good evening, my lord."

"Good evening, sir."

"Brown and Dawson! Would you like to shuttle between Bangers and London, flying business class, of course, and staying for months at a time in a first-class hotel in London and a stately home in Sussex?"

"Very well, my lord."

"QED!" the billionaire punctuated.

In London, Elizabeth Durham and Prem Surin made Dani Pi's old flat in Hyde Park Square their home, while the billionaire and his friend occupied the magnificent apartment in St. James's.

Little Primo was surprised to find that his former residence remained more or less the same. Below, in the square, the age-old plane trees, leafless now, stood in their nakedness against the bleak autumnal sky.

"Strangely enough, Lizzie, I feel as if I've come back home. It's the same degree of homecoming elation I felt in Napo on the first day of my return."

"That's a good start. Where would you like to go first?"

"Let's go to Speakers' Corner first and then totter to the Serpentine. It's such a fine day. Then we'll go to The National Gallery. But, before going inside, let's make an *acte de presence* in Trefalgar Square amidst the multitude of people from all over the world. I remember so fondly the time I was there on a bright summer day when Big Ben chimed at the same time as the bell of St. Martin-in-the-Fields on top of the sound of the fountains. It was so exuberant! After that I gravitated to Trefalgar Square when taking a stroll. Yes, it was one of those halcyon days we shared in London. We were young then! Let's be young again! Then we'd go inside The National Gallery to gawp at the portrait of Antoine Paris. While there, we should feast our eyes on Corot and Poussin and Titian and Gainsborough. The portrait of Mr and Mrs Hallett is a must-see. Later we'd pop into The National Portrait Gallery to make an *acte de presence* with Thomas Wharton Earl of Wharton and Charles Seymour Duke of Somerset and Evelyn Pierpoint Marquess of Dorchester and Sir Samuel Garth and Sir Richard Steele and J. C. Bach and Spencer Compton Earl of Wilmington, who looks similar to Robin who, without wanting anything in return, put 100 baht banknote into my shirt pocket at Wat Po where I sold souvenirs to tourists to see myself through high school and the first year at Chulalongkorn University."

"Then we'll have mocha coffee and chocolate cakes at Fortnum and Mason. Let's pretend we are tourists just for fun!"

Several days later the invigorated little chap learned that his benefactor wished to transfer the lease of the flat to him with an understanding that Elizabeth Durham had an equal right to reside in it.

Pira Sudham

Having signed a bundle of legal papers, which the lawyers required, Little Primo ceased to worry that the entire scheme could be one of Dani Pi's pranks. Indeed, it was difficult to take in the reality that he had actually acquired the lease of the three-bedroom flat in Hyde Park Square.

When PS asked why DP had made such a transaction, the big brother answered: "I want you to feel secure, to have a place of your own when you want to come back to finish your studies. I think you should go to Oxford, study and write again. Do you remember what Karl-Michael said the night we returned from Napo? *The world is full of people who let their talents go to waste.* Remember? You convinced Panya to attend Siam Music School in Bangers. I want you to convince yourself that you should go to Oxford as a mature student. I've transferred 100,000 pounds to your bank account. That should see you through Oxford. Then you can behave like an Oriental prince. Play the part. Make Oxford your stage. Shed the meek mien and timidity so that you can sit with ease and elegance at Lord Norbury's table, and you don't have to duck or bolt every time you see Lord Bewly. I've no desire to hoard all of the assets piling up here. Money from a tainted source has already soiled my hands, but I hope your high mindedness and your concept of rectitude and purity of heart will not deter you from accepting my gift. If you don't take it, it would be reverted to *them* after I'm gone."

"How about the hotel?"

"We've bought it! Karl and I shall be here for some time to set up the new management and to oversee the running of the hotel. You and Liz should return to Bangers in the middle of November to publicize the concert. Meantime, you should go to Oxford. Look around. Sniff the atmosphere and choose a college. The Michaelmas Term has just started. Go and talk to a don, a tutor and some students there. See my old college, Balliol. Visit the Bodleian Library and the Sheldonian Theatre..."

"Why not Cambridge?" ED butted in. "Academically the standards are much higher. Oxford is rife with the old boy network."

"Cambridge if you prefer. Go to Cambridge as well and then choose. By the way, Primo, I meant to ask you. Where's your watch? Threw it in the fire? Dash it! You dashed silly idiot! Buy a new one! Pop into Watches of Switzerland, and for goodness sake, buy one! Go to Simpson or Aquascutum and get a decent suit and a black tie outfit. But please, not Marks and Sparks. You too Liz! Smarten up.

150

At present I can't take you two, *yob* and slob, to Pall Mall. We'll have dinner at my club with Lord Norbury and Lord Bewly and Charles Tregonning tomorrow evening. It's black tie for you, Primo. Do shed your meek mien. Look vibrant! You know what I mean. I mean the rarefied air of an artist. Exude the vitality and artistic power! None of the timid mannerisms of an Isan peasant! I want to be proud of you. You may charm the trousers off Charles, if you haven't done so already. First, come to my flat at six. You, Little Primo, can be my butler for an hour before we totter to Pall Mall. Now, about transport! Lovely Liz! Are you listening? You have your UK driving license, have you not? Good! I'll let you drive my Rolls. Primo sits in the back and you take Piccadilly up to Piccadilly Circus then turn into Regent Street and at Oxford Circus turn left into Oxford Street to Marble Arch and Park Lane. Do that for me. For an hour I want Primo to be an Oriental prince who has a pretty English chauffeur!"

A few days later, the beautiful blond drove the pseudo prince to Oxford in Dani's Rolls-Royce. Having inspected Balloil and sniffed the academic air at Merton and at Magdalen, they continued the tour to Cambridge. After the visit to King's, Queen's and Clare College, they left, taking the M11 down south and joined the M25. Having crossed the Thames at Dartford, they headed for Ashdown Forest, and eventually entered Wealdshire Park where they were shown into a regal bedroom.

"It isn't quite right to turn a historic place like this into a business venture. It's like Claridge's," commented Prem.

"Have you slept at Claridge's?"

"Yes."

Instantly, the poet winced, reflecting the deed committed there to have one of the poems set to music.

"Thanks to death duties, many stately homes have been turned into hotels or National Trust properties," ED smirked.

PS wished to make a supportive remark, but lacking confidence, he turned it into a question:

"Otherwise, yobs and slops and the riff-raff wouldn't have a chance to set foot in it?"

But then the former herdsman of Napo was aware that he felt comfortably at home, sitting in an armchair, being warmed by the log fire.

"Liz, I think your parents would love to be here also. Let's go to Eastbourne tomorrow morning after breakfast and bring them here to spend a day with us."

"No! I know for a fact that they'd rather not. Some of us from our class don't care for a pile like this."

The next day, Little Primo put on a Daks suit, Dunhill tie and Churches shoes to emulate an English gentleman on a visit to Emma and Stanley Durham in Willingdon, a suburb of Eastbourne.

The Durhams remembered him from the previous visit to their home in Bradford. But Stan seemed reluctant to travel in that car though Emma would gladly climb into it when they were invited to lunch at the Grand Hotel.

"I know my place," said the retired butcher.

"See what I mean," whispered the daughter.

"Thanks for a nice cup of tea," the visitor bid the couple goodbye. "We'll be back to see you again."

From Willingdon, they headed towards the A22 route.

On approaching Wealdshire Park, the Rolls-Royce veered into the car park of The Coronet, an ancient public house.

"Do you actually like pub food?" Elizabeth checked.

"Of course, I do. The steak and kidney pie I had at Wuthering Heights Inn was indeed memorable. Thank you again for taking me to Haworth that year."

The landlord welcomed the couple to the bar. Seeing that the visitors were strangers in these parts, the publican recommended Sussex Ale.

"Yes, please. Half a pint," PS eagerly agreed though he did not particularly like ale. "And the same for my chauffeur."

"I'd rather have a glass of house red."

The pert and pretty driver wished to make it clear that she had her own mind and preferences. At the same time, she disapproved of her man's harmless pretense.

"I came from Siam," the Siamese of Lao extraction expanded.

"A friend of mine is in your country at present. He's somewhere in the North. Got a postcard from him this morning," the landlord responded.

A pang pierced the Isaner's heart on hearing 'somewhere in the North' where Rit Apaidham, a tribal boy, had lived on one of the hills in Chiangrai.

"At this time Northern Siam is quite cold, but not as cold as England," Surin spoke warmly.

When they had claimed a table in the dining room, the little Napotian felt an uncanny sensation that he had been to this pub many times before.

"Have we been here before Lizzie? It looks very familiar."

"A lot of pubs look more or less the same."

"It also reminds me of a forest house by the Wurm in Bavaria."

Another pang pained him as the inner eye saw Helmut von Regnitz and Reiner walk ahead of Wilhelm in the woods on their way to Muthal.

*It was a mistake to make Wilhelm go with me along the same track where Helmut and Little Reiner had taken. I should not have made him waste his precious time. Why did I do it? Was it for the sake of turning 'An Isan Lad' into a song? How puerile! I have not grown up in both mind and body after all.*

"Wait till the food comes," Elizabeth was saying. "Baked haddock and prawns, eh? I bet it'd be smothered with masses of potato with hardly any haddock and just a few tiny prawns."

"Such a charming, friendly landlord, he is too!"

"The Scots usually are."

"How do you know he's Scottish?"

"His name at the door, and the Scottish *r*."

"How clever you are."

"My father has a pronounced Yorkshire accent, and you didn't know."

"I noticed, but I thought…"

"When you go to Oxford, your upper lip will be…"

"Who said I'd go to Oxford?"

"You've already made up your mind. I know you so well that you don't have to open your mouth. You merely agreed to see Cambridge to please me. While you are at Oxford, I'll go back to SOAS. Being able to speak and write Siamese well will come in handy, especially when I go to Napo without you."

"You'd need to learn Lao for that."

When food arrived, Prem's order proved Elizabeth wrong.

"There are plenty of fish and prawns. And it's just the way I like it. How's your roast?"

"All right," Elizabeth shrugged. "Thank goodness the vegetables aren't overcooked."

"I'm surprised that you haven't had fish and chips since we arrived back in England."

"I loathe fish and chips, so oily and bland, so unimaginative! You give a Scandinavian a piece of stainless steel and he can come up with well-designed cutlery."

"Pray tell. What do knives and forks have to do with fish and chips?"

When the pro-Siam lass chose to ignore the question, the little man made an attempt at critical thinking.

"All of a sudden you've become rather critical, sneering at your own people."

"Guess where I learned it…all that talk about graft in high places in Siam and the mind-maiming teaching in Siamese schools."

"Excuse me, my dear, for changing the subject. It's been preying on my mind."

"What?"

"When your father said 'I know my place', it struck me as being rather odd. Why should an Englishman put a limit on himself? Who, if not himself, has fixed *a station in life* for him?"

"You can easily work those out for yourself. A 10-year old English boy can."

"You wouldn't help me?"

"No."

"A heartless hussy you are!"

"I'd rather be heartless than mindless. You often claim that most Siamese are mindless. Show me that you are different."

"I'm not so different. But I can try."

The little man paused, turning his maimed mind to a thinking mode.

"Right!" said he. "An Englishman who says 'I know my place', does so because it's his choice to remain where he is but he can move out of or up above his station in life, should he want to, with all the help and support he can have. There are good schools and The Open University and opportunities. If he isn't lazy, he can easily find employment and is protected by law and his trade union. There is a sense of fair play and freedom in his green and pleasant land. Should he wish to turn away from jazzy tunes and the *hoi polloi*, he can tune onto Radio 3 which broadcasts classical music and drama and commentaries. But if a Siamese peasant wants to move out of his deprived or depraved or degraded station in life, he faces suppression and the sheer weight of loads the masters and men of commerce put on him. He finds it impossible to have the bargaining power, to ask for a fair price for his produce, and for justice when he is forced to move out of his land to give way to dam construction or an eucalyptus planting, or when his rice fields and rivers are polluted with toxic waste. For a start, he doesn't know that he has any rights. He sees that all roads are blocked. He remains voiceless, dumb as a beast of burden. Poverty is his dead end. He can hardly raise himself up and out of ignorance and from suppression. He cannot avoid being swindled and taken advantage of. In misery, he succumbs to the belief that it's retribution from his bad karma committed in the past-life, so that in this life he has to suffer accordingly. In other words, he blames himself. It's *mea culpa, mea maxima culpa* rather than putting the blame on the swindlers or the authorities or the government."

"Bravo! My darling Primo, you've now become a thinking Siamese! But you need to improve your English and develop your critical thinking a little bit more. I'm proud of you!"

More guests, mostly elderly couples, began to fill the dining room.

Hence, the pair partook of their meal in silence until PS saw a notice board advertising 'OAP two courses 3.99'.

"What is OAP?"

"Old Age Pensioner. Why?"

The pub offers on Thursdays…"

"I saw it too. But we aren't OAPs. And with 100,000 pounds in your bank account, you don't look for bargains."

"Wrong again! I asked so as to show my ignorance. That's all."

But, in truth, curiosity had begun to gnaw at his developing mind.

"Haven't you noticed that most of the customers in this pub look as though they have their feet in the graves? Today is Thursday."

"Heartless you are! One day you will be an OAP too, if you are lucky enough to live that long."

On their way out, Prem said to the landlord: "We hugely enjoyed our luncheon and look forward to another visit. We're residing at Wealdshire Park."

"There you are, Ian, a satisfied customer," commented Gerry Turle, an elderly Sussex man, with an overweight bitch that answered to 'Henrietta' at his feet.

155

"What a pompous ass you are!" Elizabeth scowled. "Why on earth did you suddenly put on that horrible accent? The British won't be impressed."

"My stiff upper lip wasn't hastily put on to impress the British. After all I've had some education. This wild man from Isan happens to have an educated, refined accent. After all, it must be my patrician breeding from the previous life that has naturally come back to me now. Besides, those good people would have seen that I came in a Rolls driven by a pretty chauffeur. Most of all, I want to move out of and up above my station in life. Mind you, I too know my place but now I have had a head start, acquiring the Oxford accent! What-ho! May I inquire as to where we are going?"

"You may jolly well inquire! I'll take you to Beachy Head to dump you there, if you don't stop the nonsense. You know Beachy Head? That's where suicidal people leap. After dumping you there, I shall go to spend the rest of the afternoon with Mum and Dad, without you patronizing them, speaking with a plum in your mouth."

"Ah! That's why...that's how...the word 'plumy' came from for speaking with the stiff upper lip. Egad! One learns something new every day in old England. But, surely, you'd prefer me to speak with a plum in my mouth rather than a hot potato. And why, my dear, you are driving me back to Wealdshire Park and not to Beachy Head?"

Once on the ground of the stately home, the two lovers took a stroll along *Lovers Walk*.

They headed towards the Doric Temple.

"Lizzie, can we do something for Emma and Stan? I felt cold in their bungalow. And this is October. I can imagine what it would be like in mid winter."

"They can cope. It's much colder *oop* north. They wouldn't accept charity. This isn't Isan, you know? We've been brought up to be thinking individuals, to be independent instead of having what you call the 'hanger-on' mentality, waiting for handouts. Besides, my parents are not destitute, not yet anyway, and when they are, at least they have their pensions and the National Health Service to rely on. Our government, Conservative or Labour, is more caring in comparison. This green and pleasant land of mine is a highly developed welfare state. So let's limit our charitable deeds to the poor of Isan who have so little, and know absolutely nothing of pensions, or NHS or social welfare systems or human rights and decency for that matter."

"What have I done to deserve this lecture?"

"I haven't finished yet!"

"Can we keep moving then? I'll die from a chill if I stay still, listening to your Churchillian speech."

Near the Doric Temple, Little Primo noticed a sign that read *Wicks Walk*.

"Let's take *Wicks Walk* and go right up the knoll. Somehow I know there's a lookout there. Don't ask me how. The autumnal colours should be fantastic from the top. I wonder why it's called *Wicks Walk*. Who is or was Wicks? It sounds very familiar."

"There are plenty of Wickes Home Improvement Centres and you've also met Terry Wicks, our former neighbour in Bradford."

"Oh, yes! I remember old Wicks and his collie called Beauty and a pot of little cycad in his conservatory. You know, Lizzie, cycads grow wild in Isan woods. And old Terry paid 10 pounds for a little potted plant like that at a garden centre."

"Why bother with that blooming potted plant. It was ages ago since you made that pilgrimage to the Bronte Country."

"We were rather green then, weren't we? And I fell in love with a Yorkshire blond on Haworth Moor. Lizzie...Why do you sometimes dye your hair? I like it naturally blond. Some women would do anything to have your blond hair. But you dyed it dark brown for one of my birthday parties. True. We tend to be discontented with what we have and sometimes with the bodies we bear. Look at me! I always long for a decent height and a physique similar to Wilhelm's."

"Have you seen him naked?"

The former Buddhist priest felt compelled to break one of Buddha's Five Precepts.

"Of course not! One's third eye can see his nakedness under those conducting garbs."

Realising that such was a rather weak defence, the little liar hedged.

"I was truly grateful to you for taking me to Haworth Moor that year. If you take me back there again, I'd be more grateful. I'd like to recite memorable lines from *Wuthering Heights* over the moors."

"What lines?"

"Emily Bronte might have been familiar with the concept of the karmic force for she made Heathcliff, who had been bullied and degraded in childhood by Hindley, say to Catherine: *I seek no revenge on you. That's not the plan. The tyrant grinds down his slaves and they don't turn*

157

*against him; they crush those beneath them.* Once Heathcliff was in a strong position, he struck his perpetrator's descendants with sheer vindictiveness. I can sum up Heathcliff's vengeance as a bitter fruit of karma. The other lines I want to recite over Haworth Moor are spoken by one of Heathcliff's victims: *I'd be glad to retaliate but treachery and violence are spears pointed at both ends; they wound those who resort to them, worse than their enemies.* She wrote these in the 19th century as if to warn us. I wonder whether the concept of karmic force was alien to people in her time."

"My dear Primo, it's still alien to most of us this century."

"Perhaps, that's why we have the never-ending Palestine-Israel retaliations, wars, atrocious attacks, bombings, ethnic cleansing and shootings crop up here and there now and forever more."

"Why bother?"

It was obvious that the beautiful blond was bored with his attempt to be a thinking man.

Once more the blithering twit had to change the subject.

"I wonder whether old Wicks is alive and well."

"Alive and well for an octogenarian. He expects to live a life of a centenarian and receive a card from the Queen on his 100th birthday. Mum and Dad often talk with him on the phone."

"I wonder his dog is still alive."

"Old Terry was devastated when Beauty died. He refused to move to a care home after Joyce Wicks passed away."

"I'm sorry to hear that. I wonder who looks after him now. I wonder whether he likes meals on wheels."

"Why bother, Primo?"

"I wonder why this part of the Park is called Himalayan Garden. What is the connection? Strangely enough, I feel as if..."

"Why wallowing in your former life? Why clutter your brain with memories of the past? It's no wonder you cannot think properly. Enjoy the present to the full instead."

Having been shot down by the very one he dearly loved, the wondering man opted for silence. Hence, silently the creep delved deep within. But the introspection brought shame for having told people like Elizabeth and Dani what the seer of Napo, Tatip Henkai, had told him of his past-life.

*I've also told Charles that he was my butler in that life. The old gentleman might have thought my revelation was absolutely absurd.*

After a quick cuddle followed by forty winks in the Queen Elizabeth I Suite, the two lovers were in the throes of dressing for dinner. While putting on his necktie, the little man brought to mind draconian Dani's demand: 'You must dress appropriately for dinner at Wealdshire Park.'

"I hate to tart up!" Elizabeth whined, coming out of their bedroom in an elegant dark blue evening dress. "Look at us! Are we dining with the Queen?"

"That'd be a grand occasion. Elizabeth meets Elizabeth. My word! You look radiant. Turn round. Turn."

For once the young woman willingly obeyed.

"A pearl necklace would suit you tonight."

"I don't like wearing jewels."

"But you're wearing the diamond ring. Diamonds are not for the country."

"Oh?"

"*Upstairs Downstairs*. Remember? Come. Let's move."

Prem offered her his arm. Together the blithering twain went down the grand staircase.

Suddenly the freak stopped and muttered:

"A warm feeling has just come over me. I felt as if I had been up and down this staircase a thousand times, and Reynolds' *The Archers* over there is very familiar. Now someone unseen has just said 'Welcome back, my lord' to me! And my third eye saw..."

"Don't be ridiculous. Behave yourself. The manager is coming towards us."

Peter Channing met the couple and led them into the dining room where the residents of Wealdshire Park Hotel had been partaking of their supper.

Elizabeth played her part. Her nose in the air, she glided regally until she saw Dani, Karl, Ayumongkol, Panya, and Charles at the high table.

"It's nice to see you again, Miss," Gregory Brown and Timothy Dawson said in unison, while Brown was taking care with the chair as the lady lowered herself onto it.

"What a surprise to see you both here," Elizabeth effervescently responded.

Turning to her employer, she officiously stated: "And definitely a big surprise to see you all here. We didn't have a clue that it would be a get-together party in Sussex."

Glancing at her soul mate, she asked:

"Did you know, Primo?"

"No. I'm equally baffled. I couldn't believe my eyes!"

By now, Brown had poured the first round of the lord of the manor's choice of champagne for everyone.

"Here's Pee Surin, the lyricist, whose songs had hit the top of the charts, among us, the Philistines," Dani pontificated. "It's my birthday. Since none of you would give me a party, I had to arrange it myself."

"Khun Dani, you're a Scorpio!" Lovely Liz remarked. "I'd hate to cross you. Intuitively very sharp, very penetrating and deadly vindictive. But sharper than your intuition is that of our Pisces here. He claimed that he had been blessed with a third eye or inner eye which is in fact his razor-sharp intuition. Pisces people have sharpest intuition, believe me."

"Here we go! The sun-sign believer strikes again. That's what we get when we have a woman among us," Karl sneered.

"You! Sagittarius!" Elizabeth hit back.

She dared to challenge her lethal enemy now that she was on her home ground.

"But the Stud must have a Scorpio ascent, I fear. If you let me have your time of birth, *Horsey*, I can hit the bull's-eye. But that you wouldn't tell anyone, not even your birthplace and parentage. We had to be satisfied with what Witty would reveal. He said your *von* wasn't genuine. And we know that behind your back your colleagues call you Hitler. And you, Colonel?"

The blithering blond suddenly turned to Ayumongkol as if she did not care whether the lance she had hurled in sheer abandon, had hit the bull's-eye or not.

"What?" the Colonel looked lost as he was caught off-guard, or perhaps he did not quite follow the conversation until the amateur astrologer explained.

"I don't know my sun-sign," admitted the Colonel, a non-believer in the stars.

"When is your birthday?" Elizabeth asked.

Her voice had become somewhat protracted.

Vicious von Wittenberg fumed within, trying to suppress his urge to retaliate. However, the half-ghost's inner eye penetrated the fuming man's mind, shuddering at the hateful vibe: *Bitch! I'll get you for this! And you too, you impertinent imp! Don't pretend to be naïve with me, you cunning little cad!*

The impertinent imp also saw the devil prancing in the vindictive von Wittenberg's eyes.

*I should have warned Lizzie not to play with fire. Now it's too late; the adversary has done away with his cover.*

"The 8th of August," said the Colonel.

"A Leo! That explains everything about you! You have to be in the spotlight. Go for fame and honour and the highest rank possible. When a Leo walks into a room, you know he's a Leo. And he will not sit facing a wall or in a dark corner, skulking. He has to be seen and heard."

"Khun Panya, tell Khun Elizabeth your birthday," said Dani in an attempt to create a diversion.

Tongue-tied, Panya pleaded for help from his childhood friend. The two Napotians had to whisper.

"Dash it, Primo!" Dani barracked. "No dashed gibberish Siamese or Lao at the table or anywhere whilst Pan is with us in England. He must learn to speak English!"

"In that case, we'll never know the month when he was born."

"Point taken!"

"*Pangerdwaneyangdueneyang?*"

"*Wantisarmduenmeena*," Panya grinned.

"The 3rd of March," Prem translated. "We were born in the same week, same month and in the same year, I remember now. And, oh, we were in the same class at Napo Primary School."

"Oh dear! Two fish together!" Elizabeth screeched.

"Is that bad?" Dani asked loudly.

"It's fishy! Let's hope the two fish here swim upstream against the current to spawn...to create and to achieve their aims in life," the sun-sign believer expounded. "The Pisces sign is two fish heading in different directions. One swims upstream to attain its ambition, its goal. The other opts for an easy way out, being taken by the current downstream eventually to be lost in the oblivion of the sea of mediocrity."

"Very well put, Liz. I'm sure that the two fish here are heading upstream. Good luck to you both with your creation. To Pan with his flute and to Primo with his pen!"

The freak noticed that the enemy did not join in. He trembled at the sight seen through the inner eye. The foe's mask, which had charmed visiting royalties, in-house dignitaries and important hotel guests, had been dropped, revealing a scowling, hard face with the lips pressed and the eyes glaring viciously.

"Lobster Bisque isn't the main course," Ayu was saying to his protégé.

*Lucky Pan has guidance and protection from Ayu. Not long ago they were bent on killing each other. Now Pan is going along a path similar to the one I have taken. Only mine seems more hazardous and I have trodden carelessly with trial and error and without a military might to protect me against my adversaries, one of whom is sitting opposite me now.*

Momentarily the son of *Pramae* seemed to have forgotten that he had been protected by his Mother Goddess at all times, and that his enemies could not touch him.

"Apart from being with us on my birthday, Ayu and Pan are on their way to Munich where Pan shall have an audition," declared Dani. "Willie wants to be absolutely sure that Pan excels in Rodrigo's *Fantasia para un Gentilhombre*. If he's satisfied, he'll tell us to put it in the programme which Lovely Liz and Little Primo have yet to put together and send to the printer. So, you two, the twittering twain, will be told shortly. Be prepared to fly back to Bangers. Apart from the editing and printing the programme, you'll work with Jonas on the publicity campaign, the VIP list, the media list and send out invitations in the second week of December at the latest. It's a charity concert, and I intend to make them pay the price. I want to make the pre-concert publicity in such a way that people who think they are somebody in society have to be seen there. The proceeds go to the Napo Project for which, I'm delighted to say, Willie agreed to perform. Pan's part in the programme means that the all-German repertoire will have a token piece. At present, Willie adheres to Beethoven's Egmont Overture, Schubert's Symphony No. 8 and Beethoven's Symphony No. 7. Imagine, Pan playing Rodrigo! I can't wait to see the faces of Bangkok musical dons when they find out that the flautist has been an insurgent, a man from that forlorn Isan village called Napo. And no one has heard of him before. Charles! Khun Ayu discovered our talented young man, Khun Panya. In Siam we call each other *Khun*. *Khun* this and *Khun* that for both sexes. And we say *sawasdi krap* or in the case of Khun Elizabeth *sawasdi ka* when we greet each other. When you go to Siam, you'll have to do a lot of *krapping and wai-ing*. Talking about going to Siam, Charles, you should go at the same time with Lovely Liz and Le Petit Primo and stay with them at my Buck House for as long as you like. You'd be at home there among the things you freighted to Papa and Mama. Karl-Michael and I will definitely be with you in the City of Angels at Christmas. Sorry for keeping all of you from ordering your dinner. Let's see what the kitchen has to offer us this evening. And, by the way, Khun Pee, I meant to ask you, for the last time, to buy a watch. You two were late coming down to dinner. I had to send the manager to fetch you."

"That's because we didn't expect to meet anyone in particular for dinner. All we were told was that we'd be at the table at ...."

"Why don't you wear a watch?"

"It's a long story."

"Don't give me that! Liz, do you know why?"

"No, Khun Dhani. I barely notice whether he wears anything."

Charles afforded a smile at the remark.

"Here, take my Patek Philippe and put it on. Now!"

The incredible magnanimity caused the anima in Karl-Michael Maria von Wittenberg to flare up once again. But he silently sneered: *Yes, grab it! I'll make sure that you suffer a hell of a lot for it. You won't get away with it, you grabbing goblin,* for he knew the price of such a watch which was of the same make and model as the gift he had also received from the beloved hotel owner.

"And he has decided," Elizabeth declared, ignoring the lethal adversary.

"What will you have then, Primo?" asked the neutral mentor.

While her friend was putting on the second-hand watch, which could have commanded the same price as a brand new BMW, Lovely Liz continued:

"I mean he has decided on Oxford."

"Good! I'm delighted that our little poet will begin to swim upstream. Remember the first term, the Michaelmas, starts on the 12<sup>th</sup> of October. Have you decided on the College?"

"Yes. *Maudlin.*"

"Maudlin? You've just had a glass of champagne. You can't be tearful already," Karl-Michael mocked.

"Excellent! M-a-g-d-a-l-e-n, pronounced *Maudlin* by King Edward IV in 1481 during a royal visit – and it has stuck ever since - has a very good tutor by the name of David Westbrook."

"My old College," said Charles. "Yes, David Westbrook is very good. You'd be lucky to have him as your tutor, Primo."

All the little Piscean needed was a gentle push to put him on his upstream course.

Meanwhile, Brown and Dawson were ready to take their orders.

"Sir, if you permit me, Chef suggests *Pheasant a l'Americaine* for the main course," said Brown.

"I always have doubts when a chef or a *maitre d'hotel* suggests or recommends certain dishes," said the lord of the manor.

"But this one I also recommend, my lord. I was in the kitchen this afternoon helping Chef with the preparation of the pheasants."

"The name puts me off. Why *a l'Americaine*? And how was it done?"

"The pheasant is slit open along the back, flattened, seasoned with salt and pepper and then based with butter on both sides which are then coated with freshly made breadcrumbs that have a hint of cayenne pepper. After that the bird is slowly grilled, and served with grilled bacon, grilled tomatoes, mushrooms, deep-fried potatoes and sprigs of watercress."

"I'm tempted," said Charles.

"I'll have it, provided that the bird's well-hung," the billionaire turned on his princely charm.

"Very well-hung, sir," Dawson said with a deadpan face.

"You should be the judge, shouldn't you, Dawson?" Karl-Michael chuckled, and then added: "I wish Witty were here. He'd have taken the opening even better."

"He was invited."

"European dishes aren't to his taste," Karl explained. "The rice queen doesn't like potatoes."

"Chef said the dish has been specially created in honour of the American guests who are dining with us this evening, my lord," said Brown, slowly turning to face the mentioned table.

At once one of the Americans yelled: "Waiter!"

Brown looked quizzically at his lord and master.

Dani nodded his consent.

With aplomb, Brown went to wait on the Americans.

"That's Phil Gates," said Charles. "It's in The Daily Telegraph this morning. He came to buy a hotel. I heard that The Gleneagles is coming on the market."

"Phil Gates, the world's richest man? Well! Well!" exclaimed the 19th richest man in the world. "It'll be worth a turn to look. But, mind you, this place of mine isn't for sale. Mick, please go to find out from Reception how long Gates and his party are staying with us. Dawson! Take our orders, and more champer before we go on to Corton-Charlemagne. With our pheasants, decant three bottles of Petrus 61, and when you have a chance, tell Brown to remain at Phil's table throughout."

Karl quickly told Dawson his choices before leaving the table.

For the benefit of all present at the lord of the manor's table, Dani said:

"I wouldn't sell Wealdshire Park, for I intend to make it one of the most magnificent hotels and spas. Brown and Dawson are here not only to look after us tonight, but also to train budding butlers. When the management contract comes to an end, I won't renew. We'll bring many of our people from The Imperial Palace to show the British what service is. At present, the richest man on earth has yet to bawl for a waiter!"

"Just like King Richard III crying: 'A kingdom for a horse!'" the budding writer contributed.

Meanwhile, Karl returned to his chair, and whispered:

"Only tonight."

"What a pity. I could have put Brown as Phil's butler 24 hours a day to show him what we can do for service."

"I don't think Gates would have come only to pay for the service. Like most American billionaires, he wants to buy history," stated the antiquarian.

"We've got history, haven't we? Wealdshire Park has tons of history. King Henry the Eighth slept here on his way to and from Hever Castle. Then his daughter Queen Elizabeth I came later. The property had been in the same family for nearly 900 years until recently. Thanks to death duties."

"And Labour governments," Elizabeth added.

"To whom shall we thank when the entire British automobile industry has been gobbled up by either the Germans or the Americans? Jaguar to the Americans, and Rolls-Royce and Bentley to the Germans and Rover to the Chinese! There will soon be hardly anything British left!" Karl commented contentiously.

"How about fish and chips?" Little Primo wondered aloud.

"Even fish and chips are now mostly owned by Chinese, Italians or Greeks," DP proclaimed. "Go to any shops in Tottenham Court Road. If you see a white face behind the counter, you'd want to kiss him. The people from the subcontinent have taken over the sound equipment and computer retailing businesses and convenience stores."

Elizabeth Durham giggled.

But Charles Tregonning looked lugubrious.

"Yes! Rolls-Royce to BMW and Bentley to Volkswagen," Karl bitched.

When the main course had been served, the freak took the first bite of his pheasant. He almost spat it out, grimacing at the bird that was too pungent for him to appreciate.

"It's too well-hung for you, isn't it?" Karl sneered.

Prem decided to keep his mouth shut and his eyes averted from his enemy.

"Not my problem," said the mentor who had parted with a sizeable sum of money on a gift from Watches of Switzerland to appease the furious friend.

Previously KW had raged, having learned that a luxurious three-bedroom flat in Hyde Park Square topped with 100,000 pounds had been bestowed on the grabbing goblin.

O, *what I would give to have baked haddock and prawns.*

"A kingdom," said Elizabeth, reading Little Primo's mind into Richard III.

"That's for a horse, you dashed silly girl," the wimp bounced.

Once more Charles afforded a smile, seeing a child's play.

Ayumongkol and Panya put their heads together again, poring over the menu.

Dani concentrated on tasting the second decanted Petrus 61, unaware of what was going on.

Dawson had been too preoccupied with pouring the approved wine to keep an eye on Brown at the American billionaire's table.

Then suddenly the creep rose to his feet and left.

Dani quickly followed.

In the cloakroom, the boss said:

"Don't ask Charles about David. They've parted."

"Is that why the old man looks so gloomy?" the poet asked before vomiting.

Back at the table, the Napotian would not touch the food on his plate.

"Now you could see that my parents couldn't possibly fit in," Elizabeth whispered to her lover.

"No whispering!" Dani huffed. "You see, Charles, I work hard all day, and at the end of the day, I still have to keep my staff in good order."

"My heart bleeds for you," Karl snorted.

The creep chose to ignore the remark and looked at Panya's plate on which only some bones were left.

*He could have devoured lizards, iguanas, snakes, rotten rats in Sisurachwood.*

PS had to leave the table for the cloakroom once again.

"What's the matter with him? He's absolutely rude! " Karl exaggerated his displeasure.

"Leave him alone, will you?" Elizabeth dared to stand in the way.

They waited a while. When the little bounder did not return, the birthday boy told Dawson to present the cake.

"Primo had a trying day," Elizabeth apologized on her friend's behalf.

"What's so trying?" Karl snapped.

"He's been trying to think, to be a thinking person."

"That must be very hard for an Isan peasant!" KW sneered.

"Karl, please," Dani intervened.

*Still he cannot hold alcohol,* thought Charles who fondly remembered their early days of friendship.

Ayumongkol and Panya put their heads together again. A moment later, Panya left the table.

"What is going on?" Karl uttered harshly to stress the misconduct of the two Isaners.

"A birthday present for Dani," said the Colonel when Panya returned, holding his flute.

By the lord of the manor's table, Panya began playing Rodrigo's *Fantasia para un Gentilhombre.*

*You could hear a pin drop,* thought Elizabeth.

Karl shifted uneasily.

*Well! I'll be dashed!* Dani exclaimed in his mind.

Charles had an adoring look on his previously grim face.

At other tables, the ladies gently put down their cups and saucers, while the gentlemen absentmindedly caressed their cognac glasses.

Then at the end of *Canario,* Phil Gates rose to his feet and came over to congratulate the flautist amid hearty applause.

"Very good! Very good, young man!" said the world's richest man, vigorously shaking hands.

"You've missed Pan's wonderful performance," said Lively Liz to Little Primo when she returned to their suite and found her soul mate in a dressing gown sitting by the fire.

"Oh?" said he, looking up at her. "What performance?"

"Pan piped his flute. But both Ayu and Pan have gone to their room now, and Danny and his Stud invited Charles to their suite. And here I am, the odd girl out."

"My poor darling, I pity you for being the only woman among us. Be wary of Karl. In future, don't call him Stud or Mickey Mouse to his face. You merely rile him unnecessarily. There's no point in making him our enemy for very little."

"He's been our enemy from day one!"

"I've behaved abominably, especially on Danny's birthday. I must go to him and apologize."

"Now? It'd be better tomorrow."

"Now, or I can't sleep."

Not knowing in which suite Danny and Karl were, the miserable little man, improperly attired, had to go down to Reception first. By the time he could locate Thomas Wolsey Suite, Charles was on the point of leaving.

Dani was saying 'good night' at the door.

"I apologize for leaving the table so suddenly. I felt poorly."

"Never mind, my dear boy. We've become inured to your fast disappearing act, haven't we Charles? Why don't you have a chat with Charles, Primo? I'm sure he would greatly appreciate your company at this trying time. I must sleep soon and get up early to be in London for a meeting. Good night to both of you."

Once inside his bedroom, Dani telephoned Elizabeth.

"Don't open your door to anyone tonight. That's an order!"

"And so the grabbing goblin should be screwed well and proper!" Karl decried.

Meanwhile, Prem followed Charles to the Sir Thomas More Suite where a wood fire was blazing, sending out a warm flickering glow.

"I'm sorry to hear that you and David have parted after such a long time together."

"I'll get over it. But, for seeing you and Elizabeth, Danny and Karl, the Colonel and his concert flautist, all in such happy pairs, I was quite miserable over dinner. Alcohol didn't help."

Sitting in an armchair by the fire, Little Primo said: "And I treated you horribly in the past. I'm so sorry."

"You've been forgiven," said Charles, moving up to stand closer to the fireplace. "And I look forward to going to Siam with you. I'll book my flight as soon as you let me know when."

"It should be a great pleasure to fly away from cold and gloomy London with you, Charles, to the tropical sun."

"I'd be willing to give an arm to be with you in your country. I heard so much from Danny about your village, and what you've been doing for your people. I also want to help in any way I can."

"Lizzie and I will take you to Napo. It's not so poor and primitive as before. Now I can offer you a decent place to stay, obviously not as grand and luxurious as Danny's palatial pile, but you'll be comfortable. In Krungtep or Bangkok or Bangers to Danny, you'll enjoy meeting some of Danny's friends, particularly Dr. Prawit. We call him Witty. In a certain circle, he is Ewit partly because of his name but mostly because he is gay. He keeps a harem full of pretty boys."

The next morning, Prem had to knock hard to get Elizabeth out of bed.

"Where did you spend the night?" she asked with all the innocence in the world, brushing her long uncombed hair away from her face.

"In the Thomas More Suite. When I came back, you didn't open the door. Didn't you hear me knock? I knocked and knocked and woke up the people next door. So I had to go back and sleep in the Thomas More Suite."

"You mean you went back to pay off an old debt."

"Don't be daft."

"I meant the wicked karma from your past-life for treating your old butler so abominably, putting him out to grass and all that."

"That's right."

Over breakfast, Surin said: "If you drive me to the place recommended by your parents for luncheon today, I'll give you a pearl necklace or, would you rather have diamonds?"

"I'll make it a very expensive lunch. Diamonds!"

# Isan – The Hinterland

The beautiful blond could relax now, having finished editing the concert programme. Seeing her soul mate silently stand at the windows, she crept upon him.

"A penny for them!"

"I shouldn't have confided in you, a blabbermouth. I told you that I had burnt my poems and *The Monsoon People*. And you blurted all out to Danny."

"I didn't blabber like a blithering idiot. It was an intelligent discussion!"

"He didn't overhear that I agreed to work for him *with my eyes wide open* as he claimed. You told him that too! Can't a man tell his love a secret without being betrayed?"

"Betrayed? That's over the top!"

She hugged him.

He wriggled away.

"Oi! Tell yer wo!" Elizabeth, who could be easily irked by Prem's la-di-da, retaliated. "I'm gonna open tha very dear wine we ad wi Dun-i. I deserve i, aving slaved me arse off for the sinisterly rich."

"It's perfectly clear that you're a Cockney."

"And what are you then?"

The Isaner chose not to answer in front of the servant.

Then Tanong Komkam led the English mistress to the wine cellar.

Back in the headquarters, Lovely Liz found her lover gazing out of the window.

Ignoring the brooding Napotian, she sat at the head of the long table, observing the servant handling Penfolds *Grange*.

"Khun Dhani has taught you well!"

"*Chai krap*," confirmed Tanong, pouring some wine into one of the glasses.

"Ask him about his ribs," Little Prem mentioned.

"Ribs?"

The public relations consultant reflected: *Tanong, the mild-mannered man keeps smiling even while being abused by his master.*

"This wine is wonderful," she beamed, after having a taste. "You may pour."

The lively lass kept her sympathetic eyes on the servant as he moved forward to fill the glasses.

"What do you mean ribs?"

"His lord and master threw a paperweight at him, hitting his ribs."

"Oh dear! The poor man…"

"You don't have to oh dear him. He's one of the richest men in the kingdom."

"What are you talking about? He can't be one of the richest servants in Siam! Don't mock the afflicted!"

"You won't believe this, but according to Danny, Tanong is one of the nine senior household staff members, including the Chief of Security below us, to whom the very magnanimous minister had his assets transferred. Each of them is now worth over a billion. Billion, not million, please note. You didn't know that we've been enjoying the services in this grandiose pile from billionaires, did you?"

"Why did the Almighty give them so much? Nine billion baht can feed the poor in Isan for decades. Is it his way of distributing wealth? Cheers! To the obliging billionaires!"

"Cheers!" the former buffalo boy responded and then gulped down a mouthful, an uncouth act, which was another taboo according to Dani.

*With wine you don't swig it. You take a sip and let your taste buds savour the fruit, the texture, the oak, tannin and the balance of fruit and acidity. You should find out whether it's thin, acidic, intense, elegant or hefty as the case may be.*

Now, it could be defiance that induced the Isan peasant, in the absence of the wine snob, to swig the wine.

It seemed the oak-aged Shiraz had gone to his head and had loosened his tongue.

"Looking inward, my inner eye saw something terribly ugly. It was my maimed mind. Lizzie, I'm no better than the cowed and grovelling servants in this house and the dumb gardeners below. I've been mentally maimed on top of being abominably abused, made absolutely obedient, mindless and voiceless so as to take the suppression, injustice and brutal treatments lying down. Now, if I tell my people that their minds have aldredy been crippled, would they agree with me?"

"Of course they wouldn't. Crippled or stunted, maimed or undeveloped, deprived or famished, as you keep harping on it so often that it has become boring, the Siamese are the nicest people money can buy. Your people are far nicer than the British hooligans, knife-gangs, yobs and slobs who exist entirely on social welfare benefits."

"Talking about hoodlums, yobs, slobs, trash and the riff-raff, I'll never forget the night Danny and I, dressed in white tie for the gala performance of Bellini's *Norma*. Yes, Joan Sutherland was Norma. Now where am I? Oh yes. Outside the Opera House, with that divine aria: *Sediziose voci…Casta diva…Ah! Bello a me ritorna* still resonating in my ears, a lout made a finger-up-your…at us, shouting: *'Tarts!'* at the top of his voice. Danny told me not to take any notice. *We shouldn't lower ourselves to the gutter to be at the same level with the trash,* said he. Talking about Danny, I do miss him. Without him here, this place seems empty."

"Do you miss the Stud too?"

"When you think of Danny these days, you can't avoid seeing Karl. Please don't refer to him by any derogatory names, my dear. Don't let the Executive Vice President hear you call him Mickey Mouse either. VVK is definitely not a mouse. According to the horoscope, he's a Sagittarius with a scorpion cusp. You'd better take care. Only Danny can call him Mick and that's only when they are alone together."

"I heard Horse refer to your mother as a mangy crone."

"Lizzie, please. Horse or Horsey won't do either. Why do you want to antagonize him unnecessarily? For my sake, stop it. I have to live and work here."

"All right! Visually Virile Karl-Michal said your mother is a mangy crone. There!"

"If I told her that she'd probably laugh."

"And the toffs called your people nits and gits."

"They can call us what they like."

*Mother, a mangy crone*, the creep recalled an image of his biological mother, seeing her bashful smile and hearing her gentle laughter and remembered well the way she brushed her long hair with both hands.

"Talking about Mother, we should decide on the day we'll go to Napo."

"Today!"

"Don't be silly. We have yet to tell Charles."

"What a trick to pack the old man off to Pattaya, the present-day Sodom and Gomorrah! And then you had the cheek to ask Witty to house him in his five-star youth hostel only to get him mixed up with a coterie of Bangkok gays, throwing a party, or I should say an orgy, which was duly raided by the police. You should have seen the photo of the arrested men on the front page of the Post!"

"I saw it. One of the gays once wrote a nasty letter to me, accusing me of wallowing in sin, devoting my time and energy working for the filthy rich. His karma has quickly caught up with him…a married man too. Consequently his wife left him, taking the children with her back to Canada. I wonder why the police raided the orgy. Usually they turn a blind eye to that sort of thing."

"Didn't you read about the complaint? They were cavorting by the swimming pool in broad daylight. One of the neighbours phoned the police. Besides, it was alleged that there were under-aged boys involved."

"That's beside the point."

"What's the point?"

"The point is that Witty shouldn't have taken Charles there."

"It's your doing, handing Charles over to him in the first place."

"It was Witty's fault, taking Charles to the gay orgy. As for me I tried to be considerate. Charles is here as a visitor, not to work for Danny as we do. He'd be bored stiff if he stayed with us all the time. I'm sure he takes delight in the company of Witty's boys in the air-conditioned Garden of Eden. Talking about Charles, let's phone him and tell him that we'll go to Napo tomorrow."

"Would you let me drive your Mercedes?"

"No! If I let you, we'll certainly have an accident. Your British driving habits would make you observe all the traffic rules and regulations which Siamese drivers don't. And that could cause accidents. Should you stop for pedestrians at a zebra crossing, the way you normally do in the U.K., the car behind you could crash into the back of ours. And when an on-coming car flashes its headlights at you, in Siam, it means: *Don't you dare, I'm coming fast and I won't stop.* In the UK it means: *You can go ahead.* So bang! And here, if you drive a Mercedes, you can stay in the fast lane all the way even though you don't drive fast. If I let you drive, you'll be so correct and courteous that other drivers would think it was a waste to have a Mercedes. You drive me in the UK, and I drive you in Siam. Now, I'll phone Charles."

The Napo Project Manager hummed softly to the tune of *Home Sweet Home* as he was visualizing in his mind's eye the guesthouse that an architect and an interior decorator, friends of Prawit, had built and furnished.

The Napotian had indicated to the architect that two ancient teak houses in Ayudhaya should be bought, dismantled and trucked to Napo to be reassembled by the Mongkol Pond opposite The Napo Primary School. Since he expected Dani and Karl and Colonel Ayumongkol to visit Napo, the country house should be air-conditioned and have modern bathrooms.

The following day they were on their way to Isan.

After Korat, the party visited the 11th century stone shrine at Pimai.

Built with hewn stones in a vast walled compound, the mini Angkor stands in the centre of Muang Pimai on the banks of Moon River. It is a World Heritage Site, attracting millions of visitors from all over the country and abroad. Hence, as a tourist, Charles took delight in sightseeing, imagining that he was taking in the splendour of Cambodia's Angkor Wat.

Little Prem allowed Elizabeth to take over as a guide when they entered the outer precinct of the *Prasart*.

He observed how keen she seemed, conducting the tour, explaining the history of Prasat Hin Pimai and the heroic deed of Miss Boonlua and hundreds of the raped women from Korat on the Plain of Sumrit as if she had been an old Isan hand.

Hence, the native dropped back and sat on a fallen block of stone under an old rain tree. There, time passed pleasantly while he contemplated the details on the exquisitely carved lintels. He looked into the past and saw thousands of slaves quarrying for stones from hillocks over a hundred miles away and teams of elephants dragging the boulders from the quarry to Pimai. At the site, a myriad of skilful stone masons and sculptors worked with their chisels and hammers. The sounds of the tools were still ringing in his ears when the two English friends returned to him.

By then Elizabeth had moved on to the socio-economic aspects of Siam.

*There she goes again*, the meek little man mused. *You can't shut her up when she is on the subject.*

He remained silent on the way out of Pimai.

"Wealth is not at all evenly spread," she was repeating a common characteristic of the third world. "You've seen how people like Danny and Witty live, and soon you'll see how the poor of Isan live, at subsistence level and often in dire need. The very rich live off the sweat of the poor and hang on to every penny they have while the exploited workers beg for an increase so that their earnings would reach the minimum wage of just about a pound a day. Thousands of impoverished farmers in provinces have to march into the capital to plead the government for higher prices for their produce. Price suppression of agricultural produce at grass roots level and forced relocation of families who are in the way of dam constructions and eucalyptus plantations, among other things, are some of the major issues. Here, there is no social welfare for the unemployed, and old people don't have pensions. There is no National Health Service as we know it."

"Perhaps such scarcity might reduce the number of the unemployed in the U.K. by half," commented Charles who voted for the Tories.

Farther from Pimai, on the main route that ends at Nongkai on the south bank of the Mekong River, Little Prem took a right turn, taking a feeder road heading east via Dongkeng. They passed through hamlets and plains where reapers were harvesting their rice.

The driver also drew much pleasure from being in his county during the harvest.

Once he stopped for Charles to take photos of the reapers on the shimmering Plain of Pratay. Quietly observing the millionaire, the child of Isan stood by the vehicle, looking at the scene through the eyes of the newly arrived Englishman, and saw a pristine and romantic picture of the East.

The Isaner decided to withhold some morbid realities regarding the bare-footed reapers' risk of stepping on rats' urine from which leptospirosis could be fatal; of the farmers being prone to parasitic worms that entered their bodies through the skin of their feet or from eating uncooked fish and meat; of having to bend down, backs to the sky and faces to the soil to plant or reap rice from dawn to dusk in the mud to earn an average of 20 pounds a year.

Meanwhile, the little chap saw in his mind's eye an image of a silent little boy squatting by his father's side, waiting for their sacks of rice to be weighed at the sale yard in Muang. That child could still hear *Take it or leave it! Go away! Go! Sell your measly rice elsewhere! Go!*

Such fierce barking occurred because a desperate peasant had rustled up courage to haggle for more. He recalled also the sight of little Toon Puthaisong squatting on her heels beside a basketful of the well-washed grass, begging Chinaman Ching to buy it to feed his horse for 10 satang so that she could buy from him a pencil that was priced at the same amount, but to no avail. All was in vain. There was neither pity nor charity in the hardened heart of the money-grabbing shopkeeper. The little peasant girl might have to squat dumbly there like a Khmer stone stature for another century.

*How long would it take me to be powerful enough to help the poor so that they would have bargaining power?* Tadpole Od pondered while Charles was taking photos of the herd of buffaloes in a nearby field.

At the destination, the half-ghost drove to the guest house. There, he was overwhelmed when the ancient Ayudhaya teak house he had in mind turned out to be two new grand buildings joined by a spacious platform with a smaller structure of the same style to serve as a kitchen and a pantry.

Guru Kumjai came over to welcome the party and opened the gate for them with a key left in his care.

"Leave it to Witty and his friends and you get an imposing mini palace full of things they call *objets d'art,*" said Luke-pi. "Look at the cushions and earthenware of various sizes and shapes everywhere. The interior decorator must have a penchant for cushions and pottery. What shall we do with them? They are all over the place."

"Very charming indeed," Elizabeth crooned.

"This is exactly what I expected of a Siamese country house," Charles observed.

"Many of our people are so curious that I let them in. What impressed them most were the flushing toilets on which one sits instead of squatting, and then the gas stove, the oven and the kitchen sink, all of which they have not seen before," said the headmaster, opening the bar and the kitchen for the visitors to inspect.

They found the fitted kitchen ultra-modern and fully equipped, and the bar, which was an extension of the kitchen area, well stocked. In the refrigerator there were several bottles of wines, some tonic water and mineral water. On the bar counter Prem found an envelope under a paperweight addressed to him.

*My dear Primo,*

Pira Sudham

*I was on my way to villages in Mahasarakam. So I dropped by to have a look at the final stage of 'Bankhunlaung' (House of the Noble) before the interior decorator would leave Napo. I approved it, and so would Danny, who had a hand in the whole thing after he heard that you wanted to build the guesthouse. Now, not only Danny and VVK and Ayu will take delight in it. I also would come more often to Isan and stay here for a day or two. The cost is met by the Pi Foundation. Therefore, you don't have to worry about the extravagance. You'll find that the plumbing works, if you switch the water pump on. The water from the artesian well is drinkable. The wines in the fridge are for the house-warming party. Have a wonderful time.*

*With much love.*

*Wit.*

"Well?"

"What can I say? The architect and the interior decorator have gone over the top. That's all I can say. Witty has acted as if money is no object in this venture. Look! This is a palace in the middle of the rice fields. Nevertheless, Charles should choose his house first thing. After having settled down, we'll have house-warming drinks before we think about dinner."

On hearing the dreadful word *drinks*, Guru Kumjai said that he must go back to the school since it was almost closing time.

"The headmaster cannot bear the smell of alcohol as much as you cannot bear the smell of cigarette smoke now," Prem told Charles after Kumjai had left. "But Anucha, the assistant teacher, may drink. I'll go over to Anucha's house when the school is over, and invite him to join us. Look! Look at the way the head teacher totters. He's not old but carries himself like a wobbly old man, head bending, shoulders drooping as if he is carrying the blighted country on them."

Together the trio silently observed how the headmaster wearily trudged towards the school. Ten minutes later, before they would go inside their houses, they heard the chorus of schoolchildren reciting a ballad.

"It hasn't changed!" Prem exclaimed. "It hasn't changed at all."

The host was the first to emerge, after a shower and a change of clothes.

From a tap in the kitchen, he let the water run for a while before taking a glassful. Lifting the glass to the light, he saw how clear the water was. Then he tasted it.

178

*Since a source of drinking water has fortunately been found deep beneath Mongkol Pond, a pipeline can be laid to supply water to the villagers.*

With that scheme hovering in his mind, the wimp made his way to the school, passing schoolchildren on their way home. He said hello. The little girls rushed away, leaving one tiny boy behind.

"*Ceu-ee-yang,*" the freak asked in Lao for the boy's name.

"Kiat," said the skinny child, whose name meant little frog.

"*Hoojakkoibor?*" Luke-gop inquired whether the boy knew him.

The little frog nodded. It had also been passed on to him that the weird man had been called by several names, including Tadpole Od.

"Go and tell Grandmother Liang that Luke-pi has arrived and he will come to see her tomorrow."

The little frog hopped away from the big frog. The latter stood still, allowing the straggling bands of boys and girls to file past.

At the school, he saw Tongdum Tinthaisong closing the windows, and went up to say *sawasdi krap.*

"Guru Kumjai has made me the caretaker of the school."

The ex-insurgent seemed happy enough to exchange a knife and a gun for a broom, a rag and a bucket of water.

"And Toon cooks for the teachers," Tongdum added.

Hence, Piang had volunteered as well.

The two women called out to Luke-pi to enter Anucha's house by the kitchen door which had been left wide open to let out the charcoal fume and the smell of the cooking.

"It's *kaibaikapao,*" Toon indicated.

"Yes, it smells very much like stir-fried chicken with basil, garlic, chilli and anchovy sauce. How I remember its aroma and taste so well! Definitely *kaibaikapao* is my favourite dish."

"When we finish cooking here, we'll go over to your house, and do *kaibaikapao* for you and your guests," Piang volunteered. "When we heard that you had arrived with guests, Kiang caught three chickens and dressed them for us to bring here."

"Not too much chilli this time. The Englishman cannot eat spicy food. But Lizzie can take it quite hot. Can one do stir-fried chicken with basil without chilli? No? What a pity! Well, make it very mild then, and give Lizzie a special chilli sauce. You know: chopped chilli and garlic in fish sauce with some freshly squeezed lime juice. She loves that."

"Yes, we know. She can eat very hot papaya salad and Isan pickled fish just like us," said Piang who had cooked for Elizabeth during the previous visits.

"Well! Well! Look! Who is *beating the backside of my kitchen!*" Anucha Rajapakdi greeted the visitor.

So the Siamese from the Central Plain and the native of Isan took to each other as if they had been old friends.

Together they sauntered towards Bankhunluang.

"The headmaster usually takes a nap at this time," Anucha explained. "He comes to dine with me at sunset."

"He looks tired and older than his age," commented Prem. "Is he in good health?"

"He enjoys rude health, but suffers from the lack of a cause for which to fight. On the other hand, some people wanted him to part with the money left in the bank account. Since he wouldn't yield, they change their tactics. They asked him to spend the money to lay 500 metres of concrete road from the school to the street. But when the headmaster was told the cost, he said no. At that price, 10 kilometres of *uneaten* road could be had, he said. So they got stuck with him there."

"He tries to prevent thieves, crooks and rogues from devouring ..."

"Now you can add drug traffickers and amphetamine peddlers to the list. It's a worry nowadays. What's worse is that they are using children to deliver drugs to buyers. In the process some of the young carriers have become addicts."

Little Prem shuddered, sensing a foreboding shadow over his home village.

In Bankhunluang, the two Siamese were surprised to find the English guests sitting native style on the home-made bulrush-mat. It was Elizabeth's doing, teaching Charles to sit cross-legged.

"What has Charles done to you?" Little Prem directed the question at Elizabeth. "Why did you want to torture him, making him sit like that?"

Sitting down, the teacher shook hands with the English gentleman, saying:

"My name is Anucha, or Anu for short."

To Elizabeth, Anu made a *namuskara*, saying *sawasdi krap*.

"*Sawasdi ka,*" she responded.

The host went to the bar and returned with wine and glasses. In his mind's eye he saw himself together with Dani, Lord Bewly, Lord Norbury and Charles dining in Pall Mall.

*Alas, the journey has not ended, and now Wilhelm is coming.*

"In Napo, most homes have neither tables nor chairs. People sit on the floor just like us doing now," Anucha was saying.

"You know, Anu, where Charles comes from, to live in a house without tables and chairs is unthinkable," said the university drop-out, lowering himself down on his knees to serve his guests.

"Welcome to Napo, Charles," Little Primo toasted.

"Thank you. I'm very happy to be here."

The freak noted the old Etonian's pronunciation of 'here'. It reminded him of Marquess of Salisbury's accent.

*And to hear it in Isan!*

"Are you comfortable, sitting cross-legged on the floor, old thing?" Luke-pi worried.

"Not really," Charles admitted.

"Let's move to the lounge then."

The armchair gave much comfort to the old gentleman, who had never sat on the floor cross-legged before.

At one point Elizabeth commented: "Khun Anu's English is very good!"

"It is. Perhaps it is better than mine. He was in the final year of the Faculty of Political Science at Dhamasart University before the October 6th massacre. Charles, Anu can tell you all about that phase of the history of Siam. As for me I'll never forget that I punched Danny on the nose in the night of October 6th."

"You did what?" Lovely Liz raised her voice in amazement.

"I punched Danny on the nose and moved out to share the bed-sit with you in Earl's Court."

"Why didn't you tell me before?"

"One doesn't blurt out to people, particularly to a blabbermouth like you, that one had punched Danny on the nose."

"I'm not a blabbermouth!"

If Dani had been with them, he would have stopped the purported altercation with his pretentiously trenchant reproof: *Children!*

Since he was not, the creep made another toast:

"To absent friends."

"May they remain absent," Elizabeth quipped.

"Lizzie, that's not nice. After all, we are drinking their wine."

"And staying in their house," added Charles.

"To be honest I like all our friends, but for Witty Wit, I think he's over the top," the beautiful blond remarked.

"You mean, you can't stand the competition. Poor you! Among us, you're the odd girl out."

"With Ewit around, I'm not so sure. Look! He gave us the bubbly with the price sticker still on the bottle."

"Sorry, I should have taken it off," the wimp apologized and peered at the offending little sticker. "You know, Charles, for what one pays for a bottle of champagne in Bangkok, a man and his wife with four children can live on it for a year in Napo."

*There he goes again*, thought the alluring lady. *Once he's on the subject you can't shut him up.*

She was right.

"And for a bottle of Danny's favourite wine, they can survive for a decade. Danny drinks at least three bottles of it, on top of white and red in a day, with friends, of course."

"With friends like us," the ebullient lass sniggered.

"What are four or five bottles of fine wine a day to a billionaire?" Charles challenged. "I know an African potentate who washes his feet with single malt whisky every evening."

"And then he drinks it?" Anucha wanted to know.

While everybody seemed to be exuberant, the Napotian recalled one of the most expensive wines which Wilhelm Hagenbach had chosen at Claridge's, and suffered a pang of anxiety in anticipation of seeing HW in Bangkok.

Thus, he immediately changed the subject, asking Anucha:

"Anu, how do the children behave at school? Are they sublimely obedient like I was at their age?"

"Too obedient and too submissive," said Anucha. "Talking about our pupils, may I ask you to attend the headmaster's class, and tell me whether it was similarly conducted?"

"May I be there too?" Lizzie keenly inquired. "Perhaps Charles would like to join us as well."

"We'll frighten the little children," Little Prem protested.

"Khun Elizabeth and Khun Charles observe my class while Khun Prem becomes the headmaster's student once more."

Meanwhile, Piang and Toon arrived, carrying bags of foodstuffs. Little Prem led them to the kitchen and explained the function of the gas burners and where the utensils were. The two women, who had recently moved into the 20th century in the way of using plastic bags in place of bamboo baskets, seemed rather diffident in operating an elaborate gas cooker and in using shiny stainless steel pots and pans and cutlery. And there was no wok!

"You'll have to do *kaibaikapao* in a flat-bottomed frying pan, I'm afraid," the tadpole suggested.

Then, he went to the bar to open a bottle of New Zealand Chardonnay. Tasting the wine the way Danny had taught him, the novice in the art of wine tasting found the pale-gold liquid to his liking.

"No! You don't pour a different wine into these glasses," Elizabeth rebuked as the little bounder was about to fill her sparkling wine flute with the white wine. "Use new glasses. You'd have known by now. Danny wouldn't be amused."

"Danny isn't here, and we're neither in London nor in Bangkok, Lizzie. We're deep in the heart of Isan where I used to drink muddy water out of a coconut husk. It doesn't matter one bit if we drink white wine out of these."

"To Charles and to me, it does!"

She collected the used glasses and went to the bar.

"This is what I found uncomfortable in living in England, Charles. Your life is so strictly regulated by rules and etiquette. I had to learn from zero to avoid being a bounder. Dining at Lord Norbury's table, for instance, was a very painful experience. Danny said that he could tell a man's station in life, his background, his level of education and where he's from as soon as the man opens his mouth and the way he holds his knife and fork, or whether he knew the difference between an ordinary knife and a fish knife, between porcelain and china. Here, I feel at ease to talk, act and react to my people. If I did something out of the way, they'd say *bopeneyangdok* (It does not matter)."

"In Wit's house, I made a terrible mistake," Charles admitted. "I sat on a sofa and crossed my legs without being aware that it's unforgivably rude to point one's foot or both feet at a Siamese. I got quite a lecture from Wit."

"Oh, yes. Another thing -- you mustn't touch our heads," said Anucha. "And when you want to thank those who are older, you say *kobkhun* and to younger ones you say *kobjai,* and when you *wai* or make a *namuskara,* you bend your head rather low to your elders or those who are higher in position or VIPs, but you don't have to bend your head much to the younger, lesser and ignoble lot."

When women's chorus of laughter was heard, the Napotian looked at the English gentleman, shaking his head as if to say: *When women get together!* But he was happy with the thought that Piang had overcome the death of her husband and that Toon had been happy again with Tongdum in Napo. Momentarily he could forget the vile threat from the Drug Baron whose shadow had reached Napo and most of the villages.

Presently, Elizabeth rejoined the men, putting white wine glasses in front of her friend.

"Use these!"


How the evening mellowed.

Such was a pleasant time to be in Isan, a time of mild winter.

Now, at sunset, silent reapers were returning home from the paddy-fields, wearily trudging along the ridge of Mongkol Pond where the schoolchildren had skipped and run. Herds of buffaloes too moved homeward; their dark skin and hair were awash with the setting sun.

Little Prem left his guests for the front part of the terrace to gaze at the school in case the headmaster might be seen moving about the ground. How quiet the school seemed then. There was not a soul in sight.

"Khun Anucha escaped from the October 6th massacre at Dhamasart University and joined the *K-Force,*" Elizabeth was telling Charles.

Attracted by the topic of conversation, Luke-pi rejoined his friends, saying:

"Yes, do tell us what happened, Anu. I read in a back issue of the Post that a certain authority was to rewrite the history of the October 14th and the October 6th massacres. Before it can belie the truth, let's hear from you what actually happened."

"The truth of the matter is this," said Anucha decidedly. "A lecturer and his class of 25 students held a mock convention of a pressure group to press the junta for the promulgation of the constitution. You see, Khun Charles, the despots seized control of the country on the 17<sup>th</sup> November. Then they abrogated the Constitution, dissolved parliament and proclaimed martial law.

"But then the police burst into the classroom and arrested the lecturer and 12 students. It was claimed that the meeting contravened martial law that forbade a gathering of more than five persons. The imprisonment of the 13 brought a large number of lecturers and their students to gather in front of the prison. Day-by-day students from various universities and colleges in the capital and from Khon Kaen, Chiangmai, and Cholbury joined the rally at Dhamasart University. By the 14<sup>th</sup> of October over 125,000 students had converged at the campus until it could no longer hold the crowd. Then the mass began moving along Rajdamnern Avenue. But the move did not progress farther than the Monument of Democracy and Panfa Bridge. It is an irony that nearly 2,000 people, who wanted to have a democratically elected government, should be massacred at the Monument of Democracy, shot at by fully armed troops and tanks and helicopters. The official body count of the dead was 69, but, by us, the massacred and the missing were 1,965 persons. The nation was in shock, horrified that the despots could use the armed forces to quell the marchers as if it was a war against the people. It was the shock value that made the despots, the Terrible Trio, as they were named afterwards, leave the country. But not for long, in early October, one of the Terrible Trio sneaked back from Singapore, hiding his horrible crime under the yellow robe of a Buddhist monk. We knew for a fact that the return of the despot was celebrated in some quarters, and so we organized another rally within Dhamasart University. Once again we incited the wrath of the murderers. The force stormed the campus on the 6<sup>th</sup> of October, shooting into the crowd. The victims, males and females were killed on the spot. Many were garrotted, doused with petrol and set on fire, clubbed or stabbed to death; some female students were raped and then killed. The scene of carnage is, for me, almost unbearable to recall though years have since passed. It was as if the beasts in the hearts were released to do their worst. How could they hate us so much that they could commit such slaughter? Now, I have a fear that there will be several more massacres to come, each time more horrible, premeditated and cunningly planned. And there won't be any shock value left as it was the first time.

"Thinking that if I stayed I would be killed along with hundreds of other students, Nopadol and I covered our lecturers, Khun

Chantichar and Khun Sawitri and helped them swim across the river to safety on the Tonbury side. We hid for several days in a friend's house before we could make our way to Sisurachwood where some surviving students had already joined Kumjai's *K-Force*. The rest, I think, you already know. They can rewrite that part of our history, as Prem said they would, the truth cannot be altered or buried since the international media recorded both massacres throughout."

"Yes, I saw the broadcast on the BBC in late evening of October 6th while Danny and the Cliftons were dining at Claridge's," said Prem.

"I saw it too," said Charles.

"So did I!" Elizabeth exclaimed. "And I never thought that one day I'd meet one of the freedom fighters!"

"I'm lucky to be alive today," Anucha declared.

*But Rit did not survive the October 14th massacre.*

In his mind's eye, Prem Surin saw Rit Apaidham's forehead split from a single shot at point-blank.

"Most horrible, as all killings are, one should not try to blot them out of history, or whitewash them in order to cover the truth or make them less shameful. We'll have to live with the bitter memories and prepare for the following massacres which Anu predicted," the poet concluded.

Meanwhile Piang and Toon came out of the kitchen, saying that the meal had been prepared.

"There's no need to wait on us," said Luke-pi. "Thank you both for the cooking."

The two mothers left Bankhunluang. So did Anucha, with the excuse that by now the headmaster might have been ready to partake of dinner at his house.

# The Maimed Minds

The next day, before visiting the school, Prem and Elizabeth took Charles to visit Grandma Boonliang who remained in Surin House while Piang, Poon and older children had gone to reap their rice in a distant field.

Leaving the beautiful blond to chat with the grandmother, Luke-pi took the English gentleman to the edge of the village to see cattle husbandry and aquatic farming.

The same development scheme had been extended to create a pilot project in the form of a small vineyard on which Nikom and his wife Boonma grew the vines.

Seeing their benefactor and a foreigner approach, the couple emerged from under the clusters of leaves to squat on the soil and performed the *namuskara.*

*Unlike Russian serfs, these poor souls could scarcely plot a revolt,* Charles Tregonning entertained a tenuous thought.

He was surprised to see the landowner lower himself down, squatting like a peasant so as to be at the same level as his humble tenants.

The visitor remained standing, being anxious that he might not be able to load his16 stone onto his ankles to adopt such posture. Standing at ease the antiquarian listened to the sound of the Lao language.

A few moments later, the landlord bid the tenants goodbye and guided his friend back to the family house.

"Soon after the launching of the Napo Project, the Napotians have ample supplies of meat and fish. Now we have the very first vineyard. You see, that piece of land has been left fallow for so long. It was on high ground, unsuitable for rice planting."

"My dear boy, you're reviving feudalism, are you not?"

"If it's seen as such, then it's on a very minute scale and only during their generation. You won't see their children and grandchildren grovel in front of us. Anu is making sure of that. I let them reduce themselves to bundles of rags and cringe at our feet because they would be utterly ill at ease if I pressed them to stand up and act as our equal. They would not believe me if I told them that all of us are equal, that in your country there are such notions as human rights. They would not believe that they have any rights. For generations these people, my own parents included, have been treated as if they were subhuman. They have been cowed, cheated and taken advantage of at every turn. The fear of the masters has been force-fed to their hearts to such a degree that it seems almost impossible to expunge it. But, for now, for me anyway, there is a small victory to be had. I beat the eucalyptus promoters to that plot of land."

After collecting Lovely Liz from the family home, Luke-pi led his friends into the heart of the community, going from house to house so that Charles could observe silkworm rearing and silk weaving by the womenfolk.

During the tour, Prem stopped to ask about the ailing men, women and children who lay on mats in their houses. During his absence, there had been no volunteers to take the sick to the hospital.

"Let's go to the school after this house," Little Prem suggested. "When we've sat in the classes as Anu proposed, I'll take the most severely ill to the hospital. You see, Charles, in our modern times there are, in remote villages such as Napo, innumerable ailing persons who cannot afford medical treatment. I wish to have at least one doctor and a few nurses in this district for the sake of these people."

"That's it!" Elizabeth exclaimed. "Our Napo Project should also include construction of a hospital."

"I've read about an African bush hospital run by an aid project called *Medicine without Frontiers*," said Charles. "A similar scheme could be applied here. I'm all for it."

"Charles may help us persuade Danny to cough up another 10 million baht," the bubbly blond enthused.

"Maybe we should push the authorities to build a hospital instead of going for hand-outs from Danny all the time," the Napotian opined. "But then, it might take years if we rely on the authorities. Before the hospital could materialize, every bag of cement and every single piece of construction material would have been 'eaten', not to mention that only a certain company would be awarded the contract to build it. Meanwhile these disease-prone people have to be attended to."

The native took his visitors away from the house of the man who had been suffering from liver disease.

"Building a 30-bed hospital would be easier than pleading for a doctor and one or two nurses to come away from their beloved

Bangkok to care for the patients in what Karl called a God-forsaken Isan village like Napo," the little man expatiated.

"I can sponsor a doctor from the U.K. to come here for the first six months if you have such difficulty at the beginning," Charles proposed. "I know a retired general practitioner in Tunbridge Wells who might be prepared to lend a helping hand here."

Hence, hopes hung precariously in the air.

At the school, Prem went to Kumjai's class after Anucha had welcomed Elizabeth and Charles.

"May I be your student once again for half an hour," Prem deferentially requested.

The headmaster invited his former student into the classroom, losing no time in taking the opportunity to extol the virtues of self-improvement.

"It's all very well that we firmly believe in the force of karma. But, with us now, is living proof that one doesn't have to succumb to the belief that poverty is a result of bad deeds committed in the previous life, and that in this life the poor would remain impoverished to the end of their days. Our admirable visitor has successfully done away with the shackles. Poverty is a human condition. Like graft, it can be addressed, corrected or changed for the better. Yes, boys and girls, I've been talking to you time and again about change. Khun Prem has changed the course of his life. He has improved himself and has changed his station in life for the better. Now he can help others who are less fortunate. If it were not for him, we would not have this school and many of the parents would not have cows and oxen, ducks and chickens, fish and prawns to farm and to sell."

Bright-eyed, the children were eagerly waiting to hear more when the headmaster paused.

The visitor could see himself, a starving little boy, sitting at the back, listening attentively to Guru Kumjai's customary dictum which was being repeated now.

"Education is light to show the way in darkness. That's why every child has to come to school to learn to read and write and count. Being illiterate, you'll always be at a disadvantage. You wouldn't know how their weighing machines work and how to calculate. That's why we study mathematics and learn to read. So then, where were we? Oh, yes. Read after me: *Life of a Dragon-fly.*"

"Life of a Dragon-fly," the class repeated in unison, reading from the textbook spread in front of each of them.

"I am a dragon-fly," read the headmaster.

"I am a dragon-fly," the boys and girls repeated.

"My friends and I fly all over the paddies and marshes," uttered Kumjai in a monotone.

"My friends and I fly all over the paddies and marshes," the children parrotted.

Prem stood up and bowed to beg leave.

Then he went to Anucha's class.

It was quickly settled that Elizabeth remained in the classroom, while Little Prem and Good Old Charles departed to take the sick to the provincial hospital.

The Mercedes ably negotiated the bumpy country road.

Where the driver could not steer it away from bumps and potholes, the woman winced and moaned. The two ailing men suffered silently.

Skirting the Plain of Weeping Gula, Luke-pi mentioned:

"Charles, this plain used to be full of wild life. Now we're losing it to the accursed eucalyptus plantations. What a pity."

The Englishman did not immediately respond for he was thinking: *It is intriguing that this winsome young man, whom I met by chance in a most extraordinary circumstance in Soho, should harbour so much anger and bitterness and sorrow.* But then he said:

"My dear boy, I hope you don't mind me saying this. Though I enjoyed staying with Witty, I'd rather be with you. May I move back to Danny's place when we return to Bangkok?"

"By all means, Charles," said the driver, eyes on the ruined road. "Life with Witty could be a bit too much to take, I believe. He's over the top, as Lizzie said."

"No, it's not that. Though I've had pleasures, dwelling in Witty's marble hall, with handsome houseboys to pamper me, I came to Siam to be with you."

The driver could not find a word to say in return. So he drove silently for many kilometers. Then he stopped the car at the railway crossing before steering the vehicle slowly across the rails and heading for the hospital.

Many times he had taken the sick to this ramshackle pit of human suffering and disease. Each time he felt like a drowning man, going down into the depths of pity and despair brought about by the sight of patients and their relatives lying or sitting on the footpaths and in the corridors when the wards were full to capacity.

"We shall need three push-chairs, Charles. I fear that we have a case of acute appendicitis on our hands, so we should make for an emergency ward."

The sight of an enormous white man and a dapper native pushing wheelchairs caused one hospital staff member to move.

"It's urgent. The appendix may burst very soon," he said to the sour-faced pregnant clerk, who did not seem to care.

Though Little Prem did not know for sure that the moaning woman had appendicitis, the bluff might work to get his painful people quickly into the hospital. However, the little man forgot that the morose hospital staff had seen daily the poor souls that had died while waiting to be treated. The mere sight of a groaning crone could hardly touch a hardened heart.

Meanwhile, the perturbed millionaire, born in the lap of luxury in a welfare state and living a well-sheltered life in his green and pleasant land, was exceedingly affected by the sight and sound of the dying on the footpath and in the hallway.

Obviously, he did not appreciate the customary nonchalant tardiness and tedious procedure of admission in a state hospital. The old Oxonian went to the counter and offered his credit cards and bank notes, voicing vociferously:

"If it's a case of payment, I guarantee to pay for all."

Having made such an outburst, the art dealer looked absolutely livid.

The monsoon man tugged at the antiquarian's arm and begged him to back away from the registrar cum public relations officer, who was apparently astonished by the sight of so much money up front.

The Napotian collected the cash and cards and put them back in the wallet which he then handed to its rightful owner.

"The turtle won't move any faster regardless of any manner of prodding. I'm afraid we shall have to be patient."

But the furious foreigner, who had not been to Afghanistan or India or Pakistan or Bangladesh or Africa to familiarize his vision and harden his heart with the sight of human suffering, would rather not stand there blinking his eyes while a myriad of sufferers stared at him.

Realising that he had allowed his temper to flare, CT carefully retreated so that he would not step on the sick and their relatives sprawling on the floor as he made his way back to the car. Once there, he moved to wait for his friend in the shade of a nearby tree.

An hour later his little friend joined him.

"I'm sorry to have brought you to bear witness to all that."

"I'm the one who should apologize for deserting you at the crucial moment when you're in need of my support. But I just couldn't bear it. I felt utterly...utterly..."

"Our people would be all right. They would get medical treatment, and the old woman did have appendicitis. If we had been an hour late, she wouldn't return to Napo alive. The man with liver disease is too far gone. But he'll be given morphine. Tomorrow, I'll give money to their relatives to come to the hospital in a hired van."

In the evening, at the House of the Noble, Anucha went straight into the kitchen when he heard Elizabeth chat vivaciously with Piang and Toon. The women were so engrossed in mirthful conversation during the preparation of dinner that they were not aware of his presence until he said in English:

"I can eat *kaibaikapao* every day."

"Hello Anu! Care to join me with white wine?" Elizabeth ebulliently invited. "The two men over there declined. I don't know why they are in such a state. Do have a glass of wine with me. I hate to drink alone."

"I'd be delighted," Anucha beamed for he was extremely pleased to have another chance to speak English particularly with such a winsome blond with whom he was hopelessly in love.

Thus, he stood very close to her at the bar.

"Let's take two extra glasses with us in case I can tempt them with this luscious Kiwi ambrosia."

Meanwhile the two gloomy men in the living room were deep in a conversation.

"I don't have time to keep a journal," Charles was saying. "Now, all the antique furniture, pictures of old masters, crystal and silver in the shop mean very little to me. How futile my whole life has been. The more millions I make the emptier I feel. All the while I had to hang on to David to fend myself against loneliness."

"Excuse me for barging in," said Elizabeth. "I thought people like you would never reach such a conclusion."

"Khun Charles, you've stumbled on Lord Buddha's concept of futility and impermanence, right here, in the land of Buddhism," Anucha contributed.

The presence of the jubilant teacher did not disperse the gloom. It took some coaxing from the temptress for them to accept her offer of the well-chilled fragrant wine.

After having imbibed a glass of wine, Little Primo could chuckle at Lizzie's silly jokes with which she hoped to alleviate the sad state of minds.

She picked another funny story that involved a lawyer, a social worker, a Christian Brother and four schoolchildren in a small aircraft that was having engine trouble during the flight. The pilot said that they had to jump before the aircraft would crash, but there were not enough parachutes for all the passengers. The lawyer grabbed one. At that moment the social worker said: 'What about the children?' to which the lawyer replied: 'Screw the children!' To that remark, the Christian Brother asked: 'Do we have time?'

All except Charles laughed.

The English gentleman was thinking seriously about retiring from the business of buying and selling works of art and antique furniture. He wished he had left London years ago and lived entirely for peace in his country house in Sussex and for more meaningful activities that would enrich his heart rather than his bank accounts.

After all, the antiquarian was progressing towards his 60th birthday. Sadly, he had neither next of kin nor a soul mate now.

"Talking about schoolchildren," Anucha saw a chance to veer towards the subject close to his heart. "Khun Prem, does the headmaster teach the way he did when you were his student?"

"Yes, quite the same," Little Prem replied. "He even reiterated: *Education is light to show the way in darkness,* as he unfailingly did at the end of every academic year. Why?"

"You see, he graduated from one of the State Teachers Training Colleges. There, he was trained to become an instrument that maims the minds of the young so that the students would become mindless, obedient and absolutely subservient later on in life. Instead of developing, the minds under such an education system cannot grow. They become stunted or, in some cases, crippled. He wasn't aware of this then and isn't aware of it now, and if I tell him so, he won't believe me. He's been trained to enforce rote learning, spoon-feeding students with nonsense and on top of that he makes them recite until every word is crammed into their heads. There is hardly any room for asking questions, for either thinking or discussing or forming opinions. The concept of an inquiring mind is alien to him because he was not taught that teachers should encourage children to ask questions and seek answers, to form opinions and express them, and most of all to think deeply and critically. Curiosity is suppressed. Inquisitiveness is a crime. To ask a question is taboo. His sole aim in teaching is to enable the students to read, write and count. But these days that's not enough. I've been facing the task of changing the system so as to replace rote learning with a process of reasoning, of acquiring an inquiring mind, of critical thinking from an early age. In my class, students are encouraged to use *what, where, why, how, when, which* to form questions and ask them. And I answer them logically so that they learn a process of reasoning. To be able to ask questions should be a norm, not a dare. I believe there are thousands of teachers who punish curious children when they dare to ask questions in classrooms in Siam."

"Yes, quite true. Guru Kumjai caned me several times. Toon had a taste of his rod too. Also, in the secondary school in Bangkok, my teacher caned me for interrupting him with a question."

"If I tell you that your mind has already been maimed during your early years, would you believe me?"

Realising that he and the assistant teacher had been thinking along the same topic, using the same words, Little Primo smiled.

*For having been mentally maimed, I must learn to overcome my intellectual shortcomings and look deep within myself for certain propensities which might have escaped crippling and then develop them to their full capabilities.*

That was his determination made in London.

But now he did not want be seen as an easy touch. For argument's sake he hedged.

"I see it as being undeveloped."

"It's the same thing!" Anucha barracked.

"Is it?" asked Prem, pondering whether Anucha could have been his soul mate all these years.

Silently he eyed Elizabeth, pleading her to intervene.

Reading Prem's stunted mind, The University of London graduate said:

"*Maimed* is an ugly word. Be nice, Anu, use *undeveloped* instead. Now I understand why many Siamese politicians are infantile, speaking childishly in the House or during the interviews on television. It has always puzzled me as to why so many of them speak and act like children. The more I improve my Siamese, the more I'm convinced that they're children at heart. Anu, you hit the nail on the head. They haven't mastered the process of reasoning, and their undeveloped minds don't grow to match their ageing and bulging bodies!"

"While greed thrives boundlessly," bitterly vouched Anucha who suddenly became aware that they had moved away from the subject he wanted to discuss. So he reversed.

"All right! You can say *undeveloped* if you like. I want to ask Khun Prem this. When you realised that your mind had been prevented from developing, did you feel angry? Would you take revenge? You know perfectly well who set their hearts on stunting the minds of the young, and on making them mindless and silent so as to be tractable and easy to govern."

"I've already gone through this, Anu, not only in London and in Bangkok but also here in Napo and on the Plain of Nadhone. I deeply regret my maimed mind, but I cannot see why or how one should or could avenge it. Perhaps the priesthood has also cleansed me of such bitterness. But I did revolt. Elizabeth knew that."

"You mean you've extinguished your fire. You've stopped carrying the torch now that you've been wallowing in luxury, enjoying good food and good wines."

When Prem did not respond, Elizabeth decisively offered a buffer.

"No, he hasn't, Anu. I know he hasn't. The amber is still there."

*No, this is not a time for me to talk of resurrecting 'The Monsoon People'.*

Charles shifted, uncrossed his legs and, in the manner of a doddery Oxford don, opined sharply.

"Take care, Anu. You're holding a two-edged sword. I know for a fact that in many schools in England the teachers are so terrified of their modern-day students that they let the *yobs*, as we call the defiant, unruly youths, run the schools. Parents lose control over their children, and youth gangs and knife-gangs roam the streets, robbing and killing people. If you are not careful you'll have our yob-like mobs on your hands. Eventually you'll have anarchy. Then another series of massacres will occur as a result."

"The massacres will recur anyway. I'm not ignorant of the way British children are reared and taught, of outcries, riots, and killings. Some of your killers are in their teens."

"Oi!" Little Prem butted in. "In Sheffield a boy not older than 15 stabbed a teacher to death in the class in front of other students, not once but several times!"

But then Anu adhered to the topic he wanted to discuss.

"On the other hand, I wish to move our younger generation forward towards the middle of the scale so that they may have well-developed minds, and so they can think for themselves. Critical thinking is a radical scarcity in this country as *krengjai* is in yours."

"What is *kreng...jai?*" Charles tentatively tasted the foreign word as if it were an exotic fruit.

Prem saw his chance.

"*Krengjai* is exactly what Anu is doing. Being a good subordinate and full of *krengjai*, Anu is afraid that he would hurt Kumjai's feelings should he criticize his superior's teaching method face to face. Instead he resorts to airing his view on us, when he is slightly inebriated. Have another glass of wine, Anu. And see what more you might come up with."

"Yes, please, one for the road. Then I'll return to my lonesome house and have dinner with my superior."

# The Concert

A day before the Munich Philharmonic was to perform at The Imperial Palace Hotel, news of an encroachment on a forest reserve appeared in a newspaper.

During the morning session in the headquarters, Little Primo reported:

"The headline '**Blatant usurping of public land**' is the main point for today. A palatial mansion, being built on a knoll, is in the heart of a forest reserve."

The public relations manager paused, glancing at his employer, expecting a reaction.

Seeing none, the Napotian resumed:

"Suan Vichitra Reforestation Company was granted concessions to eight sections of degraded forest land totalling 3,500 acres in Sisawasdi District designated for planting eucalyptus. Its workers moved in to clear a ninth section before permission would be formally granted. Then they encroached on 800 acres of adjacent forest. Local forestry officials dared not stop the encroachment, or blow the whistle, because the firm belongs to Minister Prakarn's wife.

"Suan Vichitra Reforestation Company had usurped 12,000 acres of degraded forest reserves. Under the original government policy, degraded forest can be leased to concessionaires for *bona fide* projects, mostly eucalyptus planting. But any application for more than 800 acres of degraded forests requires Cabinet approval.

"Suan Vichitra circumvented this regulation by applying for fewer than 800 acres for each lease. This enables Agriculture and Forestry Minister Sanan Kajonwong to approve the applications. Minister Sanan claimed that he did not see anything wrong in Suan Vichitra's tactics, asserting that Suan Vichitra was a legitimate investment which corresponded with the government's policy of increasing commercial forests so as to cover 40 per cent of the country's arable area.

"Meanwhile, Prime Minister's Secretary General Pornpat Kittipong described eucalyptus as Siam's future leading cash crop. Both the Agriculture and Forestry Minister and the PM's Secretary General were unaware of any wrongdoings in the Company's massive operation which has enabled Suan Vichitra to have more tracts of lands than any other companies in Siam."

*Money can make some greedy men blind*, the news monitor thought of adding to the report.

Surin sounded heavy-hearted, sensing a smack of bribery and a loss of Siam's dwindling forest reserves. Once again the saddened Isaner scrutinized the billionaire's face for sentiments which might be similar to his own. He saw that the lord and master was biting his lower lip, head bent, with his eyes focusing on the shiny surface of the long table.

Then the budding writer, who was gathering 'grist to the mill', deplored:

"What hope have we to save our fast disappearing forests?"

"Don't worry about that now."

"You don't give a damn, do you? You made me spent months reading old newspapers for nothing!"

"Dash it, Primo! I know what I'm doing. You do what I say, all right? For the rest of today, concentrate on getting the appropriate people from the media to report on the concert. Are there any journalists from the English press to do intelligent or should I say 'erudite' reviews of the performances? Find that out, will you? And also you draft an action plan to generate the publicity. All right, Primo?"

"I've spent months and months reading back copies of the Post as well as monitoring news from several Siamese newspapers each day, and you haven't done anything. The forests are being illegally logged and destroyed. Ten million people have been forced to leave their homes to give way to dam constructions and eucalyptus planting. Your gigantic pulp and paper mills and factories are polluting the air, land and water, and you don't seem to take heed. The only news that seemed to excite you and to push you into taking action was the libel case against news agencies and newspapers. You sent Lizzie scurrying to Reuters and ENN and I to Khaosod Daily as if the house was on fire."

"First things first, shouldn't it be? I know what I'm doing. You just do what I say."

At first the super rich treated the news of forest encroachment as a one-off hype. But, the following day, news of the same nature cropped up in several dailies. Now that his highly-strung slave had goaded him, the heir apparent tried to seek an audience with his mother at VP Tower.

The visit was not meant to be a confrontation but when mild inquiries gradually became convoluted, the son unleashed his tempestuous nature.

"I can't understand why you must have vast properties all over the country. You hardly go to any of these grand country houses and resorts we own. Can't you ever have enough?"

"I do it for you while your Papa is in control."

"I don't want them! And I don't want to be part of your dashed wicked scheme! " Dani responded with a gesture of throwing all back to her before leaving the steely office.

Karl-Michael von Wittenberg was outside the President's office, chatting amicably with Executive Secretary Suprapada.

"Karl, come with me," Dani von Regnitz commanded, ignoring Suprapada.

The 18th richest man in the world strode hastily, oblivious of the saluting, heel-clicking guards. He did not even turn to look back to see if his dear friend was following him as he speedily entered the lift which two security officers were keeping in readiness.

Admirably the Executive Vice President made it before the lift door closed. DP did not utter a word to KW until they sat in the back of the chauffeur-driven Rolls-Royce.

"We'll partake of luncheon with Willie at The Bordeaux Grill."

Their togetherness somewhat soothed the agitated man.

On arriving at the hotel, the duo dropped in on Wilhelm Hagenbach and the orchestra during the final stage of rehearsal in the Grand Hall.

"The programme has no lieder," remarked Dani. "Why is Willie bellowing?"

"I didn't know he could sing!"

"Oh yes, he can. In fact he's a well-known baritone before he took to conducting and composing. His famous role is Papageno in *The Magic Flute.*"

In The Bordeaux Grill, the hotel owner did not have to wait for his aperitif. For now it had become a procedure. The moment the son and heir sat, the sommelier was ready to pop the cork.

Taking delight in imbibing one of the world's most expensive sparkling wines and in the nearness of his soul mate, Dani Pi did not mind waiting half an hour for Wilhelm.

"Mick! You're looking at the biggest landowner in Siam. Would you drink to that?"

"To the biggest land owner in Siam," Karl raised his glass.

Innocent as he sounded, the hotelier knew exactly what the hotel owner meant. He surmised that in less than a year he would be drinking the same wine on the expansive marble veranda of the magnificent country house, on the knoll overlooking over Nakarin Lake, at sunset.

"Mama plans to go to China to look for a girl to marry me," Dani lugubriously mentioned. "It seems Siam has run out of respectable bankers' daughters to be my wife."

"I know. Petra and I are supposed to wed on the same day, at the same time, and share the wedding reception in the Grand Hall with you and yours," Karl said affably.

"If it weren't for your involvement in Mama's scheme, I'd have gone back to London. Mick, we should make the Royal Leicester and the Wealdshire Park exceedingly *manifique*."

"I'll drink to that," Karl raised his glass again.

"Zum Wohl! To one of the world's best hotels. Tell me, Mick. What is your formula for success? Is it hard work and professionalism, or intensified advertising and public relations?"

"All of them and more. We are not in the same boat with some international hotel chains that entered this market. They believe that the short cut to success is pinching our key staff members. Little do they know! How do you think we could get hold of their marketing strategies, corporate room tariffs, travel trade rates, room occupancies and revenues from their food and beverage outlets? And you know what we can do with inside information. On the other hand, we have the tentacles of the VP subsidiaries to thank. For weeks after the opening, guests of Sukhothai Hotel could not flush the toilets and bath water flooded the rooms every time the taps were turned on. The Peninsula failed within a year of its opening, and had to sell the property to another international chain and go back to where it came from. Then, it returned to build a new five-star property only to face a devastating delay in construction. And to top the lot, a 500-bedroom hotel on the west bank of the Chaopraya River could not open after construction was completed. Do you know what happened? It was not only financial problems but the building was said to have subsided. You can guess whose construction company built it. So there you have a towering hotel standing like a Tower of Pisa, left empty for years."

His mockery yielded the true colour of his character as it did when he said previously: "I've very few friends left. They either died in jail (meaning Heinz Hermann) or of AIDS complications (meaning the Baron and Peter Halland and John Brentcross.)"

Wilhelm Hagenbach joined the chuckling pair.

"Willie, there will be a slight change in the programme," said Dani after the conductor had been served his first glass of champagne. "*Zum Wohl!* I won't make a speech. Little Primo will. He doesn't know that yet but he'd do it admirably, I'm sure."

"Absolutely," seconded Karl. "He'd do anything when he is paid handsomely."

Wilhelm smiled.

"He's told me about the development project in his home village and the plan to build a hospital."

"Oh he has already handed his begging bowl to you!" Karl bitched.

The maestro chose to ignore Karl's bitchiness.

"He said he couldn't thank you enough, Danny."

"What I've done is a drop in the ocean. It's not worth mentioning. Today I found out that I'm the biggest landowner in Siam. I can't say that I should be proud as a peacock when millions of poverty-stricken Siamese have no land of their own. And that's one of the reasons why I won't go up to the podium this evening and face the concert audience. It's a matter of conscience," Dani stated before turning to the sommelier.

"Yes, Prawin, another Krug."

"Don't worry. There won't be boos. There'll be sheer adoration when you deliver your speech," Karl assured.

"There you are, Danny. You can still adhere to the programme. I'd be pleased if you do."

"If I speak, I'll be blowing my own horn. It'd be better if Little Primo does it. Besides, let him sing for his supper. I know he's extremely shy when it comes to speaking publicly. What's more, he'd be addressing our Prime Minister! I wonder whether our little chap could charm the trousers off our bachelor PM like he did with some people."

An hour before the concert commenced. Prem Surin, immaculately dressed in white tie, headed for the Emperor Suite, leaving Elizabeth Durham to co-ordinate the public relations activities with the hotel's public relations manager.

How strange it seemed that life could have reached its full cycle in a short time. In Berlin, in a suite of the Kempinski, PS had observed WH dress for the concert.

He remembered so clearly, as if it were yesterday, that the conductor had made such a fuss about the handkerchief, the cuffs and the cufflinks and a button that came loose at the time when every minute counted. And it happened again, here in the Emperor Suite of The Imperial Palace Hotel in Bangkok! Brown and Dawson were on hand to do the mending.

"Tod," the freak absentmindedly spoke.

*Wilhelm conducted the premier of 'Tod' in Berlin.*

The reflection made the little man anxious. Rising from the chair, the public relations executive left the bedroom to join the butlers.

"Greg, would you believe, I have to speak on behalf of my boss tonight."

"You'll do very well, Khun Prem. We'll come down and listen to you from behind the curtain. For now, champagne should do you and the maestro the world of good."

"Dr Dhani Pilaskulkosol and Mr Karl-Michael von Wittenberg," Dawnson announced.

Both men in white ties entered the living room. The lord and master stood still for a moment to check whether the blighter had dressed correctly or not. Tacitly the boss approved.

"Where is Willie?"

"Getting dressed! Not without a little mishap though. A collar button came off."

"B&D could easily fix that!"

"That's what they've done. I'll see whether he's ready."

"I'm ready," said WH, in conducting outfit, coming out of the bedroom. .

"Well! I'm dashed! What have you done? You look so radiant!"

"I had my beauty sleep this afternoon. Ah! The butlers have champagne ready for us."

Once again their togetherness brought joy enhanced by the flow of wine, causing the bibulous billionaire to be charmingly voluble.

"Brown, the boys downstairs are serving Pol Roger to the cocktail reception crowd. I had to put up with it." Turning to the conductor he said: "It's quite a cult here, Willie. Angelic people of our Divine City of Angels, with glasses in hand, chat, eat and drink during the happy hours between 6.30 and 8.30 and most times it goes on to 9 or 10. That's what they're doing at the cocktail reception in your honour just now while we have to make do with Krug up here. By the way, you will be performing to a capacity audience. The Prime Minister will arrive in 20 minutes."

Dani checked his diamond-encrusted Piaget, and continued: "In 15 minutes, we'll escort you to meet the PM at the reception."

"The pleasure will be mine," replied Hagenbach.

Little Prem moved towards the window. Looking down, he saw a crowd swarming in front of the hotel, brandishing placards.

*It could be a protest!*

The riot police barred the way. Then the scrimmage and the bludgeon began. Red lights from the police cars flashed and whirled. In less than 10 minutes the public nuisance ceased, with arrested demonstrators taken away in large vans. Moving away from the ledge, the public relation executive did not mention to anyone the scene he had witnessed. Gently putting his glass down on the coffee table, he followed his friends out of the Emperor Suite.

Turning back, Dani issued an order.

"Brown and Dawson! Follow us and look after the PM. Offer him, and all of us here, and Colonel Ayu, vintage Krug."

"Yes, sir," said Brown.

"Very well, my lord," said Dawson.

The Emerald Room boasted magnificent floral art and decorative ice-carvings as well as arrays of food platters. The latter had a variety of delectable canapes, smoked Scottish salmon, caviar, prawn cocktails, duck liver pate, roast ham, smoked oysters, slices of beef Wellington, chicken satays, and steamed crab claws for 500 honoured guests. Such was the supreme gathering of angels, deep in convivial conversation, savouring the delicacies, awaiting the presence of the Prime Minister.

When the PM and his entourage arrived, the room burst into glaring light from video recorders and press photographers. Heading the reception line at the entrance, Minister Prakarn and Madame Vichitra introduced Wilhelm Hagenbach to the Prime Minister. The PM graciously chatted with the maestro in English before moving down the line to Dani Pi, Karl von Wittenberg and Colonel Ayumongkol.

Gregory Brown moved forward to offer a glass of champagne on a shining salver to the Prime Minister, obviously delighting in having another opportunity to serve the statesman.

The PR man went back stage to be amongst 60 members of the Orchestra, trembling slightly from anticipating that in a minute he would be addressing the Prime Minister and one thousand richest and most awesome people in Siam.

Meanwhile he observed members of the orchestra carrying their instruments to their seats on the stage. Little Prem sent a meek smile to the leader, who remained behind, aloof and alone with his violin. At that instant the doors of the Grand Hall opened. The secret observer, peeking from behind the stage, eyed Minister Prakarn and Madame Vichitra ushering in the Prime Minister, followed by a throng of awe-inspiring VIPs and their bejewelled wives.

How the Napotian's heart thumped!

He knew that Elizabeth would be sitting with the members of the media.

*Where is Wilhelm? Where is the soloist?*

He had never felt so forlornly alone in his adult life while the fear of this terrifying audience smothered him.

The former village mute was afraid that he might stammer and suddenly become mute as in childhood.

"Ah! There you are," said the maestro coming from back stage. "Danny is frantically looking for you. He thought you'd chickened out."

"I won't chicken out. Somehow I have to compete with Pan."

He stretched his hands to show that they were not trembling. But they were, obviously. Wilhelm saw that too and smiled.

"You'll be all right," assured the maestro. "Now go!"

A moment later, while Little Primo was delivering Khun Dhani's speech, Wilhelm moved to be near the leader of the orchestra and said:

"That's a friend of the late Helmut von Regnitz."

When the little fellow returned, the leader went forward to take his seat amid the welcoming ovation.

"Now it's your turn, Wilhelm!"

The wimp watched the maestro bow to the audience.

Then he stood ramrod while the orchestra played the Royal Anthem. When it ended, he sought the way back to the main entrance of the Grand Hall, and quietly stood among the security officers, giving full attention to Beethoven's Egmont Overture.

When there was not a single seat to be had, the Isaner remained on his feet, taking in Schubert's Symphony No. 8.

During the intermission, he went in search of Elizabeth and found her among the journalists.

"The second half is the best part," she was saying to a reporter from the Post. "What everyone is waiting for is Mozart's Flute Concerto No. 2 in D."

She flipped open the programme.

"The soloist is an ex-insurgent from a remote Isan village called Napo. He's so cute!"

After the intermission, the concert should have resumed. Somehow there was a delay. The front section of the audience had a glimpse of the agitated maestro.

Then Panya Palaraksa entered, followed closely by Hagenbach. The flautist did not bow at once, standing humbly glancing at the audience. To everyone's surprise, he left the stage, took several steps towards the front row and knelt in front of the Prime Minister to whom Panya made a *namuskara*, with his flute between his cupped hands.

The General-turned-Prime Minister brimmed, accepting the homage with his own gracious 'wai' and leaned forward to touch the former outlaw on the right shoulder.

When the soloist returned to the stage, taking his rightful place near the looming conductor, he bowed low to the audience. Those who did not know Panya's background would think that this amazing action they had just witnessed was well-coached and calculatingly performed to win hearts, including the Prime Minister's.

The flautist himself explained later: "I don't know what came over me."

The delay that caused the maestro to lose his cool was not brought about by conceit but simply by an incident which would not have happened if the soloist, while waiting in the rear, had not undone his collar button and loosened his tie. Having been a wild beast, unaccustomed to being yoked and harnessed, the tight collar had become so uncomfortable that it had to be loosened.

That done, Panya could not put on the tie without help. Fortunately Brown came to his rescue.

Panya gave the audience their money's worth, meeting the challenge of the very difficult *allegro* in the finale with sheer sentiment and brilliance that won him the heart of the conductor. He bowed low to accept the thundering accolade.

If one wished to see a hefty colonel cry, one had only to glance at Ayumongkol.

Ayu was weeping copiously, into his handkerchief, as he reflected on the pardoned youth taking a leaf and putting it in his mouth to make a delightful sound on their trek out of Sisurachwood.

The colonel had also committed to his memory a scene in Munich when Hagenbach wanted to replace Rodrigo with Mozart. Facing the issue, the young Napotian casually said: *It makes no difference, maipenrai, I can do it,* even though, at the time, the peasant turned-insurgent-turned musician was not familiar with Mozart.

Now, the flautist had to be prompted by Gregory Brown, to return to the stage front, again and again and again, to bow and bow and bow to the stupendous applause.

Then Beethoven's Symphony No. 7 became the crowning glory of the most exhilarating evening. The ovation lasted so long that the maestro, having returned to reap the honour time and again, considered that an encore would be appropriate.

He sang a Papageno aria.

Since there were only a few persons in the concert hall who knew that the conductor had been a renowned opera singer, the shock value sent the Grand Hall thundering with the applause.

Hagenbach felt fit to explain the final encore.

"*A Song of Siam* was composed by Prem Surin, a native son of E…Esarn."

*He got the pronunciation right, but he shouldn't have mentioned my name! It's slinging mud at these glittering and powerful people.*

None could refute that the concert was heart-fulfilling. Most members of the audience would agree that in the future more of such performances should follow.

As scheduled, the Pis hosted supper at The Bordeaux Grill for the Prime Minister and the cabinet members and their wives. The table settings did not have places for Little Prem and Elizabeth who were treated as staff members while Colonel Ayumongkol, Wilhelm and Panya were guests of honour.

Not being invited to join the party, the public relations executives had to be content with the coffee shop of the hotel.

"I don't mind not being invited to partake of the feast in The Bordeaux Grill, Little Prem aired. "Ayu should have coached Pan well in the etiquette. You know which knife and fork to use, and how to eat elegantly, the sort of thing that I've gone through with Danny. By the way, have you any inkling of a scuffle outside the hotel this evening?"

"What scuffle?"

"The bludgeoning and stomping and arresting that went on outside the hotel."

"I wish you wouldn't bother me with other people's problems at this moment. I've mine to bear as it is. I'm so tired. I've slaved for weeks to publicize this blooming concert. Now I'm ready to drop."

But before dropping, she asked a waiter for a bottle Coonawarra Cabernet Sauvignon.

After a long pause, Little Primo felt compelled to say:

"Pan may have to spread himself so thinly to satisfy all of his admirers now."

"How about you? Who shall fight over you?"

The poet did not reply at once while the waiter was pouring wine for the beautiful blond to taste. Following the wine tasting procedure, she accepted Leconfield Coonawarra. As the waiter was about to pour the wine into Prem's glass, the Napotian stopped him.

When the waiter had left their table, he said:

"No one! Who would want an ageing hack like me when there are thousands of teenagers to choose from? Besides, I'm a one-person man, whereas you aren't."

Since Lovely Liz did not react, the one-person man continued:

"Tonight I saw how Pan has swayed the hearts of the mighty. I want to be able to sway the hearts of myopic, rapacious, venal bureaucrats and avaricious, ruthless and unethical tycoons so that they will be ethical and humane, but not with music. I can't read the squiggles; and not through poetry either; *they* don't read poetry. I'll do it with prose. I'll go to Oxford and write books. Wo! Wo! Go easy with that stuff. You've been drinking heavily lately!"

"Write books! You haven't scribbled a single word since you burnt your poems and the manuscript of *The Monsoon People*. Don't you know that they don't read books? Most Siamese don't have a reading habit. If they do, it's newspapers, magazines and comics. You'd better write in English, hadn't you?"

"I've been scribbling in my head all along. Don't you know that an artist creates up here first," the reluctant writer tapped his forehead several times before expounding further: "A woman conceives or is impregnated. As for a true writer, he, too, conceives. Like a pregnant woman, who nurtures the foetus in the womb for nine months, the artist's conception gradually takes shape in his head."

"For you, my dear Primo, surely it's been more than nine months since you were impregnated…and I wonder by whom."

"It doesn't matter how long or by whom, my dear Lizzie. I'll get there in the end. You know, there is a saying in old Siam: *Slowly, slowly you'll get two well-forged knives. In a rush, you'll have three badly crafted knives*, or for me, three badly written books! But before that I'll have to learn how to think profoundly. It would be worth waiting till I'd have a few years at Oxford behind me."

"Have you ever thought for one minute about me? About what I would do when you are at Oxford?"

The full-bodied red wine made her pugnacious and loud over the medium-rare sirloin steak.

"You have your randy Nin and your fat bank accounts and an eight-carat diamond ring and first class air-tickets and the romps in the best hotels and the wining and dining in expensive restaurants the world over. What else do you want?"

"I want you!"

"Steady on, Lizzie!"

The little fellow looked round to see whether other diners were taking notice.

"People will think we are having a row."


"I dread a morning such as this," Little Prem muttered the following day, glancing through the front pages of several dailies, Siamese and English, with Elizabeth by his side. "I hope that Danny is sick or doesn't want to get out of bed today."

"It has to be done. It's no use postponing. Besides, it's their own doing; it has to catch up with them eventually. The nemesis always does. Then they'd have their comeuppance."

"I wonder whether we should stop the newspapers being delivered to hotel rooms today, especially to the Emperor Suite. Wilhelm should not know about it."

"Do you know what time it is?"

"Yes. It's too late for that now."

"Too late for what?" Dani asked, entering the HQ.

"Oh dear!"

"Don't you 'oh dear' me! Tell him! It's your job."

"Children! What's up?"

The public relation manager pushed the newspapers towards the lord and master.

"It's all on the front pages. The protesters clashed with riot police or, to be precise, the riot police bludgeoned the protesters in front of The Imperial Palace last night. Look! horrible pictures of women being clobbered, dragged, and bundled into the vans."

"When did this happen?"

"Just before the arrival of the Prime Minister."

"Why didn't I know about it?"

"No one inside the hotel did. Security hushed it up, I think. The protest wasn't political. It was 500 women, largely those who were injured and the relations of 188 workers who were burnt to death in the fire at one of your factories. They were enforced with scores of people from Klongdan district where your people dumped toxic waste. They rallied in the hope of receiving some compensation. They also wanted to ask the owners of the burnt factory not to obstruct the court proceedings."

"Are there any reviews or articles on the concert?"

"It's in the Post. There should be several tomorrow in the vernacular newspapers, and there is a mention of the concert related to the protest. *While the great and the good gathered in the sumptuous hall of The Imperial Palace Hotel, wining and dining before sitting down to the performance of the Munich Philharmonic Orchestra to which only the very rich and the supremely powerful were invited, 500 women, most of whom were badly injured in the Kinder Factory fire in which 188 workers died, converged on the hotel. Their rally has been supported by some 70 inhabitants of Klongdan, where radioactive waste materials belonging to VP Cobalt Co. Ltd., had been dumped.*

*The police employed heavy-handed tactics to prevent the mob from entering the hotel's public area, and injured nearly 100 protesters, while the Kinder Factory owners flaunted their great wealth by giving an extravagant party for the much-publicized concert. It is great wealth indeed, but at an enormous cost to workers.*

*Kinder Factory employed over 3,000 workers, mostly women, but there were no fire escapes or alarms and all exits were locked to prevent the employees from stealing the products. Such are the conditions for cheap production overheads in Siam.*

"You should sue the newspaper for damages. Get Witty to look into the possibility of litigation, and you might make millions out of the case," Lovely Liz suggested.

"Witty is in disgrace at present. That's why he didn't show his face at reception and in the concert hall. It was said that he leaked to the CIA a top secret file on the operators of a ship used for drug and petrol smuggling."

"I wonder whether Witty's karma will catch up with him in his life time," Little Prem pondered aloud.

# The Oxford Years

Prem Surin delayed his departure for England to attend the reception held in honour of the newly-wedded couple.

To secure the bride for her darling, Madame VP had spent a fortnight in China, searching for a match among the Hungs. The marriage had been marked in the history of the Pis and the Hungs as one of the most significant phases in the continuation of the undiluted bloodline.

The ultimate achievement Dani could make from then on was to produce a male heir.

The decorations, stage setting and catering in the Grand Hall of The Imperial Palace surpassed many grand receptions in all the hotels in Siam.

On that occasion, the Grand Hall was also the venue of another wedding reception, none other than that of Petra and Karl-Michal von Wittenberg.

Lord Bewly flew in to be Dani's best man. On that auspicious day Hung Kwan Tai became Kwanjai Pilaskulkosol.

Then the newly-weds and the pair of PR staff members flew to London. There, they held another splendid reception at Royal Leicester Hotel before the Pis and the Wittenbergs would honeymoon at Wealdshire Park.

When the celebrations were over, Prem Surin started the Michaelmas Term at Magdalen College.

Among the freshmen, the mature student was conscious of having the mind of a British teenager. His boyish looks and small build belied his age. He was aware of class distinctions and barriers between the public school educated sons of the upper classes and the scholarship winners from state schools.

Surin studied conscientiously, keeping in sight his aim to overcome his *bonsai* mind, using the learning method at Oxford to catapult himself onto new ground, hoping to become a discerning individual and an able wordsmith.

Every minute of his waking hours meant a great deal. He deplored time lost in idleness or in physical activities that would barely enrich him mentally. Therefore, he attended most of the lectures and tutorials, and was often seen in the evenings inside the Chapel at Evensong.

During these chapel services, he participated in the responses, reading from the given texts as well as singing *Gloria* along with the choir.

Towards the end of the Hilary Term, he refrained from visiting London, causing Elizabeth to take a coach from Victoria to Oxford. She took a room at the East Gate Hotel and then went in search of her soul mate.

"I came to take you out to dinner!" Lovely Liz claimed.

It was indeed a welcome break from Chaucer. The ancient wordsmith and his tales had no room in the hearts of the young lovers during their tryst.

In the evening, in a crowded restaurant, sitting opposite each other, Elizabeth leaned forward.

"Have you heard of Witty's death?"

"No!"

"He was found dead in his Mercedes; his throat cut; his chest and stomach stabbed a dozen times. It was so gruesome. The newspapers had a field day divulging his private life, his sexual acts with teenagers, his harem, and a penchant for dressing up as a beauty queen. They dragged his wife and the adopted sons and those guiltless houseboys through mud and mire."

"O poor Witty," Prem wailed. "I'm so sorry. His karma seemed to have caught up with him so soon."

"It catches up with some of us sooner these days if or when we trifle with a sinisterly rich gang."

Elizabeth's voice vibrated ominously, causing Little Primo to shudder, realising that both of them had dared to enter the dragon's den.

"But I didn't expect it to be so horribly cruel," muttered the believer in the force of karma.

In memory of the late Prawit, the twain sat silently for a minute.

Then Elizabeth changed the subject.

"Anu has written. Good news number one -- the construction of the hospital is almost finished. Danny has asked me to fly back to prepare the publicity campaign and make arrangements for the opening, like we did for the hand—over and the opening of The Napo School. Only this time he won't get you involved. Disappointed?"

"That's because he knows I've the Prelims Exam coming, and then Trinity will be crucial. As for you, a research fellow, you're free to hop off anywhere, whenever. Don't ever think for one minute that you can fool me. You go back to SOAS so as to liaise with Asian male students, the darker the better!"

"I didn't come all the way to Oxford to be insulted!"

"You sneaked up here to catch me with another Lizzie. You think I've a soft spot for a blond and blue-eyed student, particularly from *oop* north, another Yorkshire blond, what? Well, my girl, if you'd come a week earlier, you'd have caught me with Charles. He was one of the experts at the Antiques Roadshow. I had a whale of a time with him at The Randolph."

"Your ears should have been burning while I dined last night with the foursome at Caprice."

"Why do you keep calling them names? It's most improper."

"Very proper, my dear. They tend to do things together, fly back and forth between London and Bangkok together, eat out together. And now both wives are pregnant in the same week!"

"Jealousy won't get you anywhere with them."

Elizabeth ignored that remark.

"Good news number two -- Anu has married his sweetheart who studied at the same Faculty at Dhamasart. She has also become a teacher at The Napo Witayakom School, making a husband and wife team to help Headmaster Kumjai. Isn't that marvellous?"

"Marvellous for you too! I know you have a penchant for married men."

"Primo! I've had enough!"

"Steady on, Lizzie. No need to go berserk. Have some more New Zealand Chardonnay. *Drink to me only with thine eyes, and I will pledge with mine; or leave a kiss but in the cup and I'll not look for wine.* Ben Jonson that is."

"Yes, go on. Sing for your supper. Better still, write your own song. Be original."

"Some people don't want to be original these days."

"What's the point of being at Oxford then?"

"To appreciate Beowulf and to know where and when to quote Shakespeare," the little man remarked, hiding from her the truth that he intended to use Oxford as a nursery in which he might nurture his famished mind and develop a thinking ability and hone his pen.

"It's so out of touch with reality."

"What is the reality, my dear?"

"That graft is rife. Exploitation is outrageous. Social conditions are deplorable. People live in poverty. Injustice is a bane. Many brave and idealistic men and women are murdered by hired gunmen. Thousands of pro-democracy demonstrators are massacred in the streets. The ecology is being deplorably damaged. The minimum wage is lower than a pound a day. The buyers keep suppressing the paddy price so that the rice farmers have to go down on their knees to beg for a minimal increase to make five baht for a kilogramme of their precious rice."

"I don't think Danny would pay for me to study Karl Marx even at Oxford."

"I can never talk seriously with you as I can with Anu. Anu is an intellectual. You aren't."

Like a child, he stuck out his tongue at her to cover the sense of guilt that he could not relate to her, his closest ally, all the inner feelings and conceptions that had been lying in wait for his pen.


Surin dreaded the weekly tutorial in the second year, when three out of five students dropped out. With only one English student there, it was not possible to hide his timidity and lack of critical thinking.

James Barnes had been perfunctorily reading his essay, stumbling over words, uncertain of what he had to say, pretending to cough, being embarrassed at the shallowness of his opinions.

But worse than reading the essay was the moment when the work had been read and an awful silence ensued as Michael Wilding, the tutor, looked into space, avoiding eye contact with them, saying nothing.

Barnes and Surin had to wait.

After a while, Wilding cleared his throat before asking them about the topic. Looking down at the floor the students exhibited their uncertainty, afraid that what they said would show their failure to understand.

As for Barnes, it was more the lack of preparation than ignorance. Surin had difficulty in forming opinions and understanding *Paradise Lost*.

Looking at Wilding, the freak's inner eye saw the tutor in equal anguish. MW was covering his face with his hands; his legs crossed tensely under the weight of silence. It was indeed the silence of desperation, trying to think of something to say without being dismissive, without revealing his despair at having to listen to ill-prepared work.

*There is something deeply wrong with the whole system,* Surin saw.

He had resented the Siamese way, the rote learning and a passive acceptance of the teacher's authority. But there was something not quite right with this English model in which the student's ignorant and ill-formed opinions were put forward and the tutor listened.

Suddenly it came to the creep, seeing the tormented tutor there, asking them questions they could not answer. He would reverse the roles by asking the questions, starting from ignorance and demanding knowledge.

But then Wilding voiced: "Surin! What do you think? Are you with us or day-dreaming?"

The eager student smiled impishly.

"I was *thinking*, sir. Why did Milton make Satan a rebel? Isn't it suggesting that rebellion is evil?"

"Yes, good question! Satan, you'll have noticed, is presented as a leader, a military commander. He's conducted a military revolt against God. Now in Milton's view the only monarch in the universe is God. All mankind was created equal. Satan, as a commander, has tried to subvert God's supreme role. He has taken monarchic status to himself quite improperly and set up a hierarchical society. It is Milton's contention that contemporary society was corrupt as a result of rebellion against the divine. Hence, a revolution was needed to restore the true value of society."

It was obvious that Wilding was swept off his feet by the enthusiasm of his commitment.

*Good Lord! Suddenly I've found a way!*

The little imp grinned. He would steer the long-suffering tutor into delivering informed monologues. It was better for them to end the torture that way.

In the week that followed, Surin delivered his work, pronouncing each word punctiliously, with a touch of sentiment, while Wilding looked towards the ceiling.

At the end, the students expected the usual long pause and the characteristic *Hm! Erm!* But to their surprise MW leaned forward.

"You say in your essay that you find Satan a very impressive figure. I don't care whether you find him impressive or unimpressive.

What I care about is why you find him impressive. You need to give your reasons. You need to quote from the text to prove your point."

"But that's what I thought," Prem argued, and was surprised that he had raised his voice.

"You can think whatever you like as long as you can give reasons, as long as you can give evidence."

"Evidence?" the student was puzzled.

His developing mind had to work fast.

"The important thing is to give your reasons so we can see why you say it. It doesn't matter to me what you believe."

Surin was shocked. It seemed like a dismissal; it sounded so bald, so brusque, and it showed on his face.

Hence, the tutor took pity on him, toning down his voice.

"English isn't like mathematics, you know? There aren't any right answers. It's not a subject in which there's one right answer and the others are wrong. There are countless interpretations of a text. There are hundreds of different opinions about a literary work. The point is not the answer, but how you argue your case. The case you make doesn't matter. It's how you argue it."

"So I could argue anything?" the gammy-minded student sounded as if he had just discovered the eighth wonder of the world.

"As long as the arguments are good."

"I could say Satan is heroic?"

"It is often said. You may point out that the description of his shield is like Achilles' shield and how his speeches are in the tradition of other heroic speeches in literature. You might want to ask whether military heroes are good or not. You might be able to find evidence of what Milton thought about them."

"So I'm free to say anything at Oxford."

The tutor seemed bemused.

"In principle! It's acceptable as long as you don't extend your criticism too far into society because even in England some things are just not said. You're expected to know them."

Prem graduated with a first, and decided to stay on in England despite the news of Kumjai's death from the bullets of a hired gunman. He aimed to finish *The Monsoon People* before returning to Siam.

In writing, he chose to be direct and precise, moving away from a didactic and tortuous prose style.

One day he took a break from writing and took a coach from Victoria to Oxford. The graduate slowly progressed along the cloisters towards the lawn. There, he sat under the old plane tree to recall the few happy years.

In inquiring after his former tutor, Surin learned that Michael Wilding had become Professor of the Department of English at The University of Sydney, New South Wales, Australia.

For old times, he entered the chapel and imagined that he heard the choir.

*Domine Deus, rex coelestis,*
*Deus Pater omnipotens.*
*Domine Fili unigenite, Jesu Christe.*
*Domine Deus, agnus Dei, Filius Patris.*
*Qui tollis peccata mundi, miserere*
*Nobis, suspice deprecationem nostram.*
*Qui sedes ad desteram Patris, miserere nobis.*
*Quoniam tu solus sanctus, tu solus Dominus,*
*Tu solus altissimus, Jesu Christe.*
*Cum Sancto Spiritu in gloria Dei Patris.*
*Amen.*

"Amen."

*Have courage and do not tremble to pick up a pen again. In memories of Father and Guru Kumjai, I shall write on fearlessly. I owe it to you, Napo, the land of my ancestors, to your people and the turn of your seasons. So remote and forgotten, and yet you enriched me as I lived a life of a child affected immeasurably by penury and evil, ruthlessness and injustice, ignorance and exploitation, suppression and mind-maiming. You gave me a love for the desolate plains of Isan. I won't cut you off and reject my ignoble origins for I cannot grow further without you. I owe it to you, Father Kum and Mother Boonliang. I owe so much to you for what I have achieved so far. You gave me the power of imagination and a driving force from within, a force emerging from the grass roots, from the poor who have no voice so that the emergence of peasants has to happen. I owe it to you, Kiang, Piang and Toon. I am grateful to you for our lives in Napo and for our memories. I owe it to you, Kumjai. The seed you sowed in my heart has been thriving. You gave me an impetus to create and recreate all that you have lost so that you and many teachers like you do not die in vain. I owe it to you, men, women and children of Isan. You have been my strength as I forge ahead to come this far. You are my allies as well as witnesses so I can write truthfully. You are my powerful army when I face my adversaries. My gratitude is a promise that your children and grandchildren and great-grandchildren shall suffer less.*

# An Inspiration

Inspired by *The Monsoon People*, Charles Tregonning made notes.

*Having traversed the Plain of Sarabury, we ascended the Dongrak Range. Gargantuan cement factories could be seen here and there.*

The cacophony from one of the bedrooms in his St. James's flat caused the old gentleman to pause.
"Not too loud, Primo!"
"It's Beethoven's Symphony No. 9!"
The Bose sound system should also take the blame.

*After Pakchong, it seems we have left far behind the pollution and the traffic jams and the tumult of Bangkok. Soon we reached the Korat Plateau, home of the Lao-speaking Isan people.*

"It's still too loud!"
"Sorry!"

*"Welcome to my country" said my host and driver Prem Surin.*

*In late November, when the northerly wind has turned the emerald green rice fields into gold, it is hard to believe that for centuries this region has been fomenting conflicts and migration.*

*Most parts of Isan have vast salt deposits.*

*Where the earth is bare and the rainwater has run off, leaving the soil exposed to the sun, salt crusts appear on the surface. Near the ancient town of Pimai, where a monumental mini Angkor, built in the 11<sup>th</sup> century still stands, partly in ruin, Little Primo pointed out huge areas of salt farms. Here, rice fields have been made into 'beds' over which brine, evaporated by the sun, turns into salt.*

*The open salt mines, in contrast to the nearby paddies, seem to be an ugly sign of the dying earth, barren and inhospitable, yielding salt wanted for industry.*

*"The waste from salt farms discharged into streams has caused much damage to the paddy-fields. The soil becomes salty. Rice and other plants die, and suffering rice farmers sold cheaply their worthless farms to the salt mine company and moved elsewhere," PS said.*

*Along the way, ornate and glittering temple roofs and pagoda spires could be seen near and far. It seems that each village has its own Buddhist monastery, giving rise to romantic notions of the exotic East.*

Pira Sudham

*Visitors to Isan may think that way, unaware of the implication of how deforestation, eucalyptus plantations, quarries and cement factories, salt farms, pulp and paper mills, sugar factories, plywood factories and tapioca flour factories are affecting the ecology.*

*I mentioned the glorious sight of lush eucalyptus plantations, but Little Primo said: "I wish I could see the devil's lethal discus as something adorable like a lotus flower." Having delivered such remark, he delved deep in silence. Meanwhile, I recalled a passage he wrote in his pamphlet on the subject of deforestation. He had written: 'Fast growing eucalyptus trees were chosen to replace native trees, under the reforestation programme, to provide wood chips and pulp to Japan and China as well as to local paper factories. This Australian tree variety greedily depletes water in the soil and moisture in the air, causing less and less precipitation. A few years after their growth, grass and other plants cannot survive underneath them due to desiccation and acid deposited in the soil by their fallen leaves, a self-protecting and generating way so that only eucalyptus can grow among its kind.*

*The thrust to establish and expand the pulp and paper industry in Siam has brought innumerable losses and suffering to the people who have been forced to leave their holdings where concessionaires have now planted the greedy and harmful eucalyptus trees.*

*Squatters are encouraged to encroach upon national parks and forest reserves. They slashed and burnt the woods so that a few years later the once lush rain forests can be officially classified as 'degraded'. Then, the so-called 'degraded' forests could be 'granted' to concessionaires or wealthy and powerful individuals to grow eucalyptus trees or to develop resorts, housing estates and golf courses.'*

*Then why is eucalyptus chosen?*

*"Compared to other trees, eucalyptus can be harvested after five years of growth. The investors and the industrialists do not consider the damage to the ecology that the eucalyptus can cause as long as they can log them as quickly as possible," Primo expatiated.*

*In late afternoon we arrived in Nappo, PS's home village. Ban ........ combines two teak houses joined together with another section in between to serve as bar and kitchen.*

*At night I lay awake, going over in my mind the author's revelation on the subject of distilling his anger and bitterness. On this subject, PS said: "I want to turn my suffering into an inspiration and wisdom."*

*Had I not read 'The Monsoon People', I might not have any inkling of what could have caused anger, sorrow and pain in this peaceful, slumbering village.*

*Early in the morning, we went to the village market. There, enterprising folk set up on both sides of the street makeshift stalls to sell vegetables, fruits, meat,*

220

*fish, eggs and all sorts of edible roots and leaves. An enticing aroma rose with the smoke from a charcoal stove where a young woman was grilling chicken portions for sale. The business seemed brisk. Sounds of laughter intertwined with teasing remarks and bargaining utterances -- all in Lao, of course.*

*"Most inhabitants of Nappo are rice farmers, whose paddy-fields have become infertile after centuries of yielding rice," PS said. "To be productive they require a considerable amount of fertilizer and water. It isn't easy at all to eke out a living from Isan's sandy, salty soil. From the hot dry months, hardly anything can grow. You can see existing plants and trees wilt in the searing heat, and the soil cracks into a myriad of fissures. In summer, when it is too hot and arid to till the earth, most men leave their homes to find temporary employment in Bangkok and other cities. Some may pass the time in idleness or try their luck in betting at a cock-fighting pit or in a gambling den. The women spin and weave silk for their own use and for sale. Having hardly anything to look forward to but only the drudgery of toiling on their farms, growing rice, harvesting, child raising, and trying to keep body and soul together on a meagre diet, it is small wonder that some of them fall victim to gambling and borrowing money."*

*To borrow money, in many cases, land title-deeds are used as collateral, and in some cases the debt-ridden families end up losing their land. Recently, 10 families have asked PS to pay off their debts and retrieve the title-deeds from the usurers. In so doing, they have land to till and to live on.*

*The Prem Surin Trust has been set up to support poor villagers and their dependents to ensure that there is sufficient provision and medical treatment for the sick as well as providing scholarships for the young to complete their secondary school years and then further their education in colleges and universities. Sadly, PS went on to say: "Nearly all of these childrens, when they become young men and women, will leave their homes for Bangkok or other cities or lucrative beach resorts in search of employment and opportunities and new friends. Some of them may become sex workers in brothels, bars, beer gardens or become victims of cruel and ruthless factory owners who force them to slave for a pittance. I cannot stop them leaving. There is nothing here for them except to live off their limited plots of land."*

*At this juncture, one felt compelled to ask about child prostitution and the selling of children into the sex trade and into slavery, of which we have read and heard so much in the international media. PS said: "If you want to see human drama and tragedy, you have only to go to Bangkok Central Railway Station where every day, for decades, the scene repeats itself until it has now become a pattern of everyday life.*

*Each day, when trains from Isan arrive at Hualumpong Terminal, men from nearby employment agencies approach the newly arrived migrants. Some of these* men are also Isaners, exploiting the belief in Isan kinship and the Lao language to purport a genuine wish to help with jobs and accommodation.

Fleeing from poverty in search of a better life, innumerable youngsters are trapped. Then they are taken to the adjacent shop buildings where the so-called employment agencies are. Thinking that they are going to be taken to their legitimate employers, the victims are led to brothels, where some are chained and beaten. The ugly ones are destined for sweatshops, where they are forced to work 15 hours a day without pay and never allowed outside. Tragically, many parents bring their own children to the 'Divine City of Angels' to sell them to the agencies. Deals are usually for one year at approximately 50 pounds per child. In many areas in Isan, brokers are living in villages. They buy the young there and then take the bought bodies to the capital."

One day Little Primo took me along on house calls. First of all he visited the village chief to whom he presented a bottle of imported whisky. At the headman's house, I noticed a tall steel post with four loudspeakers on top. It was set up so that the people could listen to public announcements and Radio Siam.

"Starting at six o'clock in the morning, the blaring broadcast starts our day. Most of us silently endure," said PS. "But if this kind of force listening takes place in a civilized society, it will cause outcries from the people. You would not put up with it, I am sure."

Protest is unwise. Over 10 schoolteachers in Isan have been murdered by hired gunmen. Not far from Nappo, on the 28th of December 1981 Tim Booning, a teacher of Satuk School, was shot in front of his house. For fighting against injustice and corruption, his reward was a brutal death. Then, Somjai Utrawichian, teacher of Tako School, established The Tim Booning Foundation and carried on Tim's work. Four years later, Somjai was murdered by professional gunmen in his house. PS took me to meet Tim's wife and children in Satuk where the Nappo Project also extends assistance to the widow and her four children.

"It's a shame that in this country there is no room for honest, dedicated teachers like Tim and Somjai," PS said.

In Nappo, the author gave priority to the very old and the poorest of all families. He loaded his car with clothes, bottles of soy bean cooking oil (palm oil causes high cholesterol, he believes), top-grade fish sauce (without dyestuff for colour and some harmful additives that may cause cancer), and packages of paracetamol. He distributed these with some cash to each family.

Under several huts, sick people lay.

"I wish I had a magic wand," PS mentioned. "Many ailing people are too poor to afford transport to a hospital. They just lie at home waiting to recover or die. *Often I have taken the very ill to a hospital 60 miles away and in most cases I could pay for the hospital expenses. Should illness happen to strike the poor during my absence from Nappo, as it happened while we were in Bangkok, the outcome is, as you can see now, they just lay there."*

*Though one may never again see Siam with the eye of a pleasure-seeking tourist, one wants to hold on to some memorable scenes. There was something idyllically beautiful about the rice fields, seeing a small boy set fish traps in a swamp. With long bamboo poles, several men yards apart tried to hook frogs among rush stalks while some women swung their small round nets in the water to catch shrimps and small fish for food.*

*On leaving Nappo Village for the Divine City of Angels – one of the several names of Krungtep (Bangkok to me and Bangers to Danny), one wondered: What has one learned in PS's world? At first, it was most disheartening to see that his mother looked very old and terribly wizened while the author seemed to have retained his youthful looks and vigour and resilience against the evils that beset the country.*

*Having lived a well-sheltered life, one could not help but wonder at his life lived in the face of such predicaments – ignorance, suppression, superstition, forced listening, rote learning, stealing, cheating, disease, graft, scarcity, drought, disease, grinding poverty, prostitution and slavery.*

*One is aware that in his heart he cares very much for the poor and very much against the injustice in society, and for the suffering of the people as well as the murder of brave and idealistic men and women. All of these one could see as being evils which look mundane and the natural order of things on most days except when horrific tragedy strikes and political turmoil and massacres flare up such as the massacres of the 14th October 1973, the 6th October 1976 in which thousands of people were killed.*

*To combat evil and survive, PS must have patience, prudence and cunning. He employs all the surviving tactics he knows. One should not put him under any political brand name. He is not trying to revolutionize the capitalist system, only to help make it more humane. His ethics are those which emanate from the teachings of Lord Buddha. He uses the art of prose and poetry to sway the hearts of those who hold the power. Here, there is no dividing line between literature and politics, between poetic imagination and ethical integrity, between commitment and courage.*

"Scribbling! Scribbling! Mr Tregonning! At last you're working on your memoirs!" Little Primo squawked.

"Lest I forget. Already I've forgotten the name of that divine guesthouse in Nappo. Ban something."

"You mean Bankhunluang, the House of the Noble. By the way it's Napo, not Nappo. Let me read what you've scribbled."

"Don't hover over me. Go away, Primo."

"You read *The Monsoon People* long before it was published. It's not fair! Who's PS? It's I! Why do you write about me? Why waste your time and creative juice on me? I'm not worthy of them! Why don't you write about the wheeling and dealing of auction houses and allegations that Christie's and Sotheby's colluded over commission rates for buyers and sellers, about the fake furniture sold at Sotheby's and about the picture of Salome with the Head of St John the Baptist sold at Christie's for a mere 8,000 pounds. Later, it was resold at Sotheby's at a guide price of four million pounds. You knew very well how that happened. You may reveal why Christie's staff claimed that the work of art was 'from the school of Titian' when in fact it was a Titian original. How about another meaty piece involving Boris Kustodiev's *Odalisque* sold by Christie's for 1.7 million pounds to Mr Vikor Vekselberg, a Russian oil and mining magnate, who claimed later that it was a forgery and so sued Christie's over the fake, hm? I'm sure you haven't forgotten that Sotheby's sold Lord Coleridge's Tudor chain of office as a copy for 35,000 pounds but then that gold chain was resold at Christie's as a genuine article for 400,000 pounds! You know the staff member of Sotheby's who valued the chain. She'd elucidate you more, I'm sure. You could have made an exceedingly riveting revelation of the looted Mesopotamian and Egyptian and Turkish antiquities. How about the jewels and figurines illegally dug out of the royal tombs of the Yortans in Dorak? A jewel in the crowd should include an expatiation on the day a lady came to your shop, seemingly looking for a piece de resistance. Noticing that you eyed her jewels, she aired that they might be reproductions, that you might have a closer look at them. It turned out to be a ruse to have an authentication from a respected antiquarian like you. How about the disappearance of over 100 items including paintings and figurines and artefacts from the Bristol Museum? Why did you load me with the hot stuff? I dare say you wanted to purge them from the depths of your mind by airing the secrets to me. It's sort of catharsis, is it not? Helmut von Regnitz did that too before he died. He expunged a lot of secrets before he went. You don't really want to take all the secrets to your grave, do you? But, by downloading them to me, you've endangered my life. Charles, old thing, I won't write about your society. It's not my field of fire. As for you, you don't have to scrape the bottom of the barrel. Let the hot stuff pour out! Oi! Don't leave out the smuggling of Pharoah Amenhotep III's stone head out of Egypt by Jon Bearing who coated the head with plastic and carried it out of Egypt as if it were a tourist souvenir!"

"Steady on, Primo!"

"I say! To make your book awfully hot, you could add the fracas with Bearing over the boyfriend before he did his time. It's has substance of a certain Greek tragedy, what? Oh, yes, you could make it exceedingly riveting with your side of the story on life with David Sutcliff. You whined that he left you after having used you as a stepping stone. Expose him now that he has become an actor. He owes a lot to you, i.e. the roof over his head, food, clothes, cash and your accent he has managed to parrot all those years until he could speak posh enough to audition for a role in *The Ideal Husband*. I sympathize with him. Some members of your clique ravished him just because he had to be a rent boy, prostituting himself in order to accomplish his ambition. The fact that he didn't bother to hang on to you or murder you for the inheritance, proved that he is independent minded and would do anything to reach his goal. David and I are alike in this regard. Regrettably, some of us artists have to resort to prostitution to achieve our aims. But it doesn't mean that I'd fly off and away from you as soon as I became a renowned writer. I would never dream of hurting you for anything in the world since I had hurt, injured and caused hundreds of people to die in the past-life. That's why in this life, I suffer retribution. In this life I must be good and pure to deserve a rebirth in old England and regain my ancestral home as Grandpa Tatip had told me."

"Humbug! But, if reincarnation is to take place, you'd probably regret it. This green and pleasant land would be in deep recession. Thanks to Gordon Brown's Heathcliffian stratagem. Even when he publicly claimed that he was similar to Heathcliff, few people would have speculated that he might have had a hidden agenda."

"A lot of people don't know that Mr Brown is emulating the vindictive protagonist of *Wuthering Heights*. A lot of them didn't know anything about Heathcliff. Most people didn't believe in the force of karma. Though some of Mr Brown's covert ways of bringing about the Heathcliffian retribution may be known to some, they cannot do anything. They wait for it like sitting ducks. That's the force of karma. There's no reprieve, no escape. Believe me, my dear Charles, everything we do is karma. Every swing of the swords, every rape and pillage, every drop of blood, every violent deed, every harsh word or even a harmless word such as 'pleb' has effects. The *p* word caused a Tory chief whip to fall from grace. As for Mr Brown, he has obviously inherited an inherent chain reaction that has been passed on from generation to generation. One wonders whether there have been more than one Irish counterpart of Heathcliff-Brown who had taken more cogent courses of retribution following the deaths and destructions caused by Cromwell and his troops at Enniscorthy in County Wexford and the 'to hell or to Connaught' brutal relocation, not to mention the English landlords who…"

Refusing to be drawn into a sensitive domain, Charles adhered to the subject of reincarnation.

"By the time you are reborn here, this fractured society might have already gone to the dogs. Your stately home might have been razed to the ground or become a property of the National Trust. There wouldn't be anything left for you to repossess."

"That's for the future. We're talking about you. It's a mistake people like you tend to make, trying to keep someone like David."

At this point, the blithering twit realised that he had deeply wounded the old gentleman. Hence, he reverted.

"You know more than most people in the art world and in the antique trade particularly about the looted antiquities and the trafficking of stolen masterpieces from castles and stately homes and museums. You told me that you happened to see a painting stolen from Bristol Museum during your holiday in Madeira. Cor! You could write about that too! But then you don't want to rock the boat or put your life on the line. You know that trafficking in looted antiques or stolen works of art is as treacherous and iniquitous as drug trafficking and as deadly as the shadowy world of cloaks and daggers. But, old boy, you should be daring. You, a doyen of art dealers, should offer the world your work as an equal to George Orwell's *Road to Wigan Pier*. The Rotterdam's Kunsthal Museum would be more than grateful for your revelations since its treasures, worth 50 million pounds, have been stolen. You'd be one of the very few who had an inkling of where Monet's *Charing Cross Bridge*, Matisse's *La Liseuse*, Gauguin's *Femme devant une Fenetre Ouvrte*, and Picasso's *Tete d'Ariequin* would end up. You've become such a formidable authority on art and antiquities that a mere whiff of you writing a book, possibly entitled *Hot Art* or something similar, should get attention from big publishers. As for me, I had to go down on my knees, begging a publisher to read the manuscript. If I had known that some publishers were too pre-occupied, searching for another Dan Brown or another J K Rowling to pay attention to an unknown writer from the Far East, I wouldn't … "

"Write another book and I'm sure you'd be in demand."

"You write a book, Tregy! Yes, do! Write about the wheeling and dealing in the art world. Write about Sotheby's and Christie's before somebody or a magazine does it. Blimey! You could expose some of the scheming art-dealers and the ne…ne…nefarious antiquities trade. Don't you have the guts to do it? Perhaps, for a gentleman, it's not done, or you, who have been so well-bred, looked after by your governments from cradle to grave, neither have an axe to grind, nor an incentive, nor a driving force, nor a cause for which to die. You should have been driven by sheer creative force instead of greed. As for me I have done my part. I've put my life on the line."

Pausing for breath the gibbering dimwit, who was said to be no better than a lump of excrement, suffered qualms for having resorted to sarcasm, injecting 'Oi!' and 'Cor!' and 'Blimey!' into the diatribe.

For having vehemently uttered those plebian words, it seemed as if the blithering idiot had defiled the old gentleman's patrician upbringing.

Thus, the little bounder, ostentatiously covered his ignoble origins with a Dunhill suit, applied charm to smooth over the ruffled English gentleman.

"You don't have to tell me to be off a second time. Danny and Karl are waiting for me at the Royal Leicester. It's something to do with a recital. They're going to stage a recital in the hotel's Shakespeare Hall, and one of the pieces is *Song of Siam* or *Swan Song of Siam* now that the kingdom has become a shadowed country. See you later, old thing."

The lugubrious millionaire remained seated.

The pedantic pen-pusher, who had recently been appointed the executor and the sole beneficiary of Charles Tregonning's will in place of David Sutcliff, left the apartment, leaving behind a trail of TC's *eau de toilette*.

# Against Goliath

Professor Dr Andrew Turton, ladies and gentlemen:

Change is inevitable. Nothing is permanent. The mighty Pharaohs, omnipotent Caesars, awesome warlords, horrible dictators and terrible tyrants have come and gone. Then W. B. Yeats lamented: *Change, change utterly! A terrible beauty is born.* Many years later, Kumjai Chaiwankul, a schoolteacher, reconfirmed Lord Buddha's words: *Everything is transient.* The teacher expounded that agents of change could take many forms, visible or invisible. They may come silently and slowly or, at times, swiftly and explosively, in the guise of missiles, bombs, guns and grenades.

In *The Monsoon People,* I described the socio-economic and political changes that occurred in Siam during the past 30 years. The book portrays the people in transition and agents of change.

There are mixed feelings when words like 'strike', 'protest' and 'exploitation', unheard in villages in the past, are now being used arbitrarily in the mass media. These astounding words creep into our minds like ominous agents of change. How long would the old way of life last? How long could the authorities keep the populace ignorant, submissive and silent? Should I, one day, become an instrument of change?

Throughout the long history of change, we may ask ourselves: What kind of values should we strive to maintain in spite of all the changes taking place around us? In what ways are we changing?

Now people throughout the world have become alike in many ways. Men in most parts of the world wear similar clothes and use English to communicate. We eat more or less the same food, partly due to the worldwide spread of American-based food chains. The cheese used on pizzas and the potatoes for chips and crisps have gradually changed our tastes and eating habits. Until recently, there were hardly any Siamese farmers who grew potatoes which had to be imported for foreign residents and hotels. Now a large number of our farmers have become potato farmers, changing to new methods of farming to earn larger incomes from this new cash crop. Milk and cheese are some more examples. Not long ago, few Siamese people consumed dairy products. Now milk has become part of their diet, and cheese is following quickly. The dairy industry is thriving. More and more rice fields have become grazing land, and vast areas of woodland have been turned into dairy farms.

The age of electricity has reached rural Siam. What does this mean? It means television sets, telephones, computers, satellite discs, rice cookers, refrigerators, air-conditioners, washing machines and more. Each of these items has become an agent of change in its own way.

Television means that people are exposed to alternative lifestyles as well as myriads of advertised products. New products tempt consumers to change the old for the new. Hand-made Isan bamboo and tar buckets, for instance, have now been completely replaced by plastic ones. Our handicrafts are being replaced with machine-made products. Walk into any village in Siam today, if you see a man making a basket from bamboo he would be in his seventies, and probably the last of those who could produce the craft by hand.

Electrical goods such as refrigerators and rice cookers do not only reflect the financial status of their owners but also the willingness to change the old for the new.

Designed to cook white rice (*kao jaow*), the sort of rice consumed in most parts of Siam and the world, in boiling water, electric rice cookers are not for Isan glutinous rice (*kao niaw*), which is steamed. So, once, an Isan person, who usually consumes *kao niaw*, has acquired an electric rice cooker, the family will have to switch from eating *kao niaw* to *kao jaow*. This also means that rice farmers have to switch to growing more *kao jaow* too. When one eats *kao niaw*, one eats it with fingers; as for *kao jaow*, one eats with fork and spoon.

Refrigerators are also mandatory agents of change. Simply put, food can be stored for a longer period of time, causing a major change in the daily life of many refrigerator owners, who previously foraged daily for food in the woods and in the fields. They harvested what they grew, gathered wild plants, young leaves, berries, roots, and mushrooms. In the ponds and streams and swamps they caught frogs, eels, fish, and shrimps. This was part of their daily routine.

Having refrigerators can change all this since the refrigerator owners do not have to gather their food each day. Those who could afford refrigerators are likely to be the new rich, having worked in Taiwan, Korea, Japan, Singapore and the Middle East.

On the other hand, there have been great numbers of our women who have married foreigners and then returned to their villages. They are likely to forsake their age-old huts (thatched roofs, bamboo walls, wooden stilts and ladders) and build new houses of bricks and mortar.

Another aspect of change, good or bad – positive or negative, depends on us who view it or who profit from it. Those who proclaimed that planting eucalyptus trees in vast areas would greatly benefit the country are likely to be those who are involved in the pulp and paper industry or in various bilateral aid agencies, or in the packaging industry, or in paper producing equipment, or they are pulp and wood chip exporters, or shareholders of paper manufacturing companies, or eucalyptus seed importers, or eucalyptus nursery owners, or high-ranking officials of the Forestry Department. The latter has authority to grant the so-called 'degraded' forests to concessionaires to grow eucalyptus trees.

The sore losers include relocated small holders, who were brutally forced to sacrifice their properties to eucalyptus tree planting, and inhabitants severely affected by the pollution caused by the colossal pulp and paper manufacturing plants.

One should not forget to include the environmentalists among the sore losers (one of whom I happened to know personally but, alas, he was murdered by a professional gunmen. The unfortunate teacher was against handing over Changlaiwood to eucalyptus planters.

Kumjai Chaiwankul, my former teacher, fought bravely to safeguard the woods and the soil, made more arid and acidic and less fertile by eucalyptus trees. The environment has been polluted with lethal fumes and toxic waste discharged by pulp and paper factories.

Fact: In the pulping process of boiling wood chips with caustic soda, three kilogrammes of sulphur dioxcide are released into the air for each tonne of pulp produced, with potential effects on soil and water and the health of mankind.

Fact: The sulphide process that boils wood chips in an acid solution gives off five kilogrammes of sulphur dioxcide per tonne of pulp. Moreover, cellulose fibres lost during processing are discharged as waste which can deplete oxygen in the receiving rivers and streams.

Fact: The sulphur, added in the pulping process, reacts with organic chemicals present in the pulp to form unaccountable organ-chlorine pollutants, including dioxins, which are some of the most potent poisons known.

Fact: The inhabitants at large have been kept in ignorance of the harm to health and the survival of aquatic life in the polluted rivers.

When there are outcries from affected inhabitants, strong-arm tactics have been applied to silence them. For instance, in May 2003, Samnao Sisongkram, 38, was shot dead by a gunman at his home in Khon Kaen Province. Samno, the leader of Nam Pong River Conservation and Revival Group, was in the throes of leading villagers to protest against the Phoenix Pulp and Paper Company, said to have been polluting the Pong River since 1993. Three days before the murder, Samnao received several threatening telephone calls. On the following Sunday, he was shot in the head by a man who spoke with a Southern accent, possibly from Rajabury, where most hired gunmen are from. The murderer called himself Ekarin Lertsi, saying he was interested in NGO work and in joining the protest. When Samnao's wife left the room the killer shot Samnao, and then sped away on a motorcycle.

Another case of brutality against a protester is the disappearance of Suchada Kampuboot, 41. She was abducted from her home in December 1994, following her active role in protesting against air pollution from the emission of sulphur dioxide, and water pollution from toxic waste discharge from Thai Hua Pulp.

She is now presumed dead.

Each year Isan, where the large-scale eucalyptus plantations are, has become more and more arid, similar to a semi-desert state of Australia, where eucalyptus trees grow abundantly. The rivers such as Pong and Shi have been polluted with toxic waste released by pulp and paper manufacturing plants.

The thrust to expand eucalyptus plantations so as to establish the pulp and paper industry in Siam, as in several third world countries, has become one of the greatest agents of change in the 20th century.

Before that, the process of change in Siam escalated remarkably in the late 19th century. King Rama V (King Chulalongkorn) toured Europe twice during his reign to broaden his outlook and to find out the good and bad features of colonial rule. In Europe he saw much that impressed him and he brought back ideas and principles to transform or modernize Siam, especially in the area of education.

He had 76 children by 36 wives (32 sons and 44 daughters). The princes were later sent to Europe for education to prepare them for service to the State. This period was similar to Japan's drive to modernize its society by bringing in Western clothing, customs, architecture, education, industry, and Western military training and weaponry.

King Chulalongkorn realised that European imperial powers, Britain and France especially, posed a threat to the political and economic stability of Siam. His aim was to find a way to prevent the kingdom from being colonized. The modernization of Siam included the engagement of European advisers and teachers. The British produced beneficial results in education, police, surveying and railways; while the Danes were employed in the navy; the French in law and public works; the Italians in architecture and construction; and the Germans in railway construction.

The first railway line was built in 1892 to link Korat in Isan with the capital while the postal and telegraphic services were also established. In 1888, a tram appeared in Bangkok streets, to be followed by the first motorcar in 1902. On his return from his first European tour King Chulalongkorn had an avenue of five kilometres built from the Grand Palace to his new Dusit Palace after the pattern of the Champs Elysees in Paris, the Mall in London, and the Unter den Linden in Berlin. He gave it the name of Rajdamnern Avenue (Royal Progress Avenue).

For the first time, surnames were given to the people in 1913. Prior to that, the only way to identify a person was to refer to him as son of Mister so and so, or as belonging to this or that place or village. Under the king's influence, men and women adopted Western hairstyles and clothing. He also introduced football and Western dancing to the country.

The wind of change began to increase its velocity when the king sent the sons of noblemen as well as commoners' sons to study in Europe. Most of them came to the United Kingdom, where they entered schools and universities at Oxford, Cambridge, London, Edinburgh and Manchester.

In 1911, in the reign of King Rama VI, a plot to overthrow the government was hatched by a group of army and navy officers, civil servants and civilians. But the revolution did not succeed. On the 24th of June 1932, in the reign of King Rama VII, another revolution erupted. As a result a fledgling democracy was born in place of absolute monarchy. The king stepped down and left the kingdom for England where he died in exile. Out of the 15 revolutionary leaders, 13 were educated in the United Kingdom, France, and Germany.

Since then democratically elected governments have come and gone. Often, during periods of misrule, tens of thousands of the Siamese people rose in opposition, resulting in the massacres on the 14th of October 1973 and the 6th of October 1976.

I am sad to say that more massacres are yet to follow those that have happened before.

Looking back at the history of change in Siam, it is easier to gaze at the landmarks of physical change. It is unlikely that one can collate change in the minds of the people, their mentality and attitudes. Hence, I have been making an attempt to map the topography of mental change in the people for the work in progress.

Westernization presented superabundant demands. Due to the Westernizing reforms in the 19th century, Siam was one of the few countries in Southeast Asia that escaped the colonial grasp. Perhaps, this is one of the reasons why Siamese people do not feel the pangs of colonialism, and are without a chip on the shoulder, so to speak. Even today Siam welcomes influences from the West with open arms. Western or foreign ideas, technology, and institutions are taken into Siamese society without prejudice.

Now, you may ask: Is this good or not? Certainly this is a question, which confronts most intellectuals in the country. You may ask further: Are we going to change most things? What about questions of value? What shall we choose to keep and what shall we choose to change?

What I would like to see unchanged is the love and respect young people hold for their elders. Perhaps you might think me old-fashioned to place such value on seniority, filial piety and kinship. But what a pity that old people are not respected in so many countries throughout the world these days. What I truly want to see changed is the attitude that accepts corruption as a way of life. We should be a people that know the difference between right and wrong, a people of conscience.

The word 'conscience' is new to Siamese society. In a sense, it is a foreign import, perhaps deriving from Christianity. There has not been a word for 'conscience' in Siamese until recently, when few words have been coined as a translation of it. I wonder whether it would be a subversive act to plant 'conscience' in the Siamese minds as a safeguard against accepting corruption -- bribes, stealing, hankering after kickbacks, portfolio buying, vote buying and nepotism as a way of life. How else can we be respected by other peoples not only in trade but also in other spheres of our daily life?

Having said 'change is inevitable', we may go further to ask whether we have the power to influence the sort of changes that are to take place around us. Can we uphold what we believe to be valuable? Can we hold on to our heritage and also encourage changes that are necessary? We are not helpless in confronting change, but we are often confused. Who will take the initiative in guiding change? As for me, I will do what I can, as a writer and a teacher, to steer the inhabitants towards a positive course of change, when I go back to Siam next week."

"Congratulations!" Dani exclaimed. "Not bad for an Isan buffalo boy, what? I'll tell you the secret of making an interesting speech. Say one or two things that your listeners don't want to hear. Now, let's get away. Karl has something for you. It's a laptop to speed up the publication of your next book. But, don't tell Karl that I've told you. Act surprised when he hands it to you."

Dani rambled to cover the fact that KW had nothing to do with the gift. On the contrary, the Executive Vice President had been trying to prevent the billionaire from giving gifts to the grasping goblin and that Durham female.

In order to keep peace between the two camps, the 11th richest man in the world willingly parted with whatever Karl desired, after the hotelier had engineered a series of mud-raking press interviews with the author of *The Monsoon People*.

The naïve novelist was unaware that the Executive Vice President had lavishly wined and dined the journalists beforehand. Wittenberg had spiked the food and drink with insinuations to the effect that the author of *The Monsoon People* had unashamedly employed underhand tactics to coerce a certain operatic singer-composer-conductor to turn some of the poems into songs. The piddling pen-pusher had conned a gullible grandee of the old school to publish the novel. The charlatan had tricked a billionaire into financing the Oxford years. The wicked writer's wealth derived largely from a tainted source. There was not a glint of hope in the nomination for the Nobel Prize for Literature. Moreover, the shameless author had sold his body so as to achieve his ambition and his soul to the devil for fame and riches.

Dani understood Karl's deep-seated animosity. However, the victim accepted the ill will and the vicious attacks as retribution, a karmic force due to his monstrous deeds done in the former life.

*Karl could have been one of my numerous enemies in the other life. So in this life I'm destined to be at the receiving end of his bitchiness. I must not react, must not retaliate and never pass on the pain. It must stop here within me so that there won't be any chain reaction.*

"Charles, you must be famished," Dani addressed the novelist's admirer. "I told your little chap to keep his dashed boring lecture short and to the point, but he didn't follow my advice. I don't know anyone who could go on and on like that. As a result, many people yawned. I was bored stiff and fell asleep once or twice. Who would be interested in the bally eucalyptus planting and pulping and paper manufacturing and pollution and the killings of environmental activists? I've told your friend to avoid using words such as 'destructive' and 'damaging' in referring to the pulp and paper industry. But, still he couldn't resist the temptation. Luckily he didn't mention certain names. Had he disobeyed me, the nomination for the Nobel Prize for Literature would have been a waste."

Turning towards the author, the mentor barracked further:

"Primo! You, a published author, should have known that paper is crucial to the publishing industry. The whole world needs toilet tissues and facial tissues and paper!"

"If you had listened carefully, you'd have had a hint that I wasn't against paper manufacturing. It's the choice of the damaging eucalyptus trees over other plants which are not lethal to the ecology. It's the dashed inhumane way in which the land has been acquired to grow the dashed destructive eucalyptus. On top of that, it's the dashed toxic pollutants in the air, soil and water that the damaging pulp and paper mills create. It's been said that in the third world countries, the uncaring pulp and paper manufacturers spend less than three per cent, instead of the required five per cent, of their investment on pollution control measures."

By giving back to the billionaire the *d* word, the speaker thought it was a challenge which the late seer Tatip Henkai would not approve.

*O, for once, let me have the satisfaction of challenging them!*

"You can expound that in another speech, another time," Dani ended the kerfuffle. "Just go to say goodbye to Professor Turton, and then let's be off to dine with Karl at the Royal Leicester Hotel. Chop! Chop!"

# To Die in Peace at Home

"My dear boy, you've changed your mind, have you not?" Tregonning surmised, having read the first page of *The Soka Boys*, a story to be included in *Tales of Siam*.

"Read on, and you'll find out whether I wrote about paedophilia or not."

The two Oxonians were sitting in the living room of *Bankhunluang* in Napo Village where the retired art dealer intended to stay away from the English winter with an intention to render support to Dr John Stonham at Napo Hospital.

"Read the story, old thing, and then we shall visit Soka, or the remains of it. That is, if you don't mind a long trek across the Plain of Napo to the Plain of Nadhone. We shall stand silently for a minute at the site where the shanties used to be."

"What?"

"Ayu and his Insurgent Suppression Unit razed the hamlet to the ground."

"That's horrible!"

"Actually I met some of the inhabitants before the massacre and the conflagration."

"You met Dan and Kum?"

"Well, I didn't exactly meet them. They and their mothers ran away from me. They had been foraging in a creek for little frogs. My sudden appearance frightened them. Go on. Read."

## The Soka Boys

"What are they doing?" Dan asked Kum who was panting, having hopped bare foot along the hot sandy path.

Dan wanted to repeat the question but then Kum sat down on his heels. Dan squatted next to his friend.

The shade of the tamarind tree barely comforted them.

The perplexity of *why are they doing that* recurred in Dan's mind. Not being able to suppress his curiosity, he asked Kum once more. When there was no answer, Dan turned towards the congregation of monks and old men and women, crouching on the barren earth in the scorching sun, facing three priests who were chanting a mantra.

*Why must they perform such a rite in the midday sun?* For now he saw, in front of the solemn crowd, a toad tied to a stake. Terrified by the human din and the exposure to the excruciating sun, it was trying to escape, but to no avail.

The curious boy's eyebrows curved into another silent question. Eventually he beseeched Kum for an explanation once more.

The older boy made a grunting sound and then fell silent again, staring at the monks and laymen as if to immerse himself in the awesome ritual.

The grandmothers of the two boys were among the people who had been submitting themselves to the rain-begging rite.

Missing were the schoolteacher, a modern man, who did not believe in such ritual, and Chinaman Jia. The latter had already packed his goods, and was about to leave Soka. There was no more money to be had from the penurious, drought-stricken peasants in that damned village.

*We could barely walk on the hot sand today*, Dan wanted to say. *We had to skip and run. Why do the grown-ups torture themselves?*

The boy was very much moved by the sight of his grandmother as she swayed her emaciated frame to the rhythm of hopelessness. Dan recalled what Granny had said to the members of the Boontawi family that if the monsoon did not come soon there would be famine.

Her dreadful prediction fell on all ears. But none commented on or acknowledged such despair. The wizened woman had lamented further that in all her life there had never been three successive years of drought.

The whirlwind rose from the seared plain, bringing with it swirls of dust and dead leaves. Huaysai, the creek that took the water out of Sisurachwood, had become parched.

What could the accursed dwellers of Soka do? They must torture the toad and themselves so that Paya Taen, the Divine Lord in Heaven, would take pity on the toad as well as on mankind and so yield rainfall.

But Dan did not understand the meaning of it. Nevertheless, he had been taught to respect the rituals performed by monks and the devotees.

As if he could not bear the torturous rain-begging rite any longer, Kum rose to his feet, taking his little friend with him to a copse where they caught several lizards to grill. Having voraciously devoured his share, Dan decidedly asked another question.

Before airing his anxiety, Kum surveyed the surroundings and saw heat waves rise from the plain of salt pans over endless mirages.

"The monks led the people to beg Paya Taen for rain."

"Will it rain then?"

"It might."

Dan wistfully scanned the sky for the sighting of clouds. Seeing none, he clung to a hope.

"If the drought is very bad, we may stop going to school."

Dan's thought of learning under the teacher, who enjoyed flogging schoolchildren, seemed more frightening than the famine.

"It's bad enough now. We've nothing to eat and my father will sell me."

Dan was shocked. The thought that his friend would be whisked away to captivity in the capital sent fear deep into his heart.

"My father will definitely sell me. The agent has come to have a look at me. The man asked me to undress."

"No! Did he touch you?"

"He had a good look at me and asked me to pull back the foreskin. *You must always keep it clean, and now make it hard,* he said."

The youngsters knew very little about the criteria that this particular branch of commerce employed to set the terms of agreement and pricing.

Days passed.

There were no clouds to raise hope.

Meanwhile, several families left Soka for new locations.

The straggling band of inhabitants hollered parting words. Tinged with sorrow, the sound of goodbye sent tremors deep inside their wilting hearts. Sad-eyed peasants and their ragged children trekked away, carrying their belongings, leaving dust and desperation behind.

In parting, the two sides reminded one another of filial ties and kinship. The trembling voices of the aged reverberated across the gulf of despair. They wailed: "Will we ever see you again?"

Meanwhile the adults, who decided not to forsake Soka, talked of more rites and sacrifices to gain mercy from the Ruler of the Earth and the Sky for rain, life and the normal turn of seasons.

Dan wished that he could suffer in place of his grandmother. Perhaps they might let him join in the ultimate sacrificial ritual and make him a sacrifice. His suffering might help them succeed and so prevent Kum from being sold.

He envisaged himself being tied to a stake like that toad, being tortured by the burning sun and the mortifying human din.

But the little boy had not been included in any rite. The adults completely ignored him. Being a mere child, he silently watched how the men killed a pig for a votive offering to the spirits at the village spirit house.

The rain-begging rituals became more macabre seen through the eyes of the boy, who believed that the men had become utterly desperate. The fatal twist of the knives, the mortal wounds, the deadly cries of the sacrificial animals, and the flow of blood indicated that they were slipping backward towards primeval savagery and cruelty. The ancient bitterness and hatred, passed on from heart to heart since the brutal centuries of slavery and torture, to construct the Angkor temple at Pimai, had found a vent.

One day, Dan went off by himself onto the Plain of Nadhone. The vastness of the arid land made the tiny boy more minute and singular. Without Kum by his side, he feared the solitude and the great expanse. He halted several times to turn and look at Soka.

At a sandy spot, he sat cross-legged and closed his eyes and raised his cupped hands to his chest. But, since he had not been taught the art, his was a mere imitation of praying monks and supplicating elders. He swayed slightly the way his grandmother did, seeing her now in his mind's eye.

"Pity me, lord."

The experience was both enthralling and fearful. For he, so diminutive and insignificant, had dared to catch the eye of the ultimate power. The sheer silence of the plain weighed heavily on him. The sun whipped him so mercilessly that his head throbbed painfully, and what liquid there was in him became perspiration, dripping down his face and torso.

"Pity me, lord."

Gradually, courage came to him and helped him expand. Departing from himself, he saw the image of Kum being taken away by the awesome broker.

Dan silently asked: *When will it be my turn?*

He recalled happy times in a good year, seeing Kum and himself leave the plain for home, hallooing and laughing, riding their buffaloes. Then an image of Granny merged in. It was a picture of happiness when she turned to smile broadly while harrowing a ploughed paddy. Old as she was, she could work relentlessly provided that there was enough water to grow rice.

"My lord, do pity Granny. Please be merciful to her and to all of the people for I'm your sacrifice."

The blazing sun continued to beat him hard, increasing the torture as if to test the boy's capability to endure.

"Lord, have mercy on Granny and on all the old people. Granny has nothing to eat. She is old and bony. Have pity on the starving old people for they are too weak to dig for yams or chase grasshoppers or catch lizards for food."

Curiosity made him open his eyes to see the effect of the ritual. But, to his dismay, the sky remained cloudless. There was no cool breeze to herald the rainfall. Heavy with disappointment Dan sighed and shifted. Perhaps his suffering was seen as child's play, a mockery of solemn and sacred rituals reserved for priests and religious elders.

"O divine lord, the true ruler of the earth and the sky," the heavy-hearted boy made another attempt, but no more words came out of him.

He trembled at the thought that he would be punished for his fanciful action. On the other hand, he was too young to be chary of cynicism, suffering, cruelty and futility in all things.

Now it was his own serious determination that frightened him so that he shuddered. There was no way out except to commit the ultimate sacrifice or else, he feared, he would be sold.

The knife taken from his father's toolbox flashed in the glare of the sun. Only then was he convinced that he would not fail, for the sacrifice would be so great that the Ruler of the Earth and the Sky would take pity on him and so yield rains.

But the sharp metal cut into his wrist deeper than intended. Dan winced with pain, throwing the instrument aside. The flow of blood mortified him. Still, he lifted the wounded hand towards the sun for the almighty to see, till he fell.

Lying on his back, Dan tried to call out for help but could not, for his throat was utterly parched. Trembling, he saw that the Dark Lord was descending rapidly on him. Yet he strained to hear the rumbles of thunder that would mean rainfall.

Wordlessly Charles went into the bedroom.
The writer could guess why.

Sitting on the edge of the bed, the old Etonian seemed to have been overwhelmed with sadness.

Following the old gentleman into the room, the writer sat down by his side.

"It had to be written for the sake of hundreds of children who are to be sold in a few months. Nearer to Napo is Nokrian Village. I've been there and talked to a widow called Dum Namrum who has sold all of her six children."

"Yes, I would like to see the remains of Soka. For all I know, I might have come across someone at Folly Siam, who shared the same fate with Kum."

"You've been to Folly Siam! When did you do that?"

"It was during my first visit. Witty was keen to show me the night-life. We went on a binge and ended up there."

"Leave it to Witty! Yes, the late lawyer was an authority on that type of entertainment. As for me, he wouldn't mention his nocturnal haunts in my presence. Like Danny, he seemed to have put me in a slot labelled 'Prig & Prude', believing that I still uphold Lord Buddha's Eight Precepts. But we are not talking about me at present. Now, where are we? Oh yes. You met a young person at Folly Siam. Did you know him biblically as well? I hope that you didn't beget anything!"

When the retired art-dealer appeared hurt, the frivolous freak apologized:

"Sorry, I was being facetious, or childish, as Danny would say."

"You could be cruel too, Primo. Come! Give me a massage. Lately I've had aches and pains."

"Poor old thing!"

"I'll tell you whether you are as good as one of Witty's boys or not."

"I'll give you a proper massage only after you've taken off your clothes. My dear Charles, one can't give an ecstatic massage to a covered body. *But in truth, I want to see in daylight his burly body that could have been similar to mine in the past-life. I envy his patrician breeding, his noble looks and mental stature as opposed to this puny bag of bones with a gammy mind to boot.* In exchange, you can tell me about that young thing you met at Folly Siam. Yes, do, Charles. I'm curious. What did you, an English gentleman, do in a place like that?"

Lying on his back, looking up at the little masseur, Charles said:

"My dear boy, *Tregonning* is a very old Cornish name."

"Does that mean you're a Cornish gentleman?"

"You may say that I am a gentleman. To me you are Siamese through and through, though you've claimed that you are a Lao first. Whatever you are, you are beautiful. To me, small is desirable. But, you don't seem to appreciate that. I can't see why you should be attracted to gorillas and human hippopotamuses when there're so many beautiful and dainty Siamese everywhere. As a writer you should drop into some of those crowded bars and saunas. You'd meet a number of people who might give you a lot of meat for the pot. The performer, who came to sit at my table at the end of the show, had a lot to tell. After half an hour with him, I could have come up with a very interesting story, if I were a writer."

"That kind of meat I don't need. Isan is so rich with raw material that I don't have to scratch the bottom of the barrel for 'the grist to the mill'. And certainly there is no need to search nightclubs, bars and brothels or watch those *effing* shows. I leave it to sex-struck foreigners to pick that kind of meat to the bone. They never seem to veer away from writing about the low life and carnal interludes with men and women who sell their bodies."

"For a writer, you can't even bring yourself to use the *f* word. I didn't fail to notice that there's not a single *f* word or *s* word in *The Monsoon People*."

"I won't litter my work with those vulgar words to be fashionable."

"Yet, often times you opt for archaic words like 'twain' and 'nigh' and 'Pray tell'. Was it ignorance or cunning?"

"Say whatever you like. I want to be polite and proper with a touch of cunning. It's my years of reading English at Oxford."

"Do you know what Danny calls you behind your back?"

"Danny isn't the only person who calls me names to my face or behind my back. But what have you heard?"

"Mr Double Ps for Prig and Prude. As if that's not enough, he also calls you Mr Triple Ps for Prim and Proper Primo. If I didn't know you well enough, I'd say you're a ..."

"You can say it, Charles. Go on! Say it! I wouldn't mind at all. Yes, I'm a prig and a prude and, to some extent, a priest in layman's garb. A devout Buddhist monk is inside me, if you want to know, and if possible I truly want to continue observing Lord Buddha's Eight Precepts. I won't wallow in a pigsty and then convince myself that it's a fantastic place in which to be. I won't frequent those bars and watch those *effing* shows, and go to those *effing* saunas to have anonymous sexual contacts. I won't be seen in those places with an excuse for gathering 'grist to the mill'. Besides, it serves no purpose to write about low-life personalities," professed the word smith who would soon write about Nipa and Salee, the two ladies of Pattaya.

The promising pair of prostitutes would provide him with a munificent supply of raw material to write *Two Siamese Women* as a lead story in *Tales of Siam*.

"Let me challenge you," Charles was saying. "I want you to meet Mana, one of the performers who chatted with Witty and me at Folly Siam. I bet you'd want to write about him or her."

"What is this him-her?"

"There you are. You're nibbling at the bait! Very well then, I'll go to Soka with you, and then you go to Bangkok with me to meet Mana at Folly Siam."

Prem rolled off Charles' body, exhausted. Lying next to his friend, the masseur heaved and sighed: "You seem so keen to make me go back to Sodom and Gomorrah. To what end I wonder."

"To write about Mana! You silly boy! I can't do it. I'm not a writer. You are. He or she is an Isan person too. What a life he-she has been living!"

"Not sordid, is it? I won't go near the place, if it's that kind," the priggish, prudish novelist argued.

Little did he know that soon he would be composing *A Taxi Driver and a Street Food Vendor* (to be included in *The Isan People*) for having dropped into a Patpong bar and befriended Bruce Ross, an Australian from Sydney, amid myriads of naked dancers and ready women.

"For a writer, you're very narrow-minded."

"My field of fire is narrow. My subject matters are few though there are too many Goliaths for this little David. I could be tempted to write about drag queens, prostitutes, brothel keepers, sauna frequenters, adulterers and homosexuals, I still don't see any point in exploring them. The reason why I shy away from them is that they aren't really my subjects; they don't serve a purpose – my aim, that is. After a few more stories for *Tales of Siam* and *The Isan People*, I'll shut up. I would have done my stint as a writer. Then the demon that has almost driven me insane all these years might leave me in peace."

"Do me a favour, Primo. Please do. Have a chat with Mana and see whether you can come up with a story on his life. I found him hugely fascinating. I'm sure a lot of your readers would too. Do that for me, my boy."

"Why do you want me to write about this person?"

"For a start, you're not the only one who has had a hard life. Secondly, Mana was sold into the trade when he was 13 years old. He could be your Kum. He said he had heard of Napo. His birthplace in Isan sounds like Soka or Hungka, or something like that."

By now the fish was hooked. But the pen-pushing Pisces still tried desperately to wriggle free.

"If *your* Mana is like *my* Kum, then there is no point in repeating the story, is there?"

It seemed the hooked fish did not wriggle hard enough.

"I'm sure you can explore deeper, wider and find new nuances. After all Mana has lived in Germany for several years, has had a lot of German friends, has performed in a cabaret in Hamburg..."

"All right! You don't have to go on about it. Let me ask you this. Are you in love with...with this trans...?"

"Don't be silly. If I were in love with *her*, I would be with *her* at this very moment! I wouldn't be here with you, following you like a dog."

Suddenly Little David of Siam rose to his feet.

"Not like a dog, surely. My dear Charles, for an Oxonian, you are rather prosaic. *I follow you as if I were your shadow* would be more poetic. By the way, you haven't thanked me for the massage."

"Thank you. You're much better than Nid."

"Pray tell, who is Nid?"

"Nid is one of the houseboys at the late Prawit's."

"Oh! Nid! I've often wondered what has happened to him and his team mates now that Witty is no more."

Having caught sight of the English doctor, the masseur was alarmed.

"Quick! Put your clothes back on! John's here. If he catches us like this he'd believe we've just had a quickie. What would he think when he's been coping with scores of patients all day without being able to speak a word of Lao? And here we are..."

Then the telephone rang.

A moment later the Napotian yelled:

"John! Telephone!"

*Good old John! What a wonderful doctor to have for Napo.*

244

The creep grinned impishly at the volunteer who, after a quick 'thank you', went to the telephone to answer a call from Kent.

The northerly, known locally as the kite-flying wind, made the trek pleasant for the grandee, who wore a safari suit, a Panama hat and sun glasses.

Charles looked as if he was embarking on a hunt in Africa, causing the imp to grin.

"If I were not a follower of Lord Buddha, I'd have given you a gun in case we run into some wild beasts on the Plain of Nadhone."

Instead, the teaser had in his pocket a Swiss army knife, bought together with a watch at the Swiss Centre at Leicester Square that day he spent his last few hundred pounds of poetry competition prize-money.

"This is where Dan and Kum and their mothers were digging for little frogs," Prem indicated a spot at the bottom of Huaysai Creek. Let's go down to the creek bed, Tregy, and look into the fissures. You may see several pairs of shiny eyes. Those are the eyes of tiny frogs we call *kiads*. We dig deep into the cracked earth to catch them. I'll ask Piang and Toon to forage them one day so you can have a taste of *homokkiads*, one of our Isan delicacies. It would be a far cry from smoked wild salmon and champagne at Fortnum and Mason's."

The gentleman shook his head of snow white hair at the harmless mockery from a child of Isan, to whom he had become undeniably attached. The Plain of Napo had a hand in this attachment as well. It had brought the old Oxonian closer to one of the children who had roamed this land.

A queer notion that he could have been born on such land as this parched plain, in the past-life, came to his mind.

*It seems so absurd*, Charles thought. *But, being in the East now, one must keep one's mind open to all possibilities.*

As if the two exiles were on the same wave length, the half-ghost transmitted some silly phrases: "Tregy old thing! I told you some time ago in London that you had been my butler in the previous life, and that we had passed many years in India together. Remember? I hope you hadn't pinched my silver and sovereigns. Otherwise, you would have ended up paying for your bad karma by giving back to me in this life, plus interest at the rate of 19.99 per cent APR, whatever that is."

"Yes. I had the pleasure of serving you in India before being put out to grass in Sussex!"

Old Charles sounded as if he was enjoying the child's play in the land so far away from St. James's.

The freak seemed to be swept off his feet by a whirlwind of jocosity:

"All you have to do is close your eyes and concentrate, really concentrate, and channel your thoughts into a laser beam to cut through the past-time and you'll be there. I've often done just that."

TC played up to what he considered to be his young friend's folly. Surprisingly such humour could surface on the desolate plain, in the balmy breeze, under the clear blue skies of the Korat Plateau.

After all these years, Soka remained dead. By some burnt stumps they found a lean-to shelter made of branches and twigs. Judging from the wilted leaves, the shack had been made several days ago. Inside an emaciated man lay in delirium.

*We must take him to Napo Hospital.*

The question of 'how' also entered his head.

The creep had seen soldiers make stretchers from saplings and vines to carry the wounded and the dead out of Sisurachwood. Hence, he hastened into the thickets.

A few minutes later Tregonning heard sounds of branches and creeper vines being yanked and cut. Later he saw his little friend drag all out into the open.

"Thank goodness I had a mind to bring my Swiss army knife," said the wimp, heaving and perspiring.

Within an hour a roughly made stretcher was ready. The English gentleman had to hold his breath inside the lean-to because of the stench.

Then the carriers made their way back to Napo.

At the hospital, Little Prem stayed with the dying man while Charles went to *Bankhunluang* to fetch the doctor.

*John will be pleased.*

Depite the Napotian's twisted sense of humour, he seemed anxious, guessing that the doctor might have retired to his bed.

The nurse on duty was cleaning the patient now.

*How the scent of antiseptic makes one hospital smell like any other!*

Then the little man dozed off before John Stonham turned up.

"It's a case of full-blown HIV," the doctor said phlegmatically to the twain the following day.

Prem overcame his sad concern by being busy at the registration desk, helping the newly arrived patients fill the registration forms.

*This little hospital must not be as soulless and as slow as the one in the provincial town*, the Napo Project Manager determined.

At a time like this Lovely Liz would have been doing a better job. She would be chatting with the patients and their relations, giggling and teasing them in Lao.

But then one had to do without her while she was busy travelling hither and thither with TC.

Charles made a nuisance of himself, thinking that he could be helpful, keeping the lone doctor company. The two nurses on duty came and went smiling at the fatherly white-haired *farang*, whom they loved to call 'Khun Charley'.

*Khun Charley ka, Khun Charley painaima?*

In the evening, while Piang and Toon were preparing dinner in the kitchen, Good Old Charles and Little Primo were imbibing their sundowners on the open porch of the *House of the Noble*, anticipating that the doctor would come home soon.

Knowing that John Stonham was partial to sturdy red wine, Prem opened a bottle of Coonawarra Cabernet Sauvignon so that it would have time to 'breathe'. They had held back the discussion on the dead man until now.

"Now I can let my imagination run wild," opined Little David of Siam "The dead man could have been one of the sold children, taken away from the hamlet long before Ayu and his Tiger Men ransacked the shanties. Then, knowing that the end was nigh, he came home to die, not knowing that there was nothing left except some trees. Am I on the right track, Tregy?"

"Go on. Keep your thinking hat on and I'll listen."

"But to his dismay, Soka was no more. There was not a soul to welcome him home. He must have been devastated. Any energy he had left must have been spent on making the shelter under which he laid himself down. I couldn't bear the thought of him dying alone there."

"But, as it turned out, he didn't. He passed away peacefully, without pain. John made sure of that."

"For that I'm most grateful. It must have been such a deep love for his birthplace to return to die."

"You should know. You came home too."

"True. But, I'm not going to die as yet! Now the missing link is his life in the brothel in Sodom and Gomorrah!"

"There you are. If you don't wallow in the mire, how will you find out? As I said, Mana can fill you in on that, unless you want to make your own research without his or my help."

"How right you are, Charles. What can I do without you?"

Then the duo made a plan to return to Bangkok to meet Marilyn, Mana's stage name, at Folly Siam.

Meanwhile, a re-enactment of the killing of Kumjai Chaiwankul was to be staged. When Charles heard of it, he commented:

"It's rather ghoulish, is it not?"

Yet the writer determined to go ahead with the plan. For this, he sought help from Anucha to act as Guru Kumjai.

That fatal day the headmaster led his pupils, marching along the ridge of the Mongkol Pond towards the village street to protest against the scheme to turn Changlaiwood into a eucalyptus plantation.

Where the hired gunman waited for the head teacher, Prem stood in readiness to pull an imaginary trigger.

On that fatal day, Anucha had been assigned to protect the schoolchildren at the rear; therefore, he could not have seen a motorcyclist at the spot where the road on the ridge dipped to meet the village lane.

But Kumjai must have seen him, had perhaps smiled at his murderer, thinking that he had come to join the protest. As the spearhead of the parade dipped with the road, Anucha heard gunshots. The children screamed, running away from the scene while the motorcycle sped off, leaving the fatally wounded schoolteacher and its toxic fumes behind.

Following Charles Tregonning's advice, the actors agreed not to involve the schoolchildren in the reenactment of the killing scene. Alone, the new headmaster as Guru Kumjai moved conspicuously to the dip of the road.

Little Prem divided himself in two while eyeing Anucha-Kumjai approach. One was to penetrate the heart of the professional gunman with his third eye; the other became once more the son of *Pramae*, lying in wait inside Etan, the wise old mother buffalo, intensely looking at the victim and the murderer. Thus he saw and felt and suffered the evil deed.

While Etan's eyes still beheld Anucha-Kumjai, Prem shook the teacher's hand.

"I could see the real killers, and I shall hound them in my own way," Prem promised, making Charles the witness.

The chat with Marilyn enabled Little David to gather another stone. He named it *The Transvestite* to be included in *The Isan People*.

# The Extradition

Should the suspect be apprehended in New York, a bigger fish might escape the net. Thus the decision to allow him to leave the USA was to become a political issue.

To counter the demand for extradition, the Member of Parliament called a press conference. He vehemently declared his innocence; and the usual line *I have done nothing wrong* was uttered. Outside the conference room, hundreds of supporters from his constituency rallied. Eventually, the mob made a protest march to the US Embassy.

Against the protest, the US Embassy stood its ground and pressed on with the demand for extradition so the MP could be tried in the USA on drug trafficking charges.

The power-play between the world-class bully and the Siamese government was disappointing to the DEA of several countries.

What was deemed to be a possibility did not materialize. Not a single person in high authority came out to defend and protect the accused. The bigger fish did not raise a fin. The extradition took place, and a US court found the defendant guilty as charged.

# The Search

A week before the extradition would be set in motion, Elizabeth Durham disappeared without a trace.

The search for her was resumed when Stanley Durham arrived in the kingdom. The retired butcher was not satisfied with the official notification. Should his daughter be alive, in hiding, or held captive, he wished to make a plea for her return. If it came to the worst, he wanted to collect her remains.

It was reportedly said that Elizabeth was last seen at a discotheque in Pattaya. Therefore Stanley, Prem and Charles went there, and booked into The Sun & Sea Hotel. The idyllic view over the well-tended tropical garden and the shimmering Gulf of Siam did not succeed in soothing the distraught father. He paced the floor of his hotel room back and forth like a caged lion. The overwrought parent neither ventured out nor welcomed anyone into the room until he was ready to embark on the quest.

In the evening, the trio entered Disco Chicks where Elizabeth was last seen.

Starting with the bar manager, Durham showed a photo of his daughter.

"Have you seen her?"

When the response was negative, the heavy-hearted pensioner moved on to another staff member. From one to another he repeated the same question.

All in all, Stan had more of a head-shaking gesture than the outright 'no'. So he sat down at a table farther from the dance floor.

Surin suffered a prick in the heart when Old Durham acted as if he was alone, saying to the waiter: "Beer!"

Tregonning gentlemanly took the slight, and politely indicated that he and his companion should be served as well. Then the three men sat glumly in the palpitating disco.

Little Prem entwined his thought with that of Stan's.

*This is the type of place where Elizabeth ended up among whores and sex-crazed men.*

Turning to his friend, the freak silently apologized.

*Sorry, Charles, for having brought you to this.*

He also feared for Elizabeth's life.

*Would I, for knowing nearly as much as Norma, remain safe from now on? Where is Danny? In a time of great need the ringleader has also disappeared.*

Scowling, Stanley watched the prancing, wriggling, jerking and writhing bodies on the dance floor. Thank goodness Emma did not accompany him on the search, and so to this swarming, ear-splitting pit in the present-day Sodom and Gomorrah.

Then the pensioner stood up and went over to a table where a lady sat, awaiting the couple who had left her for a dance.

'May I join you?"

Accepting a photograph, Nipa, who knew only few words of English, wondered why this old *farang* had to flaunt a photo of his young and beautiful wife in order to pick up a tart.

*Not bad looking either*, Nipa could see through the hard face. This was indeed her lucky night. She leaned towards her man so closely that she could see, even under the dim light, the thicket of hair on the upper part of his chest that the unbuttoned collar revealed. Looking down, she caught a glimpse of white hair on the huge wrists and on the backs of the hands and the stems of his fat fingers.

*Ooh*...was the sound that escaped from her thick lips.

While Stan was about to repeat the question, the man and the woman who had previously occupied the chairs came back. Old Stanley rose to his feet to introduce himself to Horst and Salee.

Then all three sat down.

At Stan's request, Horst took the photo from Nipa. But because he had eyes only for dark-haired women, he peered long and hard at it to jog his beer-soaked memories. Salee took an opportunity to have a peep.

"I remember now," Salee said. She is very beautiful, very lovely, just like a film star. She sat there with VIPs."

"*Ja, ja*," Horst seconded. "They drank very expensive cognac and smoked cigars. *Ja, ja*. We sat next to them."

"They talked of going to an island close to the Cambodian bor..."

"You must leave," the manager interrupted.

"Why?"

"You're disturbing these people."

The manager pulled Stan up, and threw him out.

Back at the hotel, the troubled father gloomily went to his room and shut the door.

In the corridor Prem made a hopeless sign and led the way to their room.

All was not well.

The worst came when Little Prem told Charles of his fear for his own life now that the cover of *Operation Norma* had been blown.

In bed, the Napotian narrated details of *Operation Norma*, unaware that the Sun & Sea Hotel was one of the properties owned by the very people he feared.

"You can't die now," Charles said. "I should be the one to go first. You're the executor of my will."

"My dear Charles, if you return to London alive, you should change that. I'm likely to pop off first."

The fear of death brought them closer.

"What are we going to do? We can't leave Stan alone here. He's so dead set against the crooks, just like the late Kumjai. And you know what that amounted to. Stan doesn't know anything about the Siamese *Power of Darkness*. This is not England. We should warn him."

But it was too late. At dawn Durham's room was raided. It was alleged that pornographic materials involving young children were found there.

Thus, the suspected paedophile was arrested.

Surin panicked.

Tregonning remained phlegmatic.

Eventually one of the banks honoured the old gentleman's credit card with 300,000 baht. The amount miraculously freed Stanley Durham.

# A Curse

During the Chinese New Year festivities, Kwanjai, or Kwan as she had been fondly called by members of the Pi clan, gave birth to another son. Coincidentally Petra Wittenberg delivered a baby girl in the same week.

Karl-Michael felt as if he was on top of the world, deliriously looking down on humanity with equanimity on board the Hadyai-Bangkok flight.

At this very moment, Karl's dearly beloved keenly awaited his arrival to celebrate a full month of Little Linda's life.

His Excellency Prakarn and Madame Vichitra had been extremely pleased with the double guarantees of the continuity of the Pi lineage. Therefore, they had welcomed the Wittenbergs into the fold.

*A hotel room is certainly not a place where parents raise their children* was a pivotal point in Dani's argument.

Thus, the two divine pairs and their little darlings had been living happily together in the same apartment in VP Place.

From then on DP and KW took care that very few exceptional circumstances could interfere with their togetherness. One of them happened to be an urgent business trip that caused the Executive Vice President to fly to Hadyai to inspect a property that would soon be falling into the grasp of the VP Group.

"Very good, Tanong," the master stated when 30 candles had been lit. "Make sure you have at least thirty more candles in store. We don't want to run out of candles before the champagne toast is made."

But then the master seemed anxious.

*It's unlike Mick to be so very late.*

It was time for the wives and the children to join him.

They entered the Emerald Room, walking ahead of the baby-carrying nannies. Little Dusit and Little Mick ran ahead of their mothers when they saw Dani at the end of the hall.

"Wo! Wo! Wo!" the billionnaire exclaimed. "Careful! When you two bump into me like this, my champagne might spill!"

The boys, dressed in white, caught hold of his trouser legs and tagged themselves to him.

When the lovely mothers, also in elegant white dresses, had caught up with their sons, Tanong bowed and deferentially presented them with glasses of sparkling wine.

"Karl should be here at any moment," Dani assured them.

Instead, the grandparents entered the festive hall. The minister motioned the nannies to leave the room with the babies and the boys. The latter protested boisterously. Some seconds later they obeyed.

Even Tanong, who was never quick on the uptake, sensed a foreboding omen from the chilling expression on both hard faces.

Because Dani and his wife and Petra did not care much for the local radio and television, they had no way of knowing that the aircraft, with Wittenberg on board, had crashed.

# Friends in Need

Most times Dani sat, holding a glass of wine, in the Emerald Room, with Tanong waiting on him.

"Mick...Mick...O Mick..."

The servant seemed anxious, hearing the lament. But, when he moved forward, the billionaire looked through him.

Once, Tanong did try to make his presence known by grovelling closely. The nearness caused the lord and master to stir.

"Where are Primo and Liz? Why aren't they here yet? Must I wait for these people? Go and fetch them, will you?"

Tanong slid away to a corner. There, he stood still, watching his master with concern.

Jurg Souter, the current *maitre d'hotel* at The Bordeaux Grill had yet to be knocked into shape.

One evening the billionaire snapped, seeing that the table was set for four.

"Jurg, I did say there would be only Karl-Michael and Dr Prawit, did I not?"

Souter adroitly removed the fourth setting.

"Sorry, Witty. I had to do it. You may take revenge if you like," the 9th richest man in the world spoke to the opposite chair.

One morning Dani waved goodbye to the imaginary Mercedes-Benz in which the late Executive Vice President sedately sat.

Little Dusit rushed up to his father, crying.

"Daddy! Daddy! Who are you saying bye-bye to?"

"To your Uncle Mick, of course."

"But Uncle Mick is dead."

"No, he isn't! Look! He's leaving for work!"

Dani opened a window and lifted his son up and over the sill, keeping the child precariously dangling from his grip.

"Daddy!"

"Now you see Uncle Mick going to work. Yes?"

Kwan managed to rescue Little Dusit.

Eventually the grandparents packed the daughter-in-law and the grandchildren off to China and sent the surviving Wittenbergs to Petra's old family home.

When Tanong failed to produce Little Primo and Lovely Liz, after several demands for their company, the master made a call to Napo Village.

At the *House of the Noble*, there was no one there. Then he called a London number. When someone answered, Dani sounded surprised.

"Who are you?"

"I'm Pam, Pamela Cannington, the tenant."

"The tenant! Since when was the flat let? You sound just like Liz. Are you Liz? Where can I contact your landlord?"

"Try St. James's, or their country house. Have you got their phone numbers?"

Dani dialed Tregoning's at St. James's.

"Charles! O, Charles! My friend! What am I to do?"

"Are you all right, Danny?"

"Is Little Primo there?"

"No. As a matter of fact, he's in your flat, doing some cleaning and dusting in case you might come back to London soon."

"Good old Primo!"


To meet Dani at Heathrow, the bonded men equipped the back seat compartment of the Rolls-Royce with a first rate brand of champagne in a silver cooler and a crystal flute.

Seeing Dani stagger, the pair rushed to support their friend who shed some tears for having landed safely on the English soil.

Now the home-coming passenger on the back seat perked up after a glass of his favourite beverage.

"My dear Primo! You must be the only Oriental in London who has a white millionaire as your chauffeur. Now, pray tell, who's your tenant?"

"A lady."

"She sounds just like Liz. I thought she was Liz, if it wasn't for the fact that..."

"She will be introduced to you shortly. Then you can see for yourself whether she is Lizzie or not. Well, at least she keeps the flat clean and tidy."

"She's not one of those, is she?"

"Nothing of the kind! I may say she's a lady of leisure, having come into some big money recently."

"A football pool? A one million pound Premium Bond win?"

"Nothing of the kind!"

"A rich uncle?"

"Yes!"

"Charles!" Dani burped. "Charles! What happened to that Stonham chap. He didn't answer my call to Napo."

"John has finished his work in Isan. A young Siamese doctor is in charge while we're looking for a replacement."

"That young doctor has just graduated. Our hospital is full of guinea pigs for him!" Little Primo decried.

"We are lucky to have him, green as he is," said Charles.

"Why are you two back here and not there where you are much needed, particularly when I needed you most of all?"

"We had to flee the scene to save our lives. Your *Operation Norma* nearly killed me or both of us, Charles and I, I mean."

"Humbug! If they wanted to get you, they could have you killed anywhere."

"We had to run, hadn't we, Charles? We didn't want to be sitting ducks, did we?"

"Sitting ducks! Indeed! As long as I'm alive, they wouldn't dare!"

"We weren't so sure, were we, Charles? My dear Danny, we didn't know where you were, whether you were still alive or not. We couldn't reach you, could we, Charles?"

"It's two against one, I can see. Anyway, here we are, safe and sound, and together again, except for...."

"And here is Piccadilly. And in five minutes, you'll be home."

At home, the billionaire was delighted, seeing flower arrangements and the material possessions. They were his, all his, reflecting his taste.

Some 15 minutes later the doorbell rang, and in walked a be-suited brunette, wearing dark glasses.

"Dr Dhani, I presumed," said she, offering her hand.

"Have we met?"

"Yes, certainly," she assured, taking off the dark glasses.

"Me Liz!"

"O, Liz! My dear Liz!"

He embraced her, whimpering like a child.

Seemingly, any minute now his Mick might appear. Dani would part with half of his fortune for that reality. When there was no one at the door, he sat down, bending his head into his hands, weeping copiously.

"You thought I'd been done in, didn't you?" Ms Pamela Cannington sneered. "Well, that was the idea. I was whisked off from Pattaya in the night to an old American airbase at Utapao and a US military aircraft flew me to Okinawa. Hardly any Siamese knew what was going on. The flight ended in Los Angeles. The DEA got their man and I pocketed half a million dollars."

"The DEA didn't get their man, Liz. If only you had known how much your father had suffered, even a million wouldn't worth the pain."

"It couldn't be helped. We played the game at someone else's expense, didn't we? Look at our meek little pen-pusher here!" Pamela indicated her soul mate. "He scribbles all the time in his head, even now."

"Lizzie!" the wordsmith protested.

"If I hadn't walked into your bloody *Operation Norma* with my eyes wide open, I'd have blamed you for throwing me to the wolves."

"Liz, please, not now. I can't take it. Not now."

Though *Operation Norma* was not entirely a failure, Dani considered it was. However, in London, he felt more secure. After all it was his home ground. Thus, he planned another operation which would not involve his friends.

# The Confession

Without Karl-Michael by his side, Dani lost interest in the entire operation of the VP Group.

But he occasionally graced Wealdshire Park Hotel with his presence, as he was doing now.

This particular evening, in the resplendent dining room, the lord of the manor staggered against a table, causing glasses to tumble.

Good breeding forbade the two offended ladies to act ungraciously. However, they grimaced and rose to their feet and wordlessly went to their suite.

Then Pamela Cannington and Charles Tregonning joined the billionaire and his companion.

"Lounge suit won't do when you dine with me at Wealdshire, Charles."

"I beg your pardon."

"I had to make do with my old black tie," Little Primo chirped.

"That's because I ordered you to."

"Yes, my lord," the little fellow agreed, making eyes at Pamela whose fingers were unadorned.

"I sold it," practical Pam anticipated his question. "I don't want to be reminded of..."

"Handsomely, I trust."

"No, I fibbed. I gave it to *me* Mum," the Yorkshire lass could not resist reverting to her childhood lexicon against Mr. Pee's la-di-da.

"Imagine, Emma has an eight-carat diamond ring on her finger while shopping at the Co-op at Polgate!"

"Yes, it would be like Grandma Boonliang wearing a tiara in Napo, wouldn't it? But for all I know, Mum might never wear it. It's too ostentatious even for Eastbourne."

"Children!" Dani excoriated the blithering pair. "Concentrate on your choices and let's get the order out of the way. I have a business proposal to make."

"Thank goodness there's neither grouse nor pheasant on the menu," commented the little chap to himself rather than to his friends.

"I don't have to remind you little twit that we're in the bud of May!" the high priest of fine dining barracked.

"There's baked haddock and prawns," Pamela pointed out. "I wonder why the chef has given up on halibut and Dover sole."

"That's because I haven't been here often enough. The place has slipped. What a pity, after all the hard work Karl and I have put in," Dani paused so that the sudden pang would pass. "Even the wine list reflected mediocrity now. I must do something before going back to the Mother of Gridlock."

"You mean Bangers, another modern-day Sodom and Gomorrah," the novelist flouted.

"Cynicism doesn't become you!" Pamela would not let Mr Prim and Proper get away with it for she still loved the Divine City of Angels, with dust, lethal fumes, traffic jams, shambles, contradiction and venality.

"When are you leaving?" Charles inquired.

The old gentleman seemed anxious that Dani would take his Little Primo back to the kingdom.

"When you're ready to take off, Charles. Now, Liz, or you prefer me to call you Pamela."

"Pam, please."

"So in all the legal documents it shall be Pamela Cannington, shall it not? I'll put you in charge of the Estate while we three are back in Siam. Meanwhile my lawyers will form a trust to which I shall transfer all of my assets in England, Switzerland and Liechtenstein. It should be so watertight that no one can challenge any of you or force you to give up your shares. Individually, you cannot release any amounts without the consent of the other two partners. When all is done, both of you blithering twain should instantly become millionaires, pound not baht millionaires."

"Quick! Primo! Pinch me!"

The child's play did not go down well with the dead serious philanthropist.

"Dash it, Liz! Be dashed serious for once!"

"It could be challenged on the ground that you weren't in sound mind, could it not?" Little Primo opined.

"I've thought of that and will work on it with my lawyers."

"What would you have left then?" the wimp worried.

"Some 10 million pounds in my personal bank account here in London. And that will go to you, Primo, should I be suddenly whisked off by a spacecraft in the night or even in daytime to heaven or to hell. When I finished with the lawyers, you'd have become the executor of my will as well. But if those millions are dissipated one way or the other while I'm still alive, I can sponge off you, can I not?"

"You can have all of your money back, from me and from Lizzie."

"Speak for yourself!" Pamela snapped.

For already she had been dreaming of what to do with her millions.

"Now, get that sour-faced waiter to bring our champagne will you? Egad! Even one of the richest men in the world has to wait here to be served. I must do something pretty quickly. Charles! Now that you are just about to become a partner, I think it'd be most proper to come back to the daily grind and manage Wealdshire. I've long admired you – our gentle, straightforward grandee of the old school. We need your expertise and your good taste and connections in high places."

"I'd be delighted," assured the taciturn gentleman.

"I'll have smoked salmon to start with and then follow by baked haddock and prawns," motioned Prem who had ceased to consume red meat.

Pamela Cannington shook her head in a manner of saying: *His stomach always comes first, having starved in his childhood in Napo!*

"What did the Napotians have for dinner tonight, I wonder," said Dani, glancing at Pamela.

He looked less grim now.

"Your irony is well-taken, my lord," replied Pam.

A pause ensued.

The Napotian saw a chance to air a hidden concern, and took it.

"I'm compelled to make a confession."

"Confession! Ha! Ha!" Dani derided. "Don't look at me! Why didn't you make Witty your confessor before his demise? He had often played that role."

"You see, because Karl is not with us here now," the little chap ignored Dani's snide remark. "I mean at this table where we were all together once, with Ayu and Pan. I do miss him."

The blithering twit paused, as if to test the temperature of the steamy water in the master's bathtub, in order to ascertain its clemency prior to his lordship's immersion.

Pam and Charles were attentively waiting to hear more.

As for the lord of the manor, it was a matter of tolerating the painful reminder.

So then, under their weighty expectations, the freak continued:

"In my mind's eye, long before the Siam Airways crash, I often saw Karl and Luzzi Sarasen, in a small private aircraft. You know, the two amateur pilots took delight in flying here and there for unalloyed excitement. Sometimes they had a woman or two with them for unadulterated pleasure. Every time such a vision came to my mind I saw the aircraft spin and dive to earth despite my attempt to avert the fatal accident by altering the mental image, but to no avail. All was…"

Dani suddenly rose to his feet and left.

"Damn you, Primo!" Elizabeth swore. "You're so tactless! You open your big mouth and put your foot in it."

"Should I go after him and apologize?"

"The damage has been done. Now that you've whetted our curiosity so abominably, you'd better finish it. I'm sure Charles would agree."

Charles was amused.

"Oh well, at worst Danny will take back all the millions promised to us. With a sweep of an Isan peasant's hand…when my big mouth gapes… millions of pounds and francs are no more. I hope you two don't mind the losses. How fickle such wealth and mankind can be."

"Primo! Don't cant! Just get on with the confession!"

"Charles?"

Good old Charles smiled benignly.

"Very well then. Where was I? Oh yes. When Karl, the late Karl that is, along with 156 passengers and the airline crew perished in that crash, I feared that the vision I had was an omen. It was truly tragic to think that he took not two but over 150 people with him. I put the blame on myself for the recurring vision as if subconsciously I wished it to occur in reality. It was a kind of mental curse from my subconscious mind to retaliate against his wicked karma, for having engineered those vicious attacks from journalists, as well as against his vilification of me. You see, Charles, when young spiritual mother, who adopted me, gave me powers to curse effectively, causing illness, accidents, or, in some cases, death to those who harmed me. The adopted one has that power for self-protection when *Pramae* cannot always be at hand to protect me."

"Do you actually believe that?" Charles mildly inquired.

"Yes, he does!" Elizabeth butted in. "But it wasn't intended to be a curse, I'm sure. Primo wouldn't hurt a fly."

"But, as I said, *subconsciously* I must have. *Pramae* knows my foes. I don't have to open my mouth. She knows. Therefore, I blamed myself for what had happened. It was like putting a bomb inside the aircraft with my own hand. That's my confession."

"If only the airlines had been aware of that!" Elizabeth punctuated.

Charles smiled again as if to say: *Are you absolutely sure that it was not a puerile thought from your maimed mind, Primo?* But the noble Englishman knew that such should be left unuttered.

Nevertheless the retired art dealer was amused by the confession.

# Agents of Change

Back in Siam, Dani Pi, Little Prem and Charles Tregonning engaged in charitable activities to improve the quality of life in villages on the Plain of Napo.

While on tour of Napo Village, the billionaire remarked on signs of wealth in the form of modern houses and shops. The speed of change had been accelerated, largely due to men and women who had gone to work in Japan, Singapore, Taiwan and Korea. Furthermore many Napo-born women had got hold of *farang* admirers. As a result they could afford better and bigger homes.

"Many people from other villages have moved to Napo because of the hospital, known far and wide for having a *farang* doctor and free medical treatment, and a very good school under a progressive husband and wife team. Soon the main street will be tar-sealed and then there will be a water supply," Prem expatiated.

The Napotian drove the Mercedes here and there so that his friends could see the changes that had taken place.

"Look! That's Panya's new house. It's what one calls applied Siamese style, meaning it's Greco-Roman-Gothic architecture."

"How grotesque!" Dani snorted.

"From wherever he performed, Pan brought home eye-catching architectural style. And here are grand houses of our women who married *farangs.*"

At sunset the trio took their sundowners, sitting on rattan chairs on the open porch of the House of the Noble.

"One of the late guru's dreams was to have modern plumbing for every house," Little Prem revealed.

"Absolutely! To be hygienic, they must have proper facilities, mustn't they, Charles?"

When the Englishman remained silent, the billionaire turned to Mr Pee.

"Couldn't you pick a man whose one foot isn't in the grave!"

"I didn't pick him. He picked me. Besides, it's been said in old Siam that loving, respecting and taking care of old people gains one a lot of merit."

"You certainly need a lot of merit to deserve a rebirth in your beloved England and regain your family seat!"

*Why is it that whatever I have said and done must bounce back to wound me? Ah, I know. It's the force of karma, my monstrous karma committed in the former life and not entirely Danny's anima. Imagine what he would have said if he had known that, in childhood, I had been described as 'no better than a lump of sh...excrement'.*

"Sorry, jet lag is catching up on me," Charles apologized.

"Tricky is the English language! Is it *catching up 'on' me or 'with' me?*" the writer asked to create a diversion.

"Dash it, Primo! Here we are, talking seriously about the welfare of your village, and suddenly you switched to English grammar. No wonder Liz said you weren't an intellectual."

"I know I'm not an intellectual. I'm just an ageing hack making muffled cries from a gammy mind, a so-called freelancer, writing mundane articles for an English newspaper. However, after publishing *Tales of Siam*, several readers wrote to me saying that they were touched..."

"Do you know what we call you behind your back? A tear jerker! Ha! Ha! Ha!"

Dani's simulated laughter, meant to be a mockery, made Prem happy. He looked at the big brother and saw a glimmer of sardonic gratification.

*Even though it is at my expense, I am glad to see a rare touch of mirth.*

"By the way," said Dani, "I meant to tell you that Ayu will join us in Napo tomorrow. He can share my bedroom. You know when Witty, poor Witty, may he rest in peace, and the architect showed me the plan of Bankhunluang, I asked them to join three houses together. But they opted for two. Should Lovely Liz, I mean Practical Pam, join us, there won't be a spare bedroom for her."

"She can sleep in Surin House. She'd like that even better."

"Anyway, she isn't coming. She must put her nose to the grindstone while we three musketeers are out here."

"It's very good of you to invite Senior Colonel Ayumongkol. Why didn't I think of that?" Prem wondered.

"Because you, deep in your devious mind, still hold resentment against the military and the far right for the 14th October and the 6th October massacres. Be nice to him when he comes. I want to help him become a General in a jiffy."

*And for killing the inhabitants and burning of Yang and Soka,* added the little man in his mind, but his lips quivered.

"I've always been nice to him, haven't I? Charles? Charles! Listen, Danny. He's snoring again. The old man can't take long journeys."

"A senior colonel?" Charles perked up.

"It's equivalent to your British 'Brigadier'. We don't have 'Brigadier' in our military ranking. Have some more champagne. That would perk you up. Should I mention that Ayu will bring our world famous flautist Pan, it should perk you up even more. I know you quite like the young man. Pan is on his way back to Germany from a tour of Japan and condescended to drop in on us mortals."

"Good Lord! Pan in Napo," Little Primo rose to the occasion. "That certainly deserves a celebration. Let's have a welcome-back party for the rich and the famous. You know his wife divorced him or he her, depending on whom you talk to in this village."

"If it was the wife who wanted the divorce, she must be dim. She missed out on sharing his fame and fortune," the billionaire expounded.

"Maybe Panya has stayed away from her for too long," Little Prem attempted to reason on behalf of the poor woman. "Anyhow, a party to welcome him home should be spiffing! We shall invite Anucha and his wife and the doctor."

"Don't forget to include the headman. It's good PR," the boss enjoyed showing off that he could always be one step ahead.

"Then we might as well include Pan's band of old outlaws to see if he still wants to speak to them!"

The wimp winced inwardly, for Kumjai was no more. But he covered his sad concern with: "It's amazing! Two of us, native sons, born in the same week, same month and in the same year, could reach a little higher than Ta Sa, Ta Si, Ta Ma and Ta Mi (Tom, Dick, Harry and John) and yet none of our achievements is meant for our people. Pan plays European classical music to the Europeans and the Americans and the Japanese. I write in English. But no one in Napo has neither listened to Pan's classical music nor read my books."

"Why didn't you write in Siamese? Why didn't you address your downtrodden, battered brothers and raped sisters in their own language? Write in Siamese about vital social issues. Wake the sleepers up! Show them what their eyes didn't see, their ears couldn't hear, and their mouths couldn't utter. Make them learn to think rationally and critically."

"My dear Danny, I want to enhance peace and understanding!"

"Peace and understanding! My foot! Don't give me that crap! Who do you think I am? What do you take me for, a dashed gullible idiot? It's people like you who keep high-ranking crooks, mighty drug lords, fearsome gangsters, powerful smugglers, be-suited extortionists, unashamed bribe-takers, greedy kickback receivers, awesome vote-buyers, formidable godfathers, invincible child molesters and big gambling den operators in the House and in other high places. Do something to reduce their number or clean them up, instead of scribbling your life away in English!"

"Steady on, Danny! What a dashed tall order you're giving me. But I value my life. I don't want to follow Guru Kumjai so quickly."

"You mean you don't have the guts."

"You're in a better position to decimate them and clean up the House -- a Herculean labour to clean the infernal stable, no doubt. I'm basically a poor and struggling writer awaiting my inheritance. For all I know, you and Charles may outlive me."

"I've been doing it, haven't you noticed?"

They were interrupted by Anucha Rajapakdi.

"Isn't Khun Elizabeth here?"

As if he did not believe his eyes and ears, Anu went in search of his heartthrob in the kitchen where Piang and Toon were preparing the repast.


While waiting for Ayumongkol and Panya, the three musketeers toured Napo to observe the progress of the Napo Project.

The hospital was a showpiece.

It had two doctors, six nurses and 40 beds. The staff quarters had been refurbished and air-conditioned.

Dr Peter Sperrin was on duty. Though obviously exhausted, he was pleased to see the visitors, with whom he could speak in his own tongue. It was also the first opportunity to meet the benefactor.

With a practised smile, Khun Dhani glanced at the patients and their relatives. He ventured further to see animal husbandry, poultry farming and fish farming. But then he declined to go to the vineyard, having stepped on a pile of buffalo dung.

"I know you and Liz have done a good job, and I approve of the Kumjai Chaiwankul Foundation. I don't have to see all of the results of your activities, Primo. But, on the way back, we should call on the village chief."

The trio trooped to Chief Singhon's house which had recently been rebuilt to keep up with Panya Palaraksa's.

Not only the chief had become Mr. Ten Percent but also a vote canvasser. Therefore he could afford a grander residence.

On the porch of the Big House, the chief and his wife prostrated at Dani's feet.

"Gormless creatures!" the billionaire sneered.

Little Prem grinned impishly.

Charles was absolutely appalled.

Nevertheless the Homhauls believed that the gracious master had bestowed a blessing on them.

# A Catalyst

After the feast was over, Charles and Little Prem retired to their bedroom.

In the other house, Dani lay awake in bed, awaiting Senior Colonel Ayumongkol to emerge from the bathroom.

"Don't turn on the light, Ayu. I didn't draw the curtains."

"This is certainly an oasis of civilization in the wilderness."

"You'd have regrets, if you had razed this fast-growing village to the ground."

"We wouldn't have done that. Napo is too far from Sisurachwood. By the way, Pan wanted me to sleep in his house tonight. Because of you I had to decline his offer. Now, what is it that you want to talk to me about?"

"What's the rush?"

"It's almost midnight! And it has been a long day for me."

"Poor old thing! Now you've asked, I'll not beat about the bush. I want to sound you out about that shining General who has recently come to the fore. He's had direct dealings with the poverty-stricken Isan peasants, has he not? He will pounce when opportunity arises, will he not?"

"My dear Danny, an opportunity can be created. An ambitious General doesn't sit and wait."

"Good! Let's create an opportunity!"

"What are you talking about?"

"About an opportune moment, my dear Ayu," Dani aired and then paused.

"Go on," Ayumongkol plodded.

"Now that the military-led coup under the name of the National Peace Keeping Force will permit the formation of a new government, we can guess who will be the Prime Minister."

"Yes?" Ayumongkol's heart was pounding.

"But if the PM-to-be and his deputy had failed to obtain visa to enter the USA, wouldn't that be a chance? I'm perfectly sure that your chaps have all sorts of vital information to use on the boys in high places when it suits them."

"What do you mean, Danny? What do you mean by that?"

"If it's leaked to the media that the front-runner to take the top job has been refused entry to the US due to the drug trade, that would be absolutely shocking, would it not? Imagine the Prime Minister of Siam who could not enter the United States to meet the US President at the White House! *Sorry, Mr. President, your Embassy in Bangers refused to issue me a visa.* Then behind the scenes your chaps could coerce the US State Department to publicly support the claim, and that should disgrace the hopeful PM nominee even more. The Post would be pleased to place the US State Department's supportive statement in the front page, I am sure. And then the vacancy might not be easily filled when the hopeful candidate for the post of Deputy is in the same net. Then your General, who has already come to the fore, keenly waiting, being seen publicly comforting grieving Isan peasants and all that crap, can step in, even without having been elected. That's the short cut."

"But he has already declared that the *coup d'etat* was not meant for him to become Prime Minister, that he definitely would not take the PM's job."

"Well, he can say that he had to lie *for* the well-being of the nation, and not *to* the nation."

This time it was the General-to-be who kept his eyes open in silence and in darkness.

"And you'd be greatly rewarded, my dear Ayu. You'd be a General in no time at all. Now, old boy, you can sleep on it."

# The May Massacre

When the Army Commander-in-Chief became the Prime Minister, masses of people protested.

Since there had been attempts to rewrite the history of the 14th October 73 massacre and the 6th October 76 killing, Prem Surin intended to record the bloody revolt as factual as possible. He noted:

*On 23rd February 1991, the Supreme Commander ousted the Shunhawan government, citing love of the country as a prime reason to get rid of the most corrupt politicians. Then he set up the so-called National Peacekeeping Force.*

*The main reason for the coup d'etat is:* 'Members of the ousted cabinet and those who held high ministerial positions in the Shunhawan government had abused their power, accruing great wealth amongst themselves. For instance, the highly corrupt politicians and members of cabinet took part in lobbying and granting licenses, concessions and monopolies to various projects and business deals. Despite his awareness of rampant corruption in the government and among civil servants and senior state enterprise executives, the Prime Minister did not pay attention to solving the problem. In fact he had been saying 'there is no problem' so often that he has been named Mr No Problem. Moreover, he came out to protect the wrongdoers by insisting on evidence such as receipts to prove any case of graft.'

*Meanwhile, Parliament and the Constitution were dissolved and the country fell under the grip of martial law. The military take-over became the 16th coup d'etat since the change of absolute monarchy to constitutional monarchy in 1932.*

*To claim that graft in the government had been so rampant that it required a coup d'etat to cleanse it seemed laudable at the time. But later the Generals began to head the boards of directors of private enterprises including airlines, and took part in land-hotel-golf course deals in forest reserves.*

*(Some years later the public learned that a General among the coup leaders left behind an extra four billion baht for which his widow and a mistress were fighting.)*

*Following the coup, a naming and shaming tactic was applied to expose the extremely rich politicians. Presumably such exposure was meant to indicate how corrupt these exceedingly rich politicians had become.*

*As if the naming and shaming antic was not enough, a foreign organisation aroused attention among overseas investors regarding the venality in Siam. The finger pointing came from Hong Kong-based political and economic risk consultants, claiming that the kingdom once again earned the distinction of being rated one of Asia's most corrupt countries.*

*Taking up the report,* The Nation *commented:* The finding by the Hong Kong consultant firm will probably come as no surprise to most Siamese who go through life paying off policemen, bank loan managers and an assortment of government officials as nonchalantly as citizens in other countries pay their taxes. What may seem a surprise was the consultant company's conclusion that corruption in the kingdom increased considerably last year.

In a society where there are no real institutional barriers to graft, there is little reason to believe that greed would have been worse last year than any other. The only thing that has changed is the size of the rewards for abusing the powers.

*If becoming extremely rich through the drug trade could be counted as corruption, the rot has indeed reached so high that the prime minister-designate was under suspicion. He was refused a US visa due to an alleged connection with the drug trade.*

*On the 27th March 1992, the nominee's chance to become the next prime minister appeared dim after the Post published, on the front page, the US State Department's statement to the effect that it had refused a visa for him to enter the US due to his suspected ties with drug trafficking.*

*On 17th May, a great mass of protesters convened at the Royal Ground to demand the resignation of the non-elected Prime Minister.*

*Prior to leaving VP Place to join the rally, I pocketed the Swiss army knife.*

*"I'll go with you," Charles determined.*

*When we confront the crowd (estimated to be over 200,000 –* The Nation*), I asked Charles to go inside the Royal Hotel and wait for me there.*

*Khun Jumlong Simuang, the leader, addressed the protesters, reiterating the ultimate goal -- the resignation of the Prime Minister. He vowed to end the struggle only after the General let go of his hold on power as Prime Minister.*

*Eventually Khun Jumlong led the protesters to the Government House to demand the resignation.*

*I kept close to him, believing in his determination and sincerity. To me, he is a rare Siamese of incredible will and courage.*

*Behind Khun Jumlong's van, we marched. Many carried banners, placards, and national flags.*

*Eventually the van halted in front of the blockade at Panfa Bridge.*

*On the other side were the armed troops.*

*A number of protesters tried to storm the barricade.*

*To stop the advancing mob, the force jetted water from several fire trucks.*

*Many were struck down. But the water cannons could not deter the protestors for long. Many death-defying men broke through.*

*The leader used a loud hailer, asking the protesters to avoid using violent means, but his van could not move as the crowd surged ahead to confront the troops.*

*I saw a female photographer taking photos of an unfortunate protestor being bludgeoned. Then she became the next victim.*

*"How can you treat people as if they are pigs and dogs!"*

*It seemed she was not concerned with her own safety.*

*"They're killing him! Help him!"*

*She ran back to us still shouting.*

*"They're killing a man. Save him!"*

*One trooper roared while clubbing the fallen protester.*

*"Why do you want democracy? Can you eat it?"*

*In seconds the bullets brought down several protesters who were trying to gain control of the fire brigade.*

*The survivors begged the armed men for mercy.*

*Yet, one protester determined to fight on, yelling at the killers.*

*"You are the despot's slaves. You are worse than animals. Join us if you are decent human beings!"*

*Against that challenge, came a command.*

*"Shoot at will!"*

*Many bodies dropped. The daring photographer fell on the ground. Blood gushed from her face. She spluttered.*

*A man dared, dashing forward to carry her away from the field of fire.*

*A contingent of armed men merged in with the General's front line. Clashes ensued with heavy casualties on our side.*

*While I sensed the protective arms of Pramae, the late Napo seer's voice boomed in my ears.*

*"I told you not to challenge your foes. Now you have disobeyed me! So take great care. Use your eyes, particularly the third one!"*

*I was drawn closer to the leader as my inner eye saw him pair with the late Headmaster Kumjai.*

*Rit Apaidham, my dear friend from the Wat Borombopit years, appeared.*

*"Come, my friend! Come forward!" Rit hollered. "Now you know what Liberty means! Liberty has never been willingly granted! It has to be fought for!"*

*Still I could neither go forth nor back away. My hands clung to the side of the van.*

*At one point, the leader climbed on top of the van to warn his supporters that the military would soon come down harder on us.*

*"Take care! I beg you to avoid using violence!"*

*At that moment I saw two men on top of an ATM booth, aiming something black at our leader. I feared for his life. An image of the hired gunman pointing his pistol at Guru Kumjai flashed before my eyes.*

*"Khun Jumlong! Watch out! Two snipers there!" I cried.*

*The two men on the top of the ATM booth vehemently declared that they were journalists.*

*Then the leader clambered down the van.*

*During a lull, Khun Jumlong scribbled on a piece of paper which he later gave to one of his aides. The man climbed on top of the vehicle, using a hand-held loud speaker to relay the message.*

*"All patriotic friends, our leader intends to fight till the General let go of his hold on power as the Prime Minister."*

*Troopers fired at the surging mass.*

*"Lie down! Lie down!" the speaker on the van yelled.*

*Then he fell on top of me, rendering me unconscious. When I came to, the pain from the bullet wound seized my body. Blood soaked my shirt.*

*A whiff of smelling salts from one of the nurses revived me.*

*"Please help me," I begged a nurse who was tending to one of Khun Jumlong's wounded men.*

*"We have nothing to treat you with except some gauze and smelling salts. We came here as protesters too."*

*Losing more blood, I fainted.*

*When I gained consciousness, the leader was addressing protesters.*

*"Please do not resist. No violence, please. Be calm and let the military do what they will with me."*

*Turning my head to one side, I could see a team of foreign correspondents step over bodies, requesting an interview with Khun Jumlong.*

*As the leader was being filmed, many shots were heard. Once more, men fell around me, while several men jumped on top of Khun Jumlong, using their bodies to shield him.*

*After a while, a man started chanting the national anthem. More men joined in. The troops opened fire again. But, despite being shot, the compatriots continued singing until the end of the anthem. Then, sitting on their haunches, they clapped their hands continuously to indicate that they were unarmed.*

*I could not free myself from the body on top of me. A wounded man, wincing near me, was shot, not once, but several times.*

*Khun Jumlong's aides, who were still alive, were blindfolded, and their hands tied behind their backs. Some soldiers kicked these defenseless men until they lay flat on the ground. Alas, there was no mercy in the hearts of the mighty whose boots came down hard on their victims. Then the salvo of gunfire resumed.*

*A familiar voice told me to play dead.*

The Nation *describes the scene of carnage as follows:*

Two military police officers pulled the protest leader out from under the dead. One officer handcuffed Khun Jumlong. Khun Siriluck, the leader's wife, attempted to stop them from taking her husband away, but they ruthlessly pushed her aside. Then the troopers rounded up some 500 protesters. They were ordered to take off their shirts, bend their heads towards the ground so that they would not see the killers.

Armed men lifted the dead onto the trucks.

*I kept my eyes closed and inhaled gently so that my carrier would not detect that I was still alive.*

*He dumped me on top of the pile.*

*A sheet of some sort was spread over.*

*While the vehicle trundled, I used the Swiss army knife to slit the sheet. At a stop I escaped.*

*Some distance away I hailed a taxi. The driver seemed sympathetic when I told him that I survived the massacre on Rajdamnern Avenue. There was no way of hiding my bloody clothes from him.*

*In VP Place, Dani was in a stupor.*

*"Where is Charles?"*

*"Charles! Charles! Charles! Dash it! How about me? Me! Me! Me! Nobody cares about me! Your Charlie barged in here, asking for you. It's like playing hide-and-seek, what?"*

*"Stop drinking! The troops are killing the people! Can't you ask General Ayu to stop the massacre?"*

*"Why should I do that, hm?"*

*When I approached him, he backed away, shaking his head.*

*"No! I won't give you another chance to hit me!"*

*It was in the Hyde Park Square flat that I hit him on the nose in the night of the 6th October 1976. Now he struck my wounded arm and grounded me.*

*Blood began to flow once more.*

276

*The drunkard fell on top of me, and thus we lay clasping each other.*

*His eyes peered into mine while my inner eye penetrated his. Through the vortex, it perceived a regal white man gazing at the deceased lying in state, bidding farewell.*

*'May you rest in peace, my dear Maurice.'*

*At long last I knew that Dani was my brother from the past-life, and I was the one who said farewell to him, my dead brother.*

"O, Brother!"

"Damn you!"

"Steady on, Danny! Do something! Ask General Ayu to order the troops to stop killing the people!"

*Time should not be wasted, telling him of what Tatip Henkai, the late seer of Napo, had told me.*

*The big brother staggered, helping me up on my feet.*

*For once he did what I asked him to do.*

"Ayu! Listen! You must speak to me even for a minute! Your men have been butchering the people! Can't you stop the killing? You tell that to your friend here!"

*By the time I grabbed the phone, General Ayumongkol had already ended the call.*

"Sorry I asked. Where's Charles?"

"He went back to look for you."

"Then I must go back and look for him."

"Treat your wound first and change your clothes. You stink."

"There's no time!"

"I'll go with you."

"No, you won't! You aren't in a state to run for your life. Besides, if I don't come back, you can keep the Napo Project going."

"You'll come back. You'll survive all of us. The meek shall inherit the earth."

*Some 10 minutes were wasted while the servant washed the bullet wound on my arm with alcohol and covered it with a large gauze pad.*

"I'm very lucky, Tanong. A lot of people died around me."

"Is it necessary to go there again?"

"I have to. Khun Charles is there, looking for me. You make sure that your master stays in the house. It is not at all safe out there."

*The taxi driver would not go anywhere near the Royal Hotel. From Wat Rajabopit I walked along the road that follows the waterway.*

*Fleeing people rushed past me.*

*"Go back! Go back!" One woman shouted at me. "Go back to the Wat for protection! The soldiers are killing the protesters. Go back!"*

*Ignoring the warning, I hastened forward.*

*Throngs of people were running away from the killers.*

*A woman carrying a child bumped into me, causing me to fall.*

*Up on my feet again, I forged ahead to reach the Royal Hotel.*

*There, protesters, members of the media and hotel guests swarmed the entrance.*

The Nation reported that thousands of men and women had sought refuge inside the hotel, occupying the public areas and rooms. Several doctors and nurses had set up operating tables in the back part of the lobby to treat the wounded.

*I had to be utterly brutal to be inside the hotel. In my frantic search, a young woman stopped me.*

*"Aren't you one of Khun Jumlong's aides? I saw you by his side. Aren't you supposed to be dead? I saw a soldier…"*

*"I was near dead. Now I'm looking for a visitor from England. He should not be caught up in the revolt."*

*"Was he tall and elderly?"*

*"Yes!"*

*"White hair?"*

*"Yes!"*

*"The foreign correspondent who interviewed Khun Jumlong fell near you and a New Zealander I know dropped some paces away. That elderly man was shot, but he kept moving. I will never forget the image of his head of white hair bobbing up and down. Even after he fell, he still tried to rise to his feet until he was again hit."*

*"I shouldn't have let him come with me."*

*"You must hide quickly. If I can recognize you, some of the frontline soldiers must have seen you with Khun Jumlong. The troops will storm the hotel. This is the last stronghold of the rebels."*

*"Do you remember where he fell?"*

*"About 10 yards from you."*

*"I must go in case he's left lying there."*

*"You won't get through. The troops have gained control of the entire avenue. Those protesters who dared to resist the advancing troops have been wiped out. Besides, there won't be bodies lying around. I saw a convoy of trucks follow the soldiers to take the dead away."*

*At that moment a throng of fleeing protesters tried to enter the hotel.*

*Perhaps they believed that the presence of the hotel guests, mostly foreigners, might make the military men shy away.*

*"The soldiers are surrounding us!" one man hollered.*

*"We're under siege," the journalist said. "You must hide. Go up to Room 132 on the first floor, left hand side, at the end of the corridor. Some of my colleagues are in that room. Say you are a friend of Ladawan. They'll let you in."*

*"Aren't you going to hide?"*

*"I didn't come in here to hide!"*

*It took me some time to locate Room 132 where reporters, press photographers and several foreign correspondents were observing the movements of the military men on the street.*

*Curiosity made me beg for a space at the window.*

*A mass of resisting protesters, who could not gain access to the hotel lobby, remained defiantly on the pavement below us, singing patriotic songs. One daring man sprinted towards the encroaching army. Several shots were fired. The sprinter fell to the ground.*

*Another salvo of deafening gunfire ensued.*

*More protesters ran towards the troops, only to be shot down.*

*Several buses sped at high speed towards the army, but the rockets burst the tyres and shattered the windscreens. Then the buses burst into flames.*

*A speeding petrol tanker took the corner in front of the Public Relations Department too fast. It careened and smashed into a burning bus. A hellish explosion ensued. A huge fireball shot up. Explosion after explosion rocked the hotel.*

*Amid all this someone knocked hard at our door.*

*"Who is it?"*

*"Ed Westlake!"*

*When the door opened, Westlake rushed in.*

*I gave my place to him.*

*Bullets shattered windowpanes.*

*"My camera!" swore a foreign newshound whose tool of trade was rendered useless.*

*"You should be grateful that you weren't shot," I said.*

*"Are you from the Post?"*

*"I'm a freelancer."*

*"I saw you with Khun Jumlong. Do you know him well?"*

*"Some time ago he granted me an interview which appeared in* The Nation.*"*

*"Ah! Now I know who you are. You're the author of* The Monsoon People. *Tell me what you know about this incorruptible Jumlong."*

Pira Sudham

*I told him the gist of the 'Rare Siamese' which was included in* Tales of Siam.

*Another salvo of gunfire forced us to crouch on the floor.*

*There was a knock at the door.*

*'Ladawan here! Let me in!'*

*Inside, she said: "A naval officer told us to leave. He said the soldiers would storm the hotel very soon. He promised that the navy will make a corridor of safety and clear Pinklao Bridge for the protesters to flee across Chaopraya River to Tonbury.*

*"That's a change of heart," said one of the foreign correspondents.*

*"Can we trust the navy?" a Siamese journalist wondered.*

*"Come down and see," Ladawan said, and left.*

*I followed her down the stairs.*

The Nation reported that over 2,000 of the protesters had left the hotel for Pinklao Bridge, while 3,000 stayed on.

*Under siege, the remaining protesters sang one patriotic song after another.*

*The military met the challenge, lashing out its wrath on the men and women outside the hotel.*

*"Go back to Room 132. Warn my colleagues that the soldiers are storming the lobby," Ladawan cried while taking photos as the forces fired at unarmed protesters at the entrance.*

*Yet I could not tear myself away.*

*Then the armed men burst in.*

*It sounded like the roar of the Devil, commanding everyone to lie face down. Those who did not obey were shot. Then more troops rushed in, stepping on the bodies. They pointed their guns at the prostrating people.*

*Only then could I dodge away up the stairs, using the banisters to protect me from the bullets.*

*Gunfire and screams followed me along the corridor.*

*From inside Room 132 I heard the shooting.*

*"Do you have a press card?" One of the foreign correspondents asked.*

*"No."*

*"Here! Take this camera!"*

*As anticipated our turn came.*

*"Open the door!"*

*Ed Westlake opened it.*

*Several soldiers barged into the room, pointing their guns at us.*

*"All of us are journalists," Westlake stated.*

*In case the beasts might not understand English, he slowly said in Siamese: "Rao tung mod pen nak kao krap."*

280

*The killers looked around. One looked under the bed. Another searched the bathroom.*

*"Stay in the room," one soldier commanded. "Keep the door open but no taking photos or filming!"*

*Soon protesters in single file were herded past our door.*

The Nation *reported that the captives were ordered to take off their shirts and that their hands were tied behind their backs. Those who were slow were kicked or hit with rifle butts. Some of those who fell were stomped upon. The fallen were dragged away.*

*Down below, an eyewitness said that the soldiers destroyed all medical equipment and supplies and prevented the doctors and nurses from treating the wounded.*

*Leaving the room, we walked along the passage way, passing broken doors. There were splashes of blood in ransacked rooms. Discarded shoes littered the corridor and the stairs.*

*We cautiously left the lobby.*

*At gunpoint the multitude of half-naked, crouching captives bent their heads to ground.*

*At the sound of cameras clicking, some military men suddenly swung around, aiming their weapons at us.*

*"No filming! No taking photos!" one of the soldiers barked at us. "Go back!"*

*We remained in the wrecked and bloodied lobby until the sound of vehicles died down. Then we rushed into the street.*

The Nation *estimated that 4,500 protesters, most of whom had sought refuge in and around Royal Hotel, were trucked away. I wandered along the blood-stained avenue.*

*It was strewn with burnt vehicles and debris.*

*The foreign correspondents and reporters filmed the conflagration and the wreckage.*

*The hope of finding Charles was waning when a soldier had forbidden me to go near the Monument of Democracy.*

*Aiming his gun at me, he ordered me to go back.*

*At an intersection I found a taxi. Here the traffic was in chaos. The traffic lights had been smashed.*

*There was not a single policeman to be seen.*

*Along Charoenkrung Road, police boxes had been ruined and shops remained closed. The taxi driver made a sudden halt to avoid an accident. Some masked men were firing at the fleeing mob.*

*After dragging the bodies off the street, two gunmen came over and peered at the driver and at me.*

*We looked harmless enough to move on.*

"I am glad to see you back alive," Tanong said.

"My guardian angel protected me. Otherwise, I would have been dead. Well, Tanong, I can do with a shower and a bowl of rice soup. How is your master?"

"He is asleep, sir. Do you want me to wake him?"

"Better not. He would only complain of a hang-over."

"There is a call from Ramatibodi Hospital, sir. Khun Charles is there now."

"Where?"

"Ramatibodi Hospital, sir. The lady, who phoned, said he is in an ICU."

"I must go to him at once!"

"A shower and a change of clothes and then a bowl of boiled rice with pork may put you in a better stead. Besides, visiting the patient in an ICU immediately after an operation might not be allowed."

"How right you are."

"While you are at the hospital you may want to see a doctor and have your wound treated before it festers."

*I was allowed into the ICU.*

"Poor Tregy! The late Dr Prawit took you to an orgy that was later raided by the police. As for me, I led you into a death trap."

"It's no fault of yours, my dear boy. The fact that we are still alive is a blessing. We must find those who brought me to this hospital. I want to make it up to them."

"Yes, we must. Do you remember any of them?"

"No, but I heard a commanding voice that sounded just like Ayu's, ordering his men to carry me away."

"So much blood has been shed. Even now the trouble isn't over and the General hasn't resigned. Thousands of people rally at Ramkhamhaeng University. Their number is increasing by the hour. I fear there will be a deadly crackdown once more."

"You're not going to…"

"No. Tell me, Charles. Where would you wish to be now? Is it your magnificent manor house in Ashdown Forest or your flat in St. James's?"

"Neither."

"Where then?"

"My dear boy, can't you guess? It's Napo. What would I give to be there now? There, we're so far away from strife, bloodshed, stuffy auction rooms, from *the world's troubles, racial hatred, religious conflicts, ethnic cleansing, hypocrisy, bigotry, conceit, snobbery..."*

*"Granted!" I interrupted, anxious that the old man might run out of breath.*

*"We'll go to Napo as soon as you're discharged from hospital. As a matter of fact, I don't feel at home in Danny's place. There I was, on Rajdamnern Avenue, among tens of thousands of the revolting Siamese, blandishing damning slogans against the General and his supporters. Danny's father is among the stout supporters of the General. And under his roof, we eat his food and drink his wines."*

*"Why Danny's father is rallying around the General, who has ousted him from office?"*

*"It's obviously beyond you or anyone of your level of probity to grasp, I know. However, the result is predictable. For a price he could recover his old ministerial post. But, old boy, don't muddle your mind with our politics. Look what happened to you when you attempted to be involved."*

*"Where would you like to be this very minute if I had a magic wand?"*

*"Strangely enough, it's Napo too. It's far away from the gunfire and the screams. How could they be so cruel and so beastly? They killed even the defenseless women and fleeing children. I still hear the shooting and the rumble of tanks, the cries of the dying. I can still hear them now. Yes, even now!"*

*"Come! Come! Don't fret so. I was there too, and I saw what you saw and felt what you felt, bearing great pain from the bullet wounds, as many survivors do. Somehow the pain has made me part of Siam now."*

Siam, the land of smiles, was passing through another horrid phase of history.

Prem Surin ended his observation with a summary from The Nation's editorial, appearing on the 24th of May.

*Bullets, rifle butts and batons did not deter the people whose love for their country transcended all barriers and fears. Panfa Bridge, Rajdamnern Avenue, Democracy Monument, Sanamlaung and the Royal Hotel became the killing fields. The capital was a bloodbath, and the tyrants, drunk on the nectar of power, were hell-bent on destroying all protesters and all persons against them. The military was out in full force to protect its interests...*

When the Supreme Commander Air Chief Marshal was asked who was to be blamed for the May Massacre, he replied: "I don't know how civilized countries deal with mobs. But I think those countries use more violent measures. In self-defense, we had to open fire sometimes to intimidate the angry crowds. When the bloodthirsty mobs came near the soldiers, they had to aim their guns low and fire to intimidate them. So now all of the people in this country are together responsible for the crisis."

The newspaper responded to Supreme Commander Air Chief Marshal's remark to the effect that in any civilized society, responsibility for poor or bad decisions should move up the hierarchy, not down. Attempting to pass the blame to all Siamese showed the contempt and disdain he held for his fellow citizens. Clearly the Supreme Commander Air Chief Marshal, the General and the new Army Chief must have direct responsibility for the tragedy and be brought to trial for their crimes.

They had not been brought to trial.

In 2001, the retired General was quoted as saying: "Should I have another chance, I'd do it again."

# The Peace in Between

When the General relinquished his premiership on 24th May, peace returned to Siam.

Shortly afterward, Dani Pi invited the headmaster of the Napo Witayakom School to the City Of Angels.

The teacher harboured regrets, having missed the action. If he had known of the protest, he would have left Napo for the capital to be at the forefront in the confrontation with the military.

"Khun Charles," Anucha spoke excitedly. "I implore you to expatiate on the massacre. If only I had been with you during the protest march!"

"If I were you, I wouldn't be so chirpy," Prem responded.

"Ah, yes. That would not be any good to my students, should I have been killed. Being alive, I can continue fostering change in the mentality of the young through my method of teaching which encourages them to develop their minds so they become thinking individuals later in life…"

"Khun Anucha," Dani interrupted. "Khun Charles will go back to London in a fortnight. He won't be able to walk for a while. Prem shall be with him until he's quite well. So we shall transfer the funds from the Napo Project to the Kumjai Chaiwankul Foundation under your administration. We'll see my lawyer today. While we are there, I shall look into the matter of changing my name. At present I can't travel to certain countries. If you followed the news in the media, you'd know why."

# A Family Dispute

When the parents knew of the name change, they were adamant. Daniel Pennington determined to purge himself of the stigma.

He had not committed sinister deeds and so why must he be penalized? The couple insisted that they had done nothing wrong either, and went further to hint at the stratagem.

"I don't want any more of your filthy lucre. Furthermore, involvement in such a heinous scheme abhors me," the estranged son barracked.

He must act quickly while his friends were with him.

Since the son refused to change his new name back to the former, the father threatened to cut the heir out of the will.


"It's time to fly back to old England!" Daniel said to his friends.

Early in the evening, the Chief of Security entered the Green Parlour where the three musketeers were imbibing DP's favourite wine.

"Several Napo men came to see you, sir."

"Good!" the billionaire said. "Take them to the Blue Room. We shall see them shortly."

"Napo men!" the Napotian cried. "Something dreadful must have happened in the village. Otherwise, they wouldn't come uninvited. I must see them at once!"

"If Anu is among them, I'd like to have a word with him," said Charles.

"Don't get excited both of you. Security mistook the visitors to be Napotians. Actually they're chaps from Rajabury to see me on some matters. Primo, you keep an eye on Charles while I deal with them. Make sure he doesn't injure himself. That slip in the bathroom was nasty. You're such a lousy carer! Any more injuries may prevent us from leaving tonight. I'll be back in 10 minutes."

But Daniel Pennington took almost an hour to re-appear.

"We'll be late for the flight!" Little Prem pouted.

"I took the men to a restaurant. You should have seen the faces of the guards when they saw that the chauffeur was their own lord and master! I should have given them a good talking to for not checking the visitors on their way out. All right, no need to keep glancing at your watch. I'll have a shower in a minute. Has Tanong packed my suitcase?"

"Yes! Hurry up, will you?"

Several hours later, the trio resumed their celebration with champagne and caviar in the aircraft. Looking at his diamond-encrusted Rolex, the billionaire said to his travelling companion:

"I say, Primo! I've just done your beloved Siam a good turn."

And he raised his glass.

"To your beloved country!"

"To our beloved Siam!"

The Napotian did not inquire into the nature of such a good deed for he was concerned with Tregonning's comfort.

"Charles is sad, leaving Siam without having said goodbye to Anu." Then the duo raised their glasses towards the lugubrious gentleman across the aisle, wishing him a speedy recovery.

Meanwhile the fourth Rajabury man, whom the son had planted in the father's bedroom, spent several hours hiding in the wardrobe until the great man returned to meet his nemesis.

The eminent politician, who had survived several attempts on his life, did not die instantly from the first hacking. The killing took many painful and horrifying minutes.

When the horrible task was eventually accomplished, the assassin remained in the blood-spattered chamber waiting for the son to come and whisk him away.

At dawn, the blood-stained killer, sneaked out and slunk along the dark gallery in search of the secret door that linked the two apartments. Lost in the labyrinthine corridors for some time, the panicking murderer attempted to escape through a window. Some minutes later, he was seen scaling down the front of the house.

A burst of gunfire hurled him to the ground.

# A Plea

The assassin realised that he had been betrayed when the son did not help him escape as agreed. Such betrayal induced him to confess that he was hired to kill the great man and a cleaver was chosen to avoid making horrific noise.

The statement also included his description of how the late minister had fought for his life.

"I had to take his life for he was a very powerful man. He would have had me killed if he had remained alive. I had to hack him to death to save my own life," the murderer concluded.

In England, Daniel Pennington resorted to Wealdshire Park. In the magnificent treasure trove, the lord of the manor was found lying on a regal four-poster in the State Bedroom in which King Henry VIII had slept.

The manager, followed by the housekeeper, moved anxiously towards the bed. Having ascertained that the recluse had left our troubled world, Christian Windfore would then follow the procedure with utmost discretion.

But before leaving the chamber, he did not fail to notice an envelope addressed to *Madame Vichitra Pilaskulkosol*.

The dead man's written words were:

*Though I have been well aware that love and kindness have never entered your heart, I shall plead with you. If you try to regain the funds transferred to me in the U.K., Switzerland and Liechtenstein, or do away with the individuals under whose control the Estate has been placed, you can expect counter charges from this part of the world. I have documented the bank transfers and the killing of schoolteachers, labour leaders and environmental activists who dared to challenge your power, as well as the payments made to the manager of hired assassins.*

*I am well aware of your power over Siamese authorities including the FDA and the majority of the media to keep the consumers in ignorance. The European Union is still beyond your shadow. Therefore, I have given instructions to alert the EU concerning the import of agricultural produce from Siam. All imports would then be checked for lead, arsenic, melanin, formalin, cancer-causing chemicals, dyestuff or antibiotics banned by the EU, used in poultry and aquatic farming in Siam and in China where you also have established a vast business enterprise.*

*Most of all I have devised a way in which Operation Damage-Destroy-Take-over can be revealed.*

288

A Plea

*I plead with you to allow my friends to utilize the resources from the Trust to benefit the much-maligned people and repair the damage and destruction done to their country.*

# The Advancing Shadow

Despite the late Daniel Pennington's plea, Madame VP sent forth her emissaries to recover the hoard. Under the threat of 'coming down like a ton of bricks', Charles Tregonning, Pamela Cannington and Prem Surin held a meeting from which an agreement emerged to the effect that Wealdshire Park should become a National Trust property.

In so doing, Little Primo considered that he had prevented the family fortune from falling into the wrong hands.

*It's beyond my power to protect Siam from the take-over, but Wealdshire Park must not go to them while it's still within my power to protect it.*

"Our neighbour Hugh Stratton, the draconian landlord at Hamlinton Hall, said most of our visitors were 'ragtag'. Mind you, it was his choice of word. I wouldn't dream of using it," Little Primo opined.

"Look at him now, languishing in HMP for the death of a business partner. The roof of Hamlinton has caved in and the rainwater has ruined his so-called *palace*."

"That's the force of karma."

"One reaps what one sows."

The word 'reap' reminded the inheritor of the inheritance. At the same time, the image of Charles Tregonning, tottering inside Ashwood Manor, came to mind.

*Poor old Tregy! What can one do for him?*

Not long ago, the Napotian had teased the old gentleman due to his unquenchable desire to collect and hoard objects.

"Tregy, old thing! You won't part even with an old pair of shoes! And that's not only because you're true to your sun-sign but also you're a born hoarder! Aren't you aware that you cannot take anything with you when you eventually pop off?"

Previously this wild man from Isan were not aware that Tregonning's properties, including the manor house and the magnificent apartment in St. James's and the valuable objects in them would soon be his.

One day the grandee had said:

"To circumvent the inheritance tax, I'll make everything I own a gift to you now. But, my dear boy, don't throw me out of the house for I hate to be homeless and penniless. Another thing! Don't regard lightly the gift according to your Buddhist doctrine of detachment. I know you don't attach much value to material things. Otherwise, I'll make Ashwood Manor either a school or an animal care centre. You should also be aware that most of the valuables are extremely rare. A lot of them are priceless."

The astute collector had imparted knowledge of their values, their history and how each piece had been collected. For instance: "The Bureau du Roi was made by Riesener in 1769 for Louis XV. The one shipped to VP Place was a copy made by Dasson for the Marquess of Wilt in the 19th century. Even a copy is worth a fortune...."

When all was said and done and the gift had been legitimately handed over, the fortunate Isaner had remarked to a journalist.

"The old man pinched my silver when he was my butler in the past-life. In this life I merely recovered what had been mine plus interest at the rate of 19.99 per cent APR. The Lord has kept account, counting from the time of pilferage up to now which should be 150 years."

Little Primo's long silence caused Pamela to put the Sunday magazine down.

"Now my parents would be delighted to visit this pile."

"Oh, yes! Today the restaurant should be full to capacity in this glorious weather. I shall go down to lend a hand."

"You? A waiter?"

"Rather! It would take my mind off writing. I've arrived at a very tedious and painful part. That's when your father went to Siam to look for you."

"Why haven't you had writer's block yet? We could kill time during the doldrums, wining and dining in London. I salivate at the thought of venison with truffle cream, *foie gras* and a sprinkle of parmesan shavings at Gordon Ramsay. You'd love to imbibe Chateau Petrus 61 again, I'm sure. We haven't had a drop of it since that birthday dinner the late Dani threw for himself here. It has a price tag of 11,000 pounds a bottle at Gordon Ramsay."

"At that price, you can make a pig of yourself without me."

"There's no need to be bothered with the cost of dining in any top restaurants anywhere in the world."

"Still I wouldn't be able to swig the wine. A bottle of that costs more than the new Vauxhall Charles has just bought for the

Pira Sudham

housekeeper. Moreover, it's more than Kiang's income from selling his rice at the suppressed price for hundreds of years."

"Stop thinking like that, Primo! Otherwise, you won't be able to eat or drink anything."

"I can't bear the thought of us making pigs of ourselves in London while Charles is suffering in his lonely house. No, it won't do!"

"Are you his partner or mine?"

"Steady on, Lizzie! You'd enjoy the night out more with Godfry Archisson. He should be hugely consoled by your company now that his wife is no more. Perhaps you might be able to remedy his craving for prostitutes. The lonely widower, who should have been exceedingly randy by now, is much grander than I, a mere lord of the manor, a title that doesn't mean much these days! Old Tregy is a lord of the manor for having bought Ashwood Manor and the Manorial Rights, but he … "

"If you want to know, Stephen Morris is much grander. He's on his way to become the new Lord Mayor of London."

"My dear Lizzie! You don't have to sleep around to help me obtain a British passport. It's people like you who could create scandals. I'm not ashamed of being Siamese, you know?"

"But still, it's good to have a British passport, isn't it? Hundreds of aliens would die for it. As for you, a frequent visitor to the U.K., you can stay here definitely as my partner. I want you here with me most of the time now, now that I can't set foot on Siamese soil. Even under my new name, they could seek me out from the moment I landed."

"Look at what you've done to me, making me stay so long in the land of dark, satanic mills when I can do so much for the poor of Isan by being in Napo."

"Aren't you aware that your writings have already done a lot of good for the voiceless, the suppressed and the much-maligned in Siam? Don't you think it's much better to write here rather than scribbling away in Napo, my love?"

"Here, I'm more useful in the kitchen or in the restaurant."

"Apart from the staff, none would believe that you're lord of the manor now."

"Most people may think that I'm a refugee or an asylum seeker, or an illegal immigrant, happy to have a job that some British underclass

292

wouldn't do. By the way, do I look as if I could be an extremist, a fanatic?"

"If you do, does it matter?"

"Oh, yes, it does. I don't want to be shot dead like that unfortunate Brazilian man. Don't you know why old Tregy gave a series of dinner parties in London and garden parties at the manor house?"

"So you could make a lasting impression as an author?"

"Of course not! I gave up any attempt to impress the British a long time ago. But Charles is still trying to put me on a solid footing with a certain peer of the realm, and you-know-who in the government. Yet I can't face Lord Bewly. I still feel ill at ease at Lord Norbury's table. As for being chummy with Peter Mundoonson and his partner, I can't purport to be witty, charming, sophisticated and gay. You do quite well out off the circuit, flirting with those charming Tories. Their airs and graces rub off on you, a former labour voter! It took only one garden party at Ashwood Manor to entwine you with Godfry Archisson."

Pamela was not at all pleased, rising to her feet

"Look! There's Charles! You had better go down and help him up here, hadn't you?"

Entering the Mandalay Room, the old gentleman cut short the pleasantries.

"I propose that we give in to the demand," Charles motioned.

"How on earth are we going to raise 100 million pounds to hand over to them?" Little Primo pouted.

"I won't give a penny back!" Pamela snapped.

"Then they'll come down on us like tons of bricks. I fear it isn't an empty threat."

"We'll fight back!"

"With what, Lizzie? These people have gunmen ready to do us in. Don't you value our lives?"

"They'd gain nothing from our deaths! Can't you see? Anyway we have Danny's instruction to expose their vile karma and Operation DDT."

"I'm afraid that won't do!" Charles huffed.

"Why not?" challenged the Yorkshire lass who had survived Operation Norma. "I won't part with *my* money. You two can do what you like with yours."

"I knew we'd have problems with Lizzie, Charles. You can work out how much we have without hers."

"I've already anticipated this. We need 40 million more."

"Let's sell everything! I do mean everything! The apartment in St. James's, Hyde Park Square flat, all the *objets d'art*, the paintings, the chandeliers, cars, furniture, carpets, piano, the lot! They don't mean much to me anyway and most are from ill-gotten gains and from the blood, sweat and tears of *my* people! With your expertise, Charles, you can help jack up the bids at the auction. That should bring in a big bundle, don't you think?"

"Another thing I haven't mentioned. If we don't meet the deadline of 23rd December, they will kill your family members, one by one, one life for one week of delay. As if to prove that their threat isn't empty, Anucha has been murdered in his house..."

"What? Anu murdered?" Pamela and Prem uttered almost at the same time.

"Anu refused to hand over the funds under the Kumujai Chaiwankul Foundation. But, according to a report, his activities that might have brought about his death covered his fight against a drug lord, as well as exposing corrupt practices among the provincial bureaucrats and contractors. Haven't you visited the Bangkok Post's website today?"

"Wicked! Wicked world! Poor Anu," Pamela wailed.

"I hope his wife is safe. But I fear she won't remain in Napo after this. Who will run the school? I must go home at once!"

"I do need your signature. You can't leave till all is done, I'm afraid."

"Then let's not waste our time squabbling!"

"For the lives of the Surins, you may have mine back as well," Pamela came round and embraced her dear friend.

# Dust of Conflicts

Pamela Cannington married Godfry Archisson. The beautiful blond became Lady Archisson when her husband progressed to the House of Lords.

Later on Lord Godfry suffered from a self-inflicted (or, according to Surin's interpretation, karmic) injury that required an appropriate period of confinement.

Later Lady Archisson gave birth to a son and named him Priam.

When in England Prem stayed at Ashwood Manor with Charles.

At the Hailsham branch of Waitrose, the incongruous pair of customers looked rather conspicuous. Using a shopping trolley more or less for support, the doddery septuagenarian, who had survived the May massacre of pro-democracy protesters in Rajadamnern Avenue in Bangkok, pushed on, heading towards the cheese section. The wild man from Isan did not stray far from his friend except for once when he lingered, having sighted, on a pack of smoked salmon, a little red sticker that read 'Was 6.99 Now 3.99'.

Back in Isan, the silent little chap lived frugally under the shadow of the Dark Lord.

Then the publication of *The Shadowed Kingdom* exposed him.

Nevertheless, the novelist made use of the time he had left in this world, teaching the young at the Chaiwankul-Rajapakdi School that he built in the village as a monument to the murdered teachers.

One day, a stranger entered the classroom. Instinctively, the teacher, who had been involved in Operation Norma and well-aware of the DDT stratagem, believed that Death had come for him.

*This is it. Goodbye Charles. Goodbye Lizzie. Farewell Wilhelm. Please, J S Bach, let me hear 'Sleeper's Wake' before I go.*

When Death did not strike, the intended victim sighed. Still facing the murderer, Little David of Isan continued conducting the lesson.

The author thought the visitation was part of a gruesome nightmare until Grandpa Tatip's voice resonated in his ears.

"Do not challenge him. Be passive and compassionate."

Then the emissary of death beckoned the target to go out.

The teacher readily obeyed. It would be better, being shot outside to avoid making a bloody mess in front of the boys and girls.

When the killer and the one to be killed were some 10 paces away from the school, the gunman halted.

"They're out to kill you. Next time you might not be so lucky. I'm also an Isaner. My home village isn't far from here. For not killing you, they'll go after me. I'll hide in Lao. Perhaps you may want to do the same to save your life."

Being aware that his life might end soon, he valued each day, being alive on Isan soil.

Lines from one of Emily Bronte's poems often recurred in his mind.

*No coward soul is mine*
*No trembler in the world's storm-troubled sphere...*

Nevertheless he avoided interviews or making statements of any kind to anyone.

The meek little man picked up where the late teacher had left off, trying to counter age-old authoritarian teaching and rote learning with a devotion to nurturing growing minds of the young.

He held that their formative minds must not be stunted, crippled or deformed as his had been.

In memory of Kumjai and Anucha, the survivor established the Chaiwankul-Rajapakdi Foundation to carry on the late teachers' admirable deeds.

From time to time the writer went to England to visit the Archissons and seek solace in the company of Charles Tregonning. Under the Sussex sky, he felt free; his spirit soared.

In the U.K., there was a child to survive him.

Priam Charles Archisson should undoubtedly gain the intellectual development which Little Primo had been deprived. It was willed that after the testator's death, P. C. Archisson would inherit Prem Surin's estate.

The quiet Napotian remained single. In the shadowed country, there need not be his flesh and blood to go through the mind-maiming teaching method which brought about mindlessness and subservience so as to enable the Dark Lord to rule ruthlessly without challenge, without trammels.

*Then I shall laugh*
*my last laugh*
*in sunlight*
*without malice*
*or sadness*
*but with gladness,*
*when good deeds are done --*
*the good karma thus done.*

Prem Surin closed his journal with the following line:

**14th October: The King died yesterday.**

However, the little old man could not rest. Often the mental image of a hunter tieing down an ass to lure the tiger came to his mind. Moreover, the warning that Goliath was out to kill him compelled the writer to hasten, penning *"A War on the Streets of Bangkok"*.

# A War on the Streets of Bangkok

"Go! Go!" the village chief commanded the crowd.

Seeing a little boy by his parents's sides, the chief coaxed, "Tanom and Jinda! Take your son with you. The boy will get half of an adult's pay. Have you ever touched a thousand-baht banknote before? An air-conditioned coach from Bangkok has arrived to take all of you there."

But the villagers did not move. It needed dexterity to convince the thick-headed peasants.

"It is a chance to make money so you can pay debts to the BAAC (Bank for Agriculture and Agricultural Cooperatives)," the big man proclaimed.

The claim worked.

Thousands of men, women and children had been convening at Ratchaprasong for such a long time that Tanin, Tanom's son, wanted to go home.

"We can't go yet," said the mother. "The work isn't finished."

The woman stressed the word 'work' to emphasize the importance of the assignment.

However, her son seemed so sad that Jinda needed to explain.

"We haven't been paid yet. How can we go? No money. No bus fare. When the work is done, they will let us go."

The boy looked sadder still, knowing that his classmates, who remained in the village, had sat the examinations. He, who was absent, would not be able to move up to Class Four the next academic year.

Tanin wept, thinking of Daeng, his puppy.

"Daeng is starving for sure," he mourned.

"It won't die of starvation," Jinda consoled her son. "It may go beg for food at the wat."

The mother could not say anything further, fearing that her vegetables at the lots by Lotus Swamp had all died.

In her hurry to get into the coach, Jinda forgot to ask Aunt Bua to do the watering in her absence.

"My poor spring onions, my poor corianders and dills," the woman silently mourned.

Meanwhile, Father Tanom remained silent though his mind's eye saw his dead caged dove. But then Tanom had always been taciturn.

In all his life he hardly complained, enduring calamities, diseases and swindlers.

For instance, he and many other villagers subserviently worked one full day, cutting down indigenous trees in Changlai Forest to create a so-called 'new forest'. But the saplings provided by the officials to replace the felled trees turned out to be eucalyptus.

"We grew eucalyptus to make new forests to benefit the nation," the chief had explained.

The greatest loss in Tanom's life was being duped to pay the so-called 'Employment Abroad Agency' 150,000 baht in advance.

To be able to raise 150,000 baht, the victim had to borrow the money from a loan shark, using the title deed of his wife's rice-field as collateral.

When he landed in South Korea, it turned out that there was no one to meet him. No job. Nothing. Out of the deal, all he got was a passport and an air ticket. As a result, the loan shark took over the land.

The first urban warfare bursting out on the streets of Bangkok had happened. The gunfire, the bombing, the conflagration and the screaming of the people drove the hearts of the population in the battlefield into utter despair.

Hundreds of men, women and children were dead.

Tanom and Jinda fell on little Tanin, protecting him with their lifeless bodies.

Uncle Sa, who was still alive despite being shot, told Tanin to escape and seek protection at the nearby monastery, Wat Sabua.

"The monks there will protect you," Uncle Sa breathed his last breath.

At Wat Sabua, three monks stood still, barring several armed men from entering the chapel. However, the holy men could not prevent the hellish sounds from destroying the peace within the temple precinct.

Ten years later, a temple boy left Wat Sabua for the old battleground. There he stood at the spot where his parents had died.

Tanin trembled so much that he had to sit down. Eventually the fever forced the boy to lay on one side, wishing for the spirits of his parents to enfold him. Despite the fact that Ratchaprasong was completely deserted while the deadly virus was waging war on mankind, including monks at Wat Sabua, Tanin believed he heard the

Pira Sudham

dreadful sounds of gunfire, of burning and the moaning of the wounded.

"Father Nom and Mother Da and little Daeng come to me now," the feverish boy tried to say.

## The End

300

Printed in Great Britain
by Amazon

38355856R00172